ADMIRAL NIMITZ

THE COMMANDER OF THE PACIFIC OCEAN THEATER

BRAYTON HARRIS

palgrave
macmillan

First published in 2011 by PALGRAVE MACMILLAN® in the U.S.—a division of
St. Martin's Press LLC, 175 Fifth Avenue, New York, NY 10010.

Where this book is distributed in the UK, Europe and the rest of the world, this is
by Palgrave Macmillan, a division of Macmillan Publishers Limited, registered in
England, company number 785998, of Houndmills, Basingstoke, Hampshire RG21
6XS.

Palgrave Macmillan is the global academic imprint of the above companies and has
companies and representatives throughout the world.

Palgrave® and Macmillan® are registered trademarks in the United States, the
United Kingdom, Europe and other countries.

ISBN: 978-0-230-10765-6

Library of Congress Cataloging-in-Publication Data

Harris, Brayton, 1932-
    Admiral Nimitz : the commander of the Pacific Ocean theater / Brayton Harris.
        p.   cm.
    Includes index.
    ISBN 978-0-230-10765-6
    1. Nimitz, Chester W. (Chester William), 1885–1966.   2. World War,
1939–1945—Campaigns—Pacific Area.   3. Admirals—United States—
Biography.   4. United States. Navy.—Biography.   5. World War, 1939–1945—
Naval operations, American.   I. Title.
D767H344   2012
940.54'5973092—dc23
[B]
                                                                    2011021969

A catalogue record of the book is available from the British Library.

Design by Letra Libre

First edition: January 2012

10 9 8 7 6 5 4 3 2 1

Printed in the United States of America.

CONTENTS

PREFACE

The sea—like life itself—is a stern taskmaster. The best way to get along with either is to learn all you can, then do your best, and don't worry—especially about things over which you have no control.

—Charles Henry Nimitz

Chester Nimitz has long been overshadowed by flamboyant World War II contemporaries, men who collected colorful nicknames like "Bull" or "Howlin' Mad." These men knew how to work the media—and write memoirs—to claim credit or settle scores. Nimitz had no nickname, left no memoir, and refused all requests from authors who wanted to "help" tell his story. He had commanded the 2 million men and 1000 ships that won the war in the Pacific. He felt that was legacy enough.

Admiral Nimitz: The Commander of the Pacific Ocean Theater is the story of an unsophisticated sixteen-year-old from rural Texas who wanted to go to West Point but ended up at the Naval Academy, and learned his profession, one job at a time. Thus, the book you are holding is more than a war story: it is a guided tour of a remarkable career, covering the six afloat commands Nimitz had in his first six years of commissioned service—and his court-martial for running aground; his seminal work in developing diesel engines, underway refueling, and tactical formations; how he built the Pearl Harbor submarine base with "borrowed" World War I surplus materials; and how he set up one of the first Naval Reserve Officer Training Corps (NROTC) units in the nation. And how, as head of the Navy's personnel bureau, he helped the fleet get ready for the coming war.

Most important, to fight that war, Nimitz developed an operating philosophy that allowed his fleet to win battles, often with forces smaller than those of the enemy. A hands-off commander, Nimitz did not smother subordinates with urgent directives. He would develop a plan, pick the right people to carry it through, let them know what he expected—then get out of the way to let them do the job. He was not, however, isolated and remote, but made frequent visits to the battle zones—often, before the battle was over—to collect the assessments of his commanders and to encourage the war-fighting forces.

At the same time, he fought more subtle engagements. He was put in command of the Pacific Fleet by President Franklin D. Roosevelt, not by the uniformed leaders of the Navy. His own immediate superiors did not know him very well, and for most of the first year of the war they viewed him with suspicion, as just another "political" officer who gained stature from his connections, not skill and experience. Then, with that battle won and Nimitz fully in charge—and the war against the Japanese brought to an end—he had to fight both Secretary of the Navy James V. Forrestal and President Harry S. Truman to get the coveted career-topping job of CNO, chief of naval operations. *Then* he became embroiled in another war, over the size and shape of the armed forces—beating back efforts to eliminate the Marine Corps and submerge naval aviation under the Air Force.

I knew Admiral Nimitz, in a manner of speaking. I had lunch with him a few times exactly fifty years ago when he was about the same age as I am now. I was a junior officer on my first shore duty, at the Naval Station Treasure Island, in San Francisco Bay. Nimitz, then living in the hills above Berkeley, would often come down to our officer's club, where the manager was a longtime friend of his. Full disclosure: I don't remember a thing he said, I was too busy telling him all about *me*. I hope this modest effort to tell his story will atone for the arrogance of youth.

ACKNOWLEDGMENTS

Admiral Nimitz's daughter Catherine (Kate) Lay and grandson Chester Nimitz Lay have been most generous in sharing family archives and stories, and in reviewing my text for egregious errors.

When some of my friends heard about this project, they passed the word to some of their friends, thus enlarging the circle of people who have directly contributed comments, suggestions, and encouragement. First, staffers at the Naval War College: Evelyn Cherpak, Donald Chisholm, Carla McCarthy, and Douglas Smith. Then, fellow authors and former associates who had something to offer: Brent Baker, Eric Berryman, Ralph Blanchard, Kenneth J. Braithwaite II, Elliot Carlson, Bruce Cole, Robert Durand, Dan Ford, George Gillett, George Kolbenshlag, Bob Lewis, John Lundstrom, Jack Mayo, Jerry Miller, Philip Russell, John Shackelton, Michael Sherman, Paul Stillwell, and Bill Thompson.

Finally, thanks to my agent, Joe Vallely, and the Palgrave Macmillan editorial staff—Laura Lancaster, Luba Ostashevsky, Alessandra Bastagli, and Victoria Wallis—without whom there would be no book.

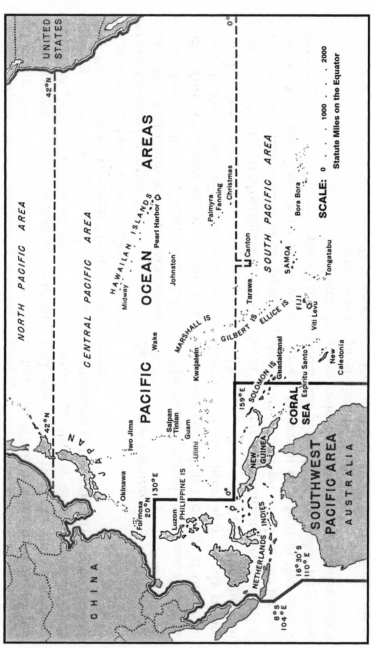

Command lines in the Pacific. The "Southwest Pacific Area" was under General Douglas MacArthur; everything else, the "Pacific Ocean Areas," was Nimitz territory.

Credit: United States Army in World War II, Office of the Chief of Military History, 1957.

CHAPTER ONE

TEXAS

Let us begin, at the beginning. Chester William Nimitz was born February 24, 1885, in the German-American settlement of Fredericksburg, Texas. He could claim a maritime heritage of sorts—both his grandfather and great-grandfather had gone to sea. For his great-grandfather, it was a full-time job; his grandfather Charles Henry Nimitz's sea time was limited to perhaps one cruise as a teenager, yet for most of his adult life he was known as Captain Nimitz. This was a military not maritime rank that came from his role as organizer of a Civil War–era volunteer militia in Texas.

Charles Henry was the most influential person in young Chester's life. One of the founders of Fredericksburg, which he and a small group of settlers built from scratch in 1846, Charles Henry was a classic entrepreneur. He set up a hotel in an eight-room sun-dried-brick building, which over time grew to offer forty-five guest rooms, a dining hall, casino, bar, brewery, bathhouse, and a combination ballroom and theatre. And, over time, the ever-expanding building came to resemble a beached steamship—complete with a mast for the flag and a crow's nest for looking out over the hills. With a bit of enlightened marketing, it became known as Captain Nimitz' Steamboat Hotel. In its heyday, the Nimitz was the last commercial hotel between the Gulf Coast and San Diego and played host to such guests as Colonel Robert E. Lee, General Philip Sheridan, and the author O. Henry, who used the hotel as the backdrop for a short story.

Charles Henry had twelve children; one son, Chester Bernard, was never really well, perhaps a combination of rheumatic fever and a congenital weakness of the lungs. Chester Bernard thought that working in the great outdoors as a cowboy, moving large herds of cows from Texas to Nebraska, would be curative. It was not, and five months after he married Anna Henke, the daughter of a cattle rancher, Chester Bernard died. Anna was pregnant with their son. She named him after his father.

Anna and baby Chester moved into her father-in-law's hotel where she worked in the kitchen. Chester grew up as a scrappy kid. His friends all had fathers, he did not. His friends enjoyed a lot of playtime, he was often stuck helping his mother in the kitchen. His light-blond hair triggered the nickname "Cottontop," which he hated so much so early in life that he once dumped a pot of green paint on his head in a that-will-show-'em! sort of move. His mother had to shave his head. Quick to anger, he got into fights with kids at school who teased or bullied him. He seems to have been pretty good at it, at least, according to relatives telling tales some seventy years after the fact, who credited him with taking on and defeating two at a time. Somewhere along the way he decided that fighting was not the best way to solve problems and learned to control his temper. Most of the time.

When Chester was not quite six, Anna married her husband's brother, Willie, and the family moved some twenty-four miles away to Kerrville, to live in and manage another hotel, owned by Chester's aunt, a widow. The St. Charles was an overgrown boarding house, with only half the guest rooms and none of the charm of the Steamboat Hotel, but it offered a place to live and work. Willie and Anna had two children, Dora and Otto.[1] Charles Henry turned day-to-day operation of *his* hotel over to his son Charles Henry Jr., drifted into politics, and was elected to the Texas State Legislature.

Willie was an engineer by education, a graduate of Worcester Polytechnic Institute, but once back in Texas, he became a professional overseer: an expert at watching other people work. He was amiable, played hotel host at times, but much to the disgust of his father, who had paid for his expensive education, Willie was never gainfully employed as an engineer. The only actual job anyone remembers him having was as a timekeeper, late in life. But Willie, to his credit, had no delusions. In an honest bit of regret, he once told his daughter, "You know, I couldn't sell gold dollars for fifty cents apiece."[2]

Chester had *his* first paying job, a dollar a week, at the age of eight, as a delivery boy for a local meat market owned by his mother's family. As he got older, he waited tables in the hotel dining room, did yard work, chopped wood and carried it around to the dozen or so stoves and fireplaces in the hotel. When he was fifteen, his aunt started paying him fifteen dollars a month. In addition to the regular chores, he became the evening desk clerk, on duty until 10 P.M.

Perhaps influenced by knowledge of his father's systemic poor health and nudged by his mother, Chester became an exercise fanatic. He swam, ran, and walked—sometimes, as much as a fourteen-mile hike to an uncle's farm. Many years later a cousin recalled, "Nothing stands out more than his utter determination to remain physically fit." The cousin added that when Chester came home for a visit some years later, "He carried a clock on his leg and he got in a certain mileage every day."[3]

His recreation was typical of boys in rural Texas: pitching horseshoes, fishing, hunting for rabbits and doves, catching rattlesnakes to harvest their rattles, going on week-long camping trips with grandfather Nimitz, or pretending to be a cowboy on the ranch where his maternal grandfather Henry Henke raised his cattle. Grandmother Henke did not speak English, so Chester became pretty fluent in German. He was also mischievous: "borrowing" a neighbor's boat for a row on the river (well, borrowed more than once, to the frustration of the neighbor who sometimes wanted to use the boat himself), and tying tin cans to a dog's tail. Fortunately, his solid Germanic middle-class background provided a few socially acceptable distractions, such as a love of classical music and skill at playing card games—notably cribbage, poker, and bridge—which would prove useful later in life.

Education? He was a quick study. The principal of Tivy High School said they "couldn't keep him busy, he was that fast." Whatever they gave him to do was quickly done, "and he was looking around for something to do . . . some trouble to get into."[4]

Confidence? A fishing party hired the cook at the hotel to go along on their river expedition and he was a no-show. Chester, barely in his teens, said, "I'll go and cook for you." The fishermen said, "What can you cook?," and Chester said, "I can cook all the fish you can get." And he did.[5]

What of the future? Horizons were limited. Young Chester was not interested in either of the family businesses, but local opportunities were few.

Traveling salesmen who stopped at the St. Charles talked of freedom on the open road; a team of surveyors described their work and suggested that Chester could become an apprentice and learn the trade, an option with some appeal. Then, one day in the summer of 1900 an army field artillery battery camped nearby. Fifteen-year-old Chester was fascinated by the pomp and circumstance and the "spanking-new uniforms" of two recent graduates of the U.S. Military Academy at West Point. They spun tales of the wonders of army life and the glories of West Point, and at that moment Nimitz decided to become an army officer.[6]

But entering West Point was no easy task. Appointments were tightly controlled, although every member of Congress had a quota. Nimitz applied to his own congressman, James Slaydon—and was devastated by the response. Slaydon's quota was filled.

However, Slaydon noted, he had an opening for the Naval Academy at Annapolis. Would Chester be interested? Chester had never heard of the place, but when he learned that it was the Navy's equivalent of West Point and that after a free college education, graduates become naval officers, he said, why not? But it was not a done deal: Slaydon had other candidates and would hold a local competitive exam in April. The winner would go on to a Naval Academy Prep School to study for an even more rigorous qualifying exam that included algebra (through quadratic equations), plane geometry, United States and world history, geography, reading, writing, spelling, and grammar—all of which had aspects that Chester, then in the middle of his junior year of high school, had probably never heard and certainly had not yet studied.

But he was game to try. His grandfather, Charles Henry, cheered him on, saying, "The sea—like life itself—is a stern taskmaster. The best way to get along with either is to learn all you can, then do your best and don't worry—especially about things over which you have no control."[7]

"Do your best and don't worry" became a guiding principle. Chester had three months to prepare; Willie, some teachers, and the high school principal volunteered as tutors. Chester's daily schedule now began at 3 A.M.; he studied until 5:30, when it was time to light the stoves. School was from 9 to 4, followed by front desk duty and homework until 10 P.M., and to bed.

Competing against seven other hopefuls, Chester came in first and soon had his first set of official orders: Report to Annapolis to get ready for the entrance exam. If he passed, he would be immediately sworn into naval service and admitted.[8]

Slaydon, headed to his congressional office at the Capitol, took the very excited young man in tow for the journey. Chester had never been more than a few dozen miles from home, had never seen a building larger than the Steamboat Hotel, had never seen, let alone ridden on, a train. It was quite an adventure.

CHAPTER TWO

NAVAL ACADEMY

Congressional enthusiasm for a larger Navy began with the start of the Spanish-American War, in 1898, when eight new battleships, six armored cruisers, and about three dozen smaller ships were authorized. Expansion of the fleet continued with encouragement from Theodore Roosevelt, who said, "There is a homely adage which runs, 'Speak softly and carry a big stick, you will go far.' If the American nation will speak softly and yet build and keep at a pitch of the highest training a thoroughly efficient navy the Monroe Doctrine will go far."[1]

As a result, the Navy needed more officers. When Chester Nimitz was sworn in as a naval cadet on September 7, 1901, it was in the largest class in the fifty-six-year history of the Naval Academy. He and his 130 classmates were in for a six-year course: four years of academics and three summer training cruises, followed by two years of service with the fleet with the rank of "passed midshipman." Then, upon positive recommendations from their commanding officers and after passing another set of exams, graduates would be promoted to ensign.[2]

The members of the teaching staff were professional naval officers, not professional educators, and their method of instruction was laissez-faire—they did not so much instruct as grade performance. At the end of each class, for instance, the instructor would assign the readings. The cadets were expected to absorb knowledge during their study time and give it back in the next class, when they would draw slips of paper on each of which was a question to be answered at the blackboard. After twenty minutes or so, the instructor would go from one to the next, critiquing the answers and only then, perhaps, offering some comment based on his own experience.

This philosophy of teaching was a reflection of the Navy's operational reality. Unlike their U. S. Army counterparts, commanding officers of warships were expected to be independent, often to operate their ships out of contact with higher command for months. They had to draw on their own initiative, intuition, and resources. They could not count on expert advice, guidance, or interference from afar. By such insistence on individual effort, the Navy expected only the strong to survive.

Then, too, there was a day-to-day regimentation that was hard for some young men to accept. Cadets marched to class, could be sanctioned for being late, for talking in formation, and for smoking anywhere on campus. In another form of testing, known far and wide as hazing, upperclassmen would verbally assault the newcomers with insults and demeaning questions. "What makes you think you're good enough to be a naval officer?" would be a mild example. Questioning a cadet's birth-legitimacy would be pushing the limits—there were rules—but was not unheard of. The answers were not as important as a demonstrated self-control. Did the cadet keep his anger in check? Was he properly respectful? The goal: to weed out those young men who could not handle pressure.

Of Chester's entering class, 114 made it through to graduation. Of those 114, Chester stood at number seven, a remarkable performance for an unsophisticated youngster who had not finished high school. From the start, he had continued his practice of early rising and had convinced his roommate to join him. They would get up at 4:30 to study, and off to a fast start, the pair were near the top of the class—until the middle of the semester when Chester caught pneumonia and spent a month in the hospital. (Vulnerability to diseases of the lungs may have been an unwelcome legacy from his father. During his lifetime, he would contract pneumonia at least three more times, and it would be the proximate cause of his death.) He was soon far behind in his classwork and catching up took native intelligence, diligence, and determination. With the help of his roommate, he was back near the top by the end of the school year. As a reward, he and his roommate were asked to split up and each room with a classmate who had not yet learned the secrets of academic success. They did so and coerced their new roommates to adopt the early-morning routine, with immediate result: everyone's grades improved.

Saturdays were for seamanship training aboard a large steel-hulled, square-rigged ship. By coincidence, the commanding officer and head of the Department of Seamanship was Commander William F. Halsey, father of Naval Cadet William F. (later known as "Bull") Halsey Junior, who was one year ahead of Chester. During Chester's senior year, the Navy's first submarine, the *Holland*, was based at Annapolis and the upperclassmen took turns going out in the bay on this curious new breed of warship. It was like a bathtub toy. None of them were much impressed.

Summer training cruises were a welcome break from routine, with new skills to be learned and new places to be visited. Chester cruised aboard two battleships and a destroyer—on which he developed an ear infection that affected him for the rest of his life. With no trained medical personnel in the small crew, the commanding officer elected to treat the infection with an antiseptic solution of boric acid squirted in the ear with a clean oil syringe. Whether from physical damage caused by the tool or the infection itself, Chester became slightly deaf in that ear. He developed some skill at lip reading to offset the handicap.

In September 1904, as they returned from their summer cruise, the seniors learned they would be graduating in January 1905, rather than June, to meet the needs of the fleet. Some classes were canceled and others doubled-up. And they were delighted to find they could move out of the makeshift Civil War–era quarters they had been occupying and into the newly built Bancroft Hall (then—and still—the largest dormitory building in the world). Nimitz, now a three-striper company commander, was assigned a private bedroom and an adjoining study he shared with another student. Several classmates quickly discovered a niche on part of the roof where they could gather, unseen from the street below or, for that matter, from any other vantage point inside or outside of the building, and drink beer.

One Saturday, the boys decided to have a beer bust, and Chester was the go-to guy to fetch the main ingredient. This led to an adventure that could have ended his hopes of a naval career, overnight. The seniors were now allowed to make trips into town to be fitted for uniforms, and Chester knew that he could get beer from his tailor. He carried a suitcase—as would anyone going to pick up some clothing—and headed right for the back room of the shop, where the suitcase was quickly loaded. He noticed someone else in the back room, a stranger, probably just another customer who was busy with his own business.

Chester lugged the suitcase back through the main gate, protected by the insignia of his exalted rank from challenge by the Marine on duty, and a grand party was had by all.

Monday morning, Chester marched his section into navigation class—to see, waiting in front of the classroom and wearing the uniform of a lieutenant commander, a new member of the faculty, the stranger from the tailor shop. He could not possibly have failed to recognize the curly-headed blond midshipman wearing three stripes on his sleeves, but he said nothing, then, or ever. Nimitz would later write, "This escapade . . . taught me to look with lenient and tolerant eye on first offenders."[3]

Another lesson Nimitz learned at Annapolis became the linchpin of his career. The Sampson-Schley controversy roiled the Navy—and soiled the Navy—just as Nimitz entered the academy. It started as a simple argument over who deserved credit for the defeat of the Spanish fleet at Santiago, Cuba, during the Spanish-American War. On one side was Rear Admiral William T. Sampson, commander of the Atlantic Fleet, who was away on other business when the battle erupted. On the other side was Commodore Winfield Scott Schley, the on-scene commander. After Sampson refused to acknowledge Schley's role in the battle, friends of Schley raised a ruckus and friends of Sampson said Schley did not deserve the honor. In a new Naval Academy textbook, the author accused him of cowardice and Schley demanded a court of inquiry to clear his name. Thereupon began the real circus. In September 1901, just as Chester was settling in, the Navy convened a three-officer court headed by the senior officer in the Navy, Admiral George Dewey. The court ran for forty-five days and collected 2,300 pages of testimony. There was daily, almost verbatim newspaper coverage, especially in the *Washington Post*, which favored Schley and ridiculed everyone else.

In the end, the court found against Schley two-to-one with Admiral Dewey in dissent. Schley refused to accept the verdict and appealed to President Theodore Roosevelt, who replied: "There is no excuse whatever . . . for further agitation of this unhappy controversy. To keep it alive would merely do damage to the Navy and to the country."[4] Throughout, the Navy was humiliated and Chester Nimitz made a vow: He would never be party to partisan, personal, or petty invective. Even four decades later, he refused to sign a battle report that denigrated a senior officer. "What are you trying to do," he said in a note to the author of the report, "start another Sampson-Schley controversy? Tone this down."[5]

As graduation day approached, the classmate who provided the Nimitz write-up for the Naval Academy yearbook, *Lucky Bag,* borrowed a few words from the poet William Wordsworth, "A man of cheerful yesterdays and confident tomorrows," and added, using the colloquial expression for Deutsch (German), "Possesses that calm and steady-going Dutch way that gets to the bottom of things."[6]

CHAPTER THREE

A PHILIPPINE ADVENTURE

C hester Nimitz spent his two years as a passed midshipman aboard the battleship *Ohio,* which was commissioned in October 1904 and sent to duty as flagship of the Asiatic Fleet. Nimitz and classmate Bruce Canaga reported for duty as the ship sailed from San Francisco on April 1, 1905, destination Manila.

They were sailing into a war zone, Russia versus Japan, although the *Ohio* was not going to be involved. Russia had been expanding its holdings in the Far East, obtaining a warm-water port (Port Arthur) from the Chinese, which it turned into a major naval base. It then moved forces into Manchuria and Korea. Meanwhile, Japan had emerged from centuries of isolation and transformed itself into a modern, industrialized nation.[1] It had about the same territorial ambitions as Russia, and soon the two were in conflict. Negotiations had failed, and in February 1904 Japan declared war but attacked the Russian naval base three hours before the declaration of war was delivered to the Russian government.

Russia's Baltic Fleet was sent to do battle, to reclaim lost territory, or at the least to salvage national dignity. After steaming 18,000 miles the ships were in desperate need of resupply, but the only available port was Vladivostok, far to the north. To get there, the Russian fleet had to sail between Korea and Japan, where Japanese Admiral Heihachiro Togo was lying in wait. With a slightly inferior but significantly better prepared force and an intelligence system assisted by the new technology called wireless telegraphy, Togo virtually annihilated the Russian fleet in the Battle of Tsushima Strait, May 27–28, 1905. The Russians lost eight battleships and more than 5,000 men. The Japanese lost three torpedo boats and 116 men.

President Theodore Roosevelt volunteered to act as mediator in a peace conference, held in August and September 1905, at the Portsmouth Naval Shipyard in Kittery, Maine. For his effort, Roosevelt was awarded the 1906 Nobel Peace Prize. He also earned the enmity of the Japanese government, which, though it agreed to the terms, was dissatisfied with the details. Among others, they expected reparations from the Russians. The war had cost them a lot of money; it didn't matter much that they had started it; the fabric of international diplomacy is often a very tangled web. Resentment would linger.

Admiral Togo was honored with a grand garden party at the imperial palace in Tokyo. It was quite an affair; several hundred tables well-stocked with Russian champagne captured at Port Arthur and a broad range of guests. The *Ohio*, which was in port, was invited to send a delegation. None of the senior officers were interested, so Nimitz and five other passed midshipmen represented the ship. They were seated at a table at the back, and when they spotted Admiral Togo slipping out of the party a bit early, Nimitz made so bold as to stand up and invite him to join them for a moment—which he did, for a brief but cordial conversation and a ceremonial sip of champagne. It was a most impressive gesture that Nimitz never forgot: the honorable admiral honoring the midshipmen.

Otherwise, the job of a newly arrived passed midshipman was to run errands, stand watch, learn as much as he could, and stay out of the way of the senior officers. Nimitz's first quarterly report rated him "Satisfactory." In the next report, after he had been assigned some actual duties that included serving as boat officer and assistant officer of the deck, the commanding officer wrote, "an excellent officer and I cheerfully commend him to the very favorable consideration of the Academic Board."[2]

At about the time Togo trounced the Russians, a flurry of anti-Japanese discrimination hit San Francisco. The good citizens were angry that immigrants from Japan were willing to work for low wages, thus upsetting the labor market. In a fit of stupidity, the San Francisco School Board announced a new policy designed to prevent "our children" from being "placed in any position where their youthful impressions may be affected by association with pupils of the Mongolian race." Japanese students would be taken out of "white" schools and moved to the "Oriental school" then serving the Chinese population.[3] In his annual address for 1906, President Roosevelt decried "mutterings" against the Japanese "because of their efficiency as workers," and affirmed his belief that "To shut them out from the public schools is a wicked absurdity."[4] The school board order was reiterated a week later, sparking violent protests in Japan. With some effort, Roosevelt negotiated a "gentleman's agreement" with Japan, which promised to restrict travel to the United States. The school board canceled the segregation order and things seemed to settle down.

When the *Ohio*'s tour as a flagship had ended, she returned to the United States; Nimitz and Canaga stayed behind in Manila. In February 1907 the newly promoted ensigns were assigned as commanding officers of a pair of gunboats, both of which had been captured from the Spanish in 1898. Nimitz had the *Panay*, and Canaga, the *Paragua*. Their mission was to show the flag to any restless natives who had not quite accommodated themselves to being under American control.[5]

These assignments are a good example of the U. S. Navy's way of testing young officers. As with the method of instruction at the Academy, it was a lot like throwing someone into the pool to see if they could swim. Of course, Nimitz and Canaga were not untrained innocents—they had been on summer cruises and had served almost two years in the fleet. But it was a bizarre assignment: the *Panay* and the *Paragua* were free to cruise around the southern islands of the Philippines, wherever Nimitz and Canaga chose, and they frequently operated together. The *Panay* had a crew of thirty sailors and two officers, Ensign Nimitz and Passed Midshipman John S. McCain (U.S. Naval Academy Class of 1906; later a vice admiral, and grandfather of the 2008 Republican presidential candidate). Nimitz also was in charge of a detachment of twenty-two Marines at a small facility on Mindanao.

The *Panay* was a bit cut off from the outside world (mail service was spotty) and was largely dependent on the local economy for food. Fresh duck—which the crew hunted themselves—was a favorite at first, but gradually wore out its welcome. One of the seamen told Nimitz he "couldn't look a duck in the beak again." Nimitz suggested they might try catching some eels, which, he understood, tasted like rattlesnake. "I have eaten rattlesnake," he said, "and it tastes pretty good." It seemed that duck was just fine after all.[6]

The assignment was a great start for a young officer; as Nimitz wrote his grandfather, "I can practice piloting and navigation and so forth . . . and besides it should teach me a certain amount of self-reliance and confidence."[7]

Meanwhile, back in California, the gentleman's agreement was not holding, and there were anti-Japanese riots in the streets of San Francisco. Immigrant workers were beaten by mobs. A few politicians in Japan called for war. Californians were thrown into a panic, fearful that an emboldened Japanese navy would appear offshore, and petitioned Roosevelt to send battleships to guard the coast. He replied that the purpose of a navy was not to scatter ships guarding harbors and seacoast cities but to remain as an element of offense. "The ships must be kept together and their objective made the enemy's fleet."[8] Nonetheless, to placate the nervous Californians, Roosevelt announced that he would send the entire battle fleet—sixteen battleships, plus accompanying auxiliaries—from Hampton Roads, Virginia, to San Francisco on a "training" cruise. But it would take some time, measured in months not weeks, to assemble the fleet and bring the ships around the southern tip of South America.

That provoked another panic, but this was in Manila, where naval authorities presumed that the Philippines were now a prime and immediate target. The American battle fleet was easily half again as large as the Japanese navy and, once in the Pacific, could serve as a check against Japanese adventuring. As the *New York Times* opined, "The moment the American fleet is stationed on the Pacific Coast Japan is absolutely stopped from sending her fleet away from home and there will be no expedition against the Philippines."[9]

But what might happen before the fleet reached the Pacific? Japan had already demonstrated, by destroying much of the Russian navy at Port Arthur before the Baltic Fleet had arrived on-scene, that it knew how to utilize a divide-and-conquer strategy. If Japan subdued America's Asiatic Fleet and occupied the Philippines before the main battle fleet arrived in the Pacific, would the United States go to war?

No one could know the answer, but after some ten months of cruising and duck hunting, the *Panay* was recalled to Manila. Time to regroup. There had been so much talk of war, and with the *Panay* so often out-of-touch, Nimitz didn't know what to expect as he approached the Cavite naval station. He was relieved to see it was still in American hands and prepared himself for the obligatory formal call on the senior officer present, Rear Admiral Uriah R. Harris. Admiral Harris was known as an unbending, by-the-book commander, and Nimitz reported in the appropriate dress white uniform, with sword.

Admiral Harris skipped the formalities and got right to the point: Ensign Nimitz was to take command of the destroyer *Decatur,* then swinging at a buoy in the inner harbor. His first challenge was to get the ship to dry dock at the Subic Bay Naval Station at Olongapo, some sixty miles away, within forty-eight hours.[10] Admiral Harris had a launch standing ready to take Nimitz—sword and all—out to the ship.

Commissioned in 1902, the *Decatur* was a state-of-the-art destroyer: 250 feet long, with two 3-inch guns, two 18-inch torpedo tubes, and a top speed of 28 knots. But it was not love at first sight; *Decatur* had been neglected for about a year. Everything was musty. Bits of equipment had been pinched off for use somewhere else. There was no fuel, no water for the boilers, no provisions for the crew—actually, there was no crew. Nimitz was greeted by a pair of Filipino watchmen. While he was looking around, a bit overwhelmed, the first members of a new crew, which soon would number three officers and seventy-three enlisted men, arrived in another launch.

Nimitz was being tested in an even better example of the navy way—throw the ensign in an empty pool and see if he could climb out. It was a rare honor for the 22-year-old Nimitz to be given command of a destroyer, although it was in large part a gift from the Japanese. He happened to be in the right place at the right time.

The first step was to get some help. Back in February, while the *Panay* was being readied for service, Nimitz spent time playing poker with some warrant officers at Cavite. They knew their way around the navy, how to cut through the red tape and deliver, and when Nimitz asked them for assistance, he got it by the bargeload: replacements for missing equipment and tons of coal and water. He and his crew turned-to with a will, loading, stowing, and installing, and within a day and a half were able to raise steam in one boiler. Enough to get to Olongapo.

Under the pressure of time, Nimitz did not run down the normal checklist before getting underway. He detached from the buoy and called for one-quarter-speed astern on the engine order telegraph—a mechanical device connected with the engine room—and the *Decatur* moved ahead. He called for full-speed-astern and the ship leaped forward. The telegraph had been hooked up in reverse.

Embarrassing, but no harm done. The problem was easily fixed, and despite sailing through unfamiliar waters with inadequate charts and running through a squall, Nimitz brought the ship to the navy yard at Olongapo on time. Challenge met.

Two weeks later, Nimitz had another challenge. Secretary of War William Howard Taft was visiting the Philippines as part of an around-the-world goodwill tour, and the *Decatur* was assigned to carry his party from Olongapo to Manila. The weather was nice and the guests would be sitting on deck chairs topside, enjoying the view. However, Taft was a very large man, plus or minus 300 pounds, and would not be comfortable in any navy standard-issue chair. Nimitz had a solution: He sent the ship's carpenter ashore to get two wicker lounge chairs and create one double-wide by removing the inside arms and lashing the chairs together.

Decatur was now ready for war with Japan, but Japan was not ready for war with the United States. The moment Roosevelt announced the fleet was headed for San Francisco, angry Japanese rhetoric was transformed into rational diplomatic discourse—big stick diplomacy at work. Then, in December, once the ships were actually underway from Hampton Roads, Roosevelt announced what had been his intention all along: The fleet was going to sail around the world. This would send a signal to navies everywhere that the United States had become a major player on the international stage. It would also, without doubt, be a great training exercise. Nothing like this had ever been attempted. Because the ships were all painted white—the normal peacetime dress for the U.S. Navy—the mission was known as the cruise of the Great White Fleet.

The announcement prompted fleet-visit requests from many nations, most notably Japan. Roosevelt was delighted; this was just what he had hoped for and perhaps had engineered with a bit of behind-the-scenes nudging. When the fleet arrived in Tokyo Bay in the middle of the next October, the Japanese could not have been nicer. Privately, the Japanese set the U.S. Navy as the one potential enemy they must become strong enough to defeat.

In the meantime, Nimitz and his ship were sent back to the cruising grounds he had just left, but with a bigger mission than duck hunting and showing the flag. For a time, the *Decatur* served as the flagship for the governor of the Sulu

Archipelago, the southernmost of the Philippine islands. Part of the governor's job was to adjudicate local disputes. With the governor aboard, the ship would drop anchor off a Sulu village, fire off a few rounds to impress the locals, then welcome a delegation aboard for a meeting.

In May, the *Decatur* sailed across the South China Sea to visit the capital city of French Indochina, Saigon. As Nimitz wrote to his grandfather, "The French there made a good deal of us, and we enjoyed ourselves immensely. They were interested a great deal in the *Decatur* and admired her very much on account of her size. Their largest torpedo boat destroyers are about half the size of the *Decatur*." In the same letter, he noted the downside of the trip: "Coming back from Saigon, I encountered my first, and I hope it may be my last, real live typhoon, and although my ship behaved remarkably well, for one of its size, we spent three very uncomfortable days."[11]

Not long after, Nimitz faced a more consequential challenge. Coming into Batangas Bay, 60 miles due south of Manila on the evening of July 7, 1908, he did not take bearings to verify his position but merely guessed. The leadsman on the bow was calling up soundings as usual, until he shouted, "We're not moving, sir!"

The ship was stuck on a mud bank, and as the tide was going out, it was going to remain stuck for some time. As his grandfather once told him, "Don't worry about things over which you have no control." So Nimitz set up a cot on deck and went to sleep.[12] Early the next morning, the *Decatur* attracted the attention of a passing steamer, which tossed over a line and pulled her off.

Although no damage was done, Nimitz had to report the grounding, which was one of the more serious categories of command error. He was immediately detached from the *Decatur* to await court-martial for "culpable inefficiency in the performance of duty." The court was sympathetic; the accused had a flawless record and the charts for Batangas were known to be inaccurate and incomplete. So Nimitz was found guilty but of a reduced charge, "neglect of duty." He was sentenced "to be publicly reprimanded." In approving the sentence, the convening authority wrote: "The promulgation of these findings and sentence will be regarded as constituting in itself a public reprimand, as required by the sentence of the court."[13]

The war scare had ended, and now out of a job, Nimitz was headed home. He thought he might join the Great White Fleet when it arrived in Manila, but

the fleet would not reach the Philippines for two months. Instead, two weeks after the court was finished, Nimitz sailed as a watch officer bringing the 35-year-
old sail/steam *Ranger* home from the Philippines. She could barely make 9
knots under power, maybe 10 knots if at the same time the sails were hoisted
to a favorable wind. The trip via Singapore, the Suez Canal, and the Mediterranean took just over three months. Even so, he beat the Great White Fleet back
by about ten weeks. Nimitz enjoyed a visit home to Texas—the first in almost
four years—and was ready for his next assignment.

He requested duty on a battleship.

CHAPTER FOUR

CHANGE OF COURSE

It may or may not have been punishment, but instead of coveted duty on a battleship, Nimitz was sent to submarines, then considered the dregs of the maritime community. In truth, a British admiral had declared that the submarine was "underhand, unfair, and damned UnEnglish." The government, he wrote, should "treat all submarines as pirates in wartime . . . and hang all crews."[1]

By 1909 the U.S. Navy did have a growing undersea fleet, with twenty-seven submarines in service or on order, but this was courtesy of Congress, which liked their low price tag. The Navy was not in thrall. At a congressional hearing, one admiral said submarines were merely interesting novelties. Another admiral opined that the thought of "those craft moving underwater would wear people out."[2] Not quite a ringing endorsement. Submarines, however, were not exactly novelties, but had been around for more than one hundred years with some degree of success.[3] Author Jules Verne celebrated the breed with *Twenty-Thousand Leagues Under the Sea*, published in 1870.

Nimitz's first submarine command, *Plunger,* was the second American submarine, which had been commissioned in 1903. It was 64-feet long with one torpedo tube, three torpedoes, a skipper, and six sailors. With remarkable good humor, Nimitz described his new charge as a "cross between a Jules Verne fantasy and a humpbacked whale."[4] After a period of instruction he settled in with this new challenge. And it was, a challenge. At one point, after a two-day open-ocean transit, *Plunger* was inspected by a medical officer. It was not a happy moment. The doctor reported, among other findings, that although the boat had only been at sea for 45 hours, her sanitary condition was far from satisfactory. Indeed, in all of the early boats, habitability was problematic. Inside the hull there was only one space, with no interior bulkheads to create separate compartments. There was a toilet, but it was out in the open. Fresh air for running the gasoline engines used for surface propulsion (and to recharge the batteries used when submerged) was sucked down through the conning tower and passed through the crew quarters; it was not ducted directly to the engines. In winter, as a consequence, the crew got very cold. Mattresses on the bunks were thin, usually damp, and always uncomfortable. Gasoline fumes, heavier than air, collected in the bilges, and there was always the danger of an explosion. Just breathing the fumes hour after hour was a health hazard, one not fully recognized at the time. Nimitz became a champion for switching from gasoline to more stable diesel engines, which would at least eliminate the explosion hazard.

Nimitz was promoted to lieutenant in January 1910 and a month later went to his next command, *Snapper,* a floating test bed for new technologies that included radio, a submarine signaling apparatus, and different types of batteries. In November 1910 Nimitz became commanding officer of the submarine *Narwhal* and briefly—at the end of his one-year tour—had additional duty as commander of the Third Submarine Division, Atlantic Torpedo Fleet. He was learning the trade.

In April 1911 Nimitz suffered a deep personal loss when his grandfather died at the age of 84. Nimitz received an inheritance that he passed to his mother, to whom he had been sending twenty-five dollars a month ever since he was commissioned—about 25 percent of his pay. Money was never a major factor in his life.

The Navy decided to try a diesel drive with a new boat, *Skipjack,* and with great logic assigned diesel-champion Nimitz as her first commanding officer. However, by the time he took over in February 1912, the Navy had decided to redesignate all submarines, replacing the traditional names with letters signifying a design class. Thus, *Skipjack* became E-1 (the first boat in the E-class).[5] By this time Nimitz had had six afloat commands in six years. Short tours of a year or less were about the norm for seagoing command. The idea was to cycle as many officers as possible through a variety of assignments, increasing knowledge and capability while establishing a record of performance. But the Nimitz record of six afloat commands in six years may well be unique.

Each of Nimitz's four submarine commands was a significant improvement over the last. Size increased from 64 feet to 134 feet, crew from six to nineteen, armament from one torpedo tube to four (with eight torpedoes in the ammunition locker), surface endurance from less than 600 miles at 8 knots to 2,090 miles at 11 knots. But the latest model German "undersea boat," or U-boat—about the same size as E-1—had a range of 7,800 miles (a round trip from Europe to New York with more than 1,000 miles to spare) at 8 knots. It was as if the U.S. Navy was merely experimenting, hoping to get it right, while the Germans knew exactly where they were headed.

At this point, Nimitz had gained a fair amount of experience in submarine operations and was invited to address the Naval War College. He chose as his topic, "Defensive and Offensive Tactics of Submarines." His basic premise (shared with most experts) was that because of limited mobility and armament, submarines were best suited to coast defense and harbor protection. He offered an innovative method for forcing enemy ships away from safe areas and into submarine-patrolled waters: "Drop numerous poles, properly weighted to float upright in the water, and painted to look like a submarine's periscope."[6]

For Lieutenant Nimitz, 1912 was a seminal year. In March, he saved the life of one of his crew who had fallen overboard while E-1 was moored at the Fore River Shipyard in Massachusetts. The man was not a good swimmer, and Nimitz jumped into the frigid water and found himself fighting both the panicked sailor and the heavy current. He managed to keep the man afloat but was not having much luck with the current until, headed out to sea, the pair was spotted by someone aboard the battleship *North Carolina*, which quickly mounted a rescue. For his effort, Nimitz was awarded the Treasury Department / Coast Guard Silver Lifesaving Medal. It may have been his most cherished award, because cause and effect were so directly related.

In May Nimitz became commander of the Atlantic Submarine Flotilla.

In August, in a more significant promotion, he became engaged to twenty-year-old Catherine Freeman, who lived in Wollaston, a few miles from the shipyard. They had met some months earlier when Nimitz and a friend from the Naval Academy, a neighbor of the Freemans, were invited in for a round of bridge. Nimitz was "paired" with Catherine. From that point forward, whenever he was out at sea or out of touch, Nimitz would write Catherine about a letter a day, even if the letters couldn't be mailed until sometime later. This was a practice he continued for the rest of their lives. They were married in April 1913.

At about the same time, satisfied with the performance of small diesel engines in submarines, the Navy decided to test them in a large surface ship. However, it had only been sixteen years since Rudolf Diesel had perfected his commercially viable engine and no one then connected with the Navy knew anything about the construction and installation of large diesel engines. Nimitz and two civilians from the New York Navy Yard (located in Brooklyn) were sent on a fact-finding and training mission to Germany, the heart of the diesel world. Nimitz was selected for his experience in operating a diesel power plant—but also because he spoke German.

Nimitz and his bride sailed on a commercial liner in May. Call it a working honeymoon, with visits to five cities in Germany and a side trip to Denmark and Sweden. It was also a period of hard work and long hours, with much to learn in a short span of time. Nimitz found the German naval officers with whom he sometimes conferred to be cold, arrogant, and unbending, until they learned that he too was a naval officer, when they became a bit more accommodating.

Chester and Catherine returned home in late summer, their family of two about to become three: Daughter Catherine, nicknamed Kate, was born February 22, 1914, followed just a year later by a son, Chester Junior. Later, two more daughters would join the family: Anna, nicknamed Nancy, in 1919, and Mary in 1931.

CHAPTER FIVE

THE GREAT WAR

Back at the New York Navy Yard by late summer, 1913, Nimitz was assigned to the Machinery Division. His job: to supervise the manufacture of two 2,600-horsepower diesels to be installed—also under his supervision—in the *Maumee*, a 14,500-ton oiler (the Navy version of a commercial tanker) then under construction. The ship would enter service toward the end of 1916.

Nimitz enjoyed showing off the new diesel engines. One time, a group of especially important visitors came to see the ship, so he put on his dress white uniform, complete with gloves, the fingers of which were about an inch longer than his hand. One of the visitors asked a technical question, and to illustrate his answer, Nimitz gestured toward a set of rotating gears without really looking at them. His gesture was too close. The gears grabbed the glove and started pulling his hand into the works. He was saved from disaster by his Naval Academy class ring, which jammed the machinery long enough for him to pull his hand back out, now missing part of a finger. He was rushed to the dispensary where the wound was treated. Nimitz, his system in shock and his hand totally numb, was anxious to get back to his guests and finish his demonstration. The doctor suggested he might want to wait just a bit. Sure enough, he was soon hit by excruciating pain and sent to bed.

As the military market for diesels grew, engine manufacturers saw a need to hire diesel-qualified executives with military experience and contacts, a rare combination. The Busch-Sulzer Brothers Diesel Engine Company of St. Louis was not involved with the *Maumee* but was aware of Nimitz's work on the project. One day in 1915, a company recruiter stopped by to offer him a job at $25,000 a year with a five-year contract. Nimitz said, "No thank you, I do not want to leave the Navy." The recruiter said, "Money is no obstacle to us. Write your own ticket." After a brief pause, Nimitz repeated, "No, I don't want to leave the Navy." At that time, his annual salary was $3,456, and that $25,000 today would be well over half-a-million. Money was never a major factor in his life.[1]

During the three years that it took to build the *Maumee*, much of the western world—the United States not yet included—went to war and the lowly, widely despised submarine came into its own. In June 1914, just before hostilities began, a rather prescient British admiral proclaimed, "As the motor car has driven the horse from the road, so has the submarine driven the battleship from the sea." He was roundly attacked and his prediction called "a fantastic dream."[2]

It wasn't long before the "dream" became a nightmare. The submarine came of age on September 22, 1914, when one German U-boat sank three British cruisers in just over 90 minutes. Germany, which began the war with twenty-six operational U-boats, went on a building spree.

On November 2, 1914, Great Britain established a naval blockade against Germany—a country heavily dependent upon imports, even for food. But Britain was every bit as dependent on imports as Germany, which sent forth its U-boat fleet in a counterblockade.

Using submarines in a blockade against merchant ships was problematic: Under international law, a warship could stop and search a merchantman. If found to be carrying contraband cargo in support of the enemy, the merchant ship could be captured and a "prize crew" would then be set aboard to sail her to an appropriate harbor. Under some circumstances, the ship could be sunk, provided that the ship's crew had been allowed to take to the lifeboats first. A submarine, however, did not carry enough sailors to make up a prize crew, so its only option was to sink the merchant ship. But, if the submarine came to the surface to give fair warning, she herself became vulnerable to attack by ramming, by concealed guns, or by warships rushing to the rescue. German policy went through several cycles, "warn" or "not warn." They tried to play by the rules, but, while the growing U-boat fleet was sinking British merchant ships faster than replacements could be built, the submarine losses were high.

In February 1917, the German government announced total "unrestricted" submarine warfare. In a note to the secretary of state, the German ambassador to the United States offered justification: "England is using her naval power for a criminal attempt to force Germany into submission by starvation." The legal requirement for "fair notice" was met, in theory, by declaring a specifically designated war zone around the British Isles within which all vessels were subject to attack "by every available weapon and without further notice."[3] On April 6, 1917, after U-boats sank several American merchant ships operating within the zone, the United States declared war on Germany.

In the meantime, the *Maumee* had been at sea for six months, with Commander Henry C. Dinger as skipper and newly promoted Lieutenant Commander Nimitz in the dual role of chief engineer and executive officer. They were operating on the south side of Cuba to provide support to the Atlantic Fleet, then on winter maneuvers. At first, the ships were refueled in a manner similar to that which had been employed when ships burned coal, rather than oil: the oiler and the customer were moored side-by-side in a sheltered bay or harbor, and the oil was transferred by hose from one to the other. But in this period, Nimitz and Dinger developed a revolutionary method of pumping oil between ships while both were underway, with the oiler towing the other ship astern.

Upon the declaration of war, *Maumee* was ordered to take up a position 300 miles south of Greenland to provide fuel to destroyers headed for Ireland. This would be the first operational test of the underway method, and despite heavy weather, bitter-cold winds, and drifting icebergs, the system worked. Thirty-four destroyers were refueled and the underway method was validated.

By February 1918, Nimitz had been promoted to commander and was assigned as chief of staff to Rear Admiral Samuel S. Robison, commander of the Atlantic Fleet submarine force. The pair headed off to Europe to gather information about British and French submarine operations that could be passed along to American crews. But the war ended before American submarines could have much impact. By late summer, 1918, much of Germany was in rebellion; the Allied blockade had cut off almost all imports, people were starving, sailors were refusing to go into battle, and the government moved toward armistice.

The years of carnage in the trenches of France made the headlines and the history books, but the effect of the Allied blockade transcended all; the war might well have been settled without the muddy bloodshed.[4]

Germany started the war with those 26 operational boats, the crash building program added 390, and the Allies and accidents cost them 173. It was an astonishing casualty rate, but so was their success: U-boats sank more than 4,000 ships, more than 11 million tons—fully one-fourth of the world's total supply.

Nimitz next served six month's duty in the office of the Chief of Naval Operations as a member of the Board of Submarine Design, which was focused on developing a submarine for operation in the Pacific Ocean—a submarine that could handle heavy weather, with exceptional range, high reliability, and a reasonable level of habitability. Next, Nimitz finally got his battleship duty, a one-year tour as executive officer of the *South Carolina,* helping to bring back the thousands of soldiers remaining in Europe. The ship carried about one thousand men per trip. It was important but dull work; Nimitz spent much of his time working on a Naval War College correspondence course.

In 1920 he was assigned as commander of Submarine Division 14, sixteen brand-new R-class boats based at Pearl Harbor. That name was not some romantic tag to charm the tourists; the area teemed with pearl-producing oysters until the Hawaiians began turning the Pearl River into a commercial port. The U.S. Navy was granted rights to use the harbor in 1887, and began developing the area about ten years later. Those efforts did not include a submarine base, and it was up to Nimitz to build one for his boats. This was an interesting challenge: He was given no particular budget for the project, but authorized to locate, acquire, and ship appropriate items of war surplus from the East Coast to Pearl Harbor.

For starters, Nimitz found a number of single-story bungalow "house kits," in which all materials were precut and numbered for easy erection. At Pearl Harbor, the houses were assembled end-to-end in long rows, their kitchens and bathrooms eliminated and interior partitions modified to provide more than a dozen warehouses and shop buildings.

That was easy. The hard part was to gather the components for a complete machine shop and foundry from East Coast shipyards. Understandably, shipyard commanders were loath to part with materials that someday, maybe, they might use. Nimitz was allowed to take some things, but not as much as he needed. With a bit of logistic legerdemain, a team of four chief petty officers— members of a group known for being forehanded, ingenious, and at times unscrupulous—filled in the gaps. On occasion, under cover of darkness, a truck might back up to a warehouse or storage yard and "liberate" items that for the most part were not carried on any accountable inventory—they were simply things left over from the war. It wasn't as if the team was stealing; the items all remained property of the U. S. government. Nimitz avoided knowing what was being taken and from where, and it wasn't until he arrived in Hawaii that he learned his personal kit included one non-war-surplus staff car formerly assigned to the commander of a Navy base. If the loss was ever reported, the information never made it to Pearl Harbor.

Submarine crews were pressed into duty preparing the ground, uprooting large cacti, smoothing out small hills, and filling in gullies. By the time Nimitz arrived, that work was well underway. Awaiting him also was the cruiser *Chicago*, which had transported most of the materials from the East Coast and was now assigned as the immobile receiving ship and floating barracks for the submarine base. (In 1928, the proud old ship was renamed *Alton*, thus freeing up the name of the nation's second city for a new-construction cruiser, put in service in 1931.) With most of the construction now being handled by qualified contractors, Nimitz could turn his attention to the needs of his division.

He heard that some of his R-class boats were having trouble with their diesel engines, so he invited the division engineer officer in for a conversation. The officer started right out complaining—the engines don't work right, the design is all wrong, etc. Nimitz let him ramble on, then offered some perspective. "You know, I was in on the design of those engines. I supervised the construction. I supervised the test and evaluation. I don't remember any problems such as you describe." The problems seemed miraculously to disappear.[5]

Another incident involved skipper Stuart S. Murray, who was having trouble parking his R boat alongside another submarine; this was no surprise since the R boats, at 186 feet, two-thirds the length of a football field, were the longest model to date but were significantly under-powered. Either the nose would bang into the other boat, or the tail would bump—usually bending some propeller blades. That was Murray's fate, and he had to report the damage to "Commodore" Nimitz.[6]

Nimitz accepted his report, and said, "Every one of my submarine commanders has a starting credit: one tail and one nose, or two tails, or two noses. If he uses up that credit, he will be in trouble with me. You are only half gone, you only used one tail, now go back and try not to take the rest of your credit."[7]

Typical Nimitz. Murray (who retired as a four-star admiral in 1956) took that advice and learned how, with great care, to come alongside without mishap.

CHAPTER SIX

CHANGE AND CHALLENGE

W hile Nimitz was replacing fields of cacti with support for a flotilla of submarines, the Navy was reorganizing the fleet into two main components: the Battle Fleet—the newest battleships and destroyers based in the Pacific (to counter that most likely threat, Japan); and the Scouting Fleet—older battleships and destroyers, based in the Atlantic. A third force was the very limited Asiatic Fleet, based in Manila. Each fleet had its own commander in chief.

In 1921 the Navy tested the effectiveness of aerial bombs on warships. The old battleship *Indiana* was one of the first test ships. It sank, as expected, from controlled detonations of bombs positioned on or near the ship. Although no aircraft were involved, on hearing this news, Brigadier General William L. "Billy" Mitchell, assistant chief of the Army Air Service, told the Congressional Committee on Naval Affairs, "We can tell you definitely now that we can either destroy or sink any ship in existence today . . . give us the warships to attack and come and watch it."[1]

Nonetheless, the Navy tests continued—involving both gunfire and aerial bombing. One test used dummy bombs against a radio-controlled ship. Eighty-five bombs were dropped by twenty-four planes with two hits. In a similar British test, 114 bombs were dropped with no hits. Whatever General Mitchell *believed*, in reality, the standard bomber of the day was not an effective weapon against maneuvering ships. These lackluster results led the Navy to develop two types of antiship aircraft, the dive bomber and the torpedo plane. The pilot of a dive bomber pointed his plane at the target and waited until the last moment before releasing the bomb. The torpedo plane launched a self-propelled weapon at the side of the ship. Both would play a major role in World War II.

Mitchell accused the Navy—in the public press—of avoiding a true test, and demanded an opportunity to participate. Under some pressure, Secretary of the Navy Edwin Denby agreed. Soon enough, several ships had been sunk. Most sinkings were unremarkable, but one has been preserved forever in dramatic motion picture footage: The anchored German battleship *Ostfriesland* sank in only ten minutes on July 21, 1921. Planes could sink ships. As of that moment, Mitchell assumed, the Navy was obsolete.

In reality, the *Ostfriesland* had been under attack by U.S. Army, Navy, and Marine Corps aircraft over a period of two days, on the first of which fifty-two bombs were dropped at point-blank altitudes from 1,200 feet (about the height of the Empire State Building) to 2,000 feet. They had thirteen hits, of which only four exploded. The ship was immobile, had no antiaircraft protection to ward off attackers, and no crew aboard to control damage. The hull was leaking before the test and weakened with each attack; the ship began flooding, overnight, all night, without operating pumps. A bombing run the next morning added to the damage and *Ostfriesland* was finished off later in the day by six 2,000-pound bombs. There were no hits, but three near-misses did the job. The ship rolled over and sank ten minutes after the last bomb. This was some twenty-four hours after the first attacks had been made, but Mitchell and his supporters were not about to let the facts get in the way of a good story.[2]

Just as the bombing tests were ending, the Navy began testing a new type of warship, the aircraft carrier. This was a concept pioneered by the British and adopted by the U.S. Navy with the experimental carrier *Langley*, which entered service in 1922.

And, while the U.S. Navy was planning for the future, the world's navies embarked on a course of limited self-destruction known as the Washington Naval Treaty of 1922. The treaty, it was hoped, would prevent an unfettered naval arms race by limiting the number and size of warships, and the number of men in the service. The two largest maritime nations, Great Britain and the United States, were each allowed 525,000 tons of battleships and heavy cruisers and 135,000 tons of aircraft carriers. The treaty forced the United States to retire some older ships, to limit new shipbuilding programs, and to scrap some that were already underway. The hulls of two planned cruisers were converted to become the first U.S. Navy aircraft carriers built to the purpose, the *Lexington* and the *Saratoga*, which would enter service in 1927. Japan could have 315,000 and 81,000 tons, respectively; France and Italy each 175,000 and 60,000 tons. No single ship could exceed 35,000 tons. Japan, insulted at being relegated to the second tier, was the first to pull out of the treaty in 1934, and the rest followed soon after.

In this period of great ferment, Chester Nimitz spent the academic year 1922–1923 at the Naval War College, studying history and simulating war games. There, Nimitz would later write, "The enemy of our games was always—Japan."[3] The reasons were not xenophobic but geopolitical. Not only had Japanese-American relations deteriorated following the Russo-Japanese War, the post–World War I expansion of Japanese holdings to formerly German-held islands in the Marshalls, the Carolines, and the Marianas threatened the American-held Philippines.

Nimitz and his classmates pondered the problem. If each major island had an airbase, what was the likely range of operation? Would the whole ocean be covered or were there gaps? Where might the aircraft carrier, as yet untried, fit in? And most important: How would the operating fleet be supported over the vast reaches of the Pacific? Postwar, Nimitz would tell a colleague that "the courses were so thorough . . . that nothing that happened in the Pacific was strange or unexpected," and that "each student was required to plan logistic support for an advance across the Pacific."[4]

He wrote his thesis on the World War I Battle of Jutland, which involved some 250 ships divided between Britain's Grand Fleet and Germany's High Seas Fleet. Jutland had no impact on the war, but it had a major influence on future operations. The cruising formation of the British fleet of twenty-four battleships was in six parallel columns, protected from submarines by a cloud of destroyers and preceded by a scouting force of cruisers and destroyers stretching out for twenty miles. Changing course was a nightmare. Smoke and mist often obscured visibility so much that it could take ten minutes for a signal from the flagship in the vanguard to reach the last ship in line. Then, as action neared, commanders had only minutes to make decisions based on minimal information. Where was the enemy? In what force? On what course? In what formation?

For the Royal Navy, Jutland sparked the development of the aircraft carrier, initially not as an attack vehicle but for reconnaissance, to get the eyes of the fleet much farther out in advance of the force.

For the United States Navy, the problem of large fleet maneuvering sparked the development of a radical approach, the circular formation. One day, working on the game board, War College classmate Commander Roscoe C. McFall set up a plot with the battleships in the center, surrounded by cruisers and destroyers in expanding concentric circles. At a signal from the flagship at the center, which could be read by all ships at the same time, changing course became a simple evolution. At the time, of course, it was just a War College exercise.

Just as Nimitz's academic sojourn was ending in June 1923, Admiral Samuel Robison became commander in chief of the Battle Fleet and took Nimitz as his flag aide, assistant chief of staff, and tactical officer. Nimitz's studies at the War College were largely theoretical; serving as a senior staff officer with the Navy's major operating fleet would be the ultimate in professional education.

Nimitz soon saw an opportunity to test the circular formation. The concept was rejected out-of-hand by Admiral Robison and many commanding officers—they were not comfortable with the idea. In a traditional formation, each ship is either directly ahead, astern, or abeam of one or more other ships, and maintaining the assigned position was a simple matter of staying lined up, aided by a hand-held distance-measuring instrument, the stadimeter. In the circular formation, you were not lined up with other ships but were stationed at a set point on a line of bearing from the guide ship, which was sitting in the center. Measuring and maintaining the bearing took some effort even in daylight and was a real problem at night.

After some mild arm-twisting, Robison agreed to a trial. The circular formation was a revelation. Upon a signal from the guide, all ships would change course at the same time, right, left, or reverse, all in unison. Antisubmarine and antiaircraft assets were always on the periphery, completely surrounding the battleships. Off and on over the next few years, the fleet played with, but did not formally adopt, the concept. Old habits die hard.

In 1924 the Battle Fleet tested the defenses of the Panama Canal, joined the Scouting Fleet in tactical exercises, worked with the Army, and supported the Marines in amphibious exercises. One exercise tested the ability of the fleet to conduct extended, transoceanic operations, and underway replenishment was a key component. Two variations were employed: towing astern for destroyers and alongside for larger ships (the first time this method was used during actual fleet maneuvers). The Marines tested prototype landing craft and methods of assault and found there was much room for improvement. A Marine Corps historian would later write, "The 1924 Fleet Problems . . . were well worthwhile, because almost every possible mistake occurred." Which is, of course, why you have such exercises. Another historian noted, "There were serious problems in terms of command relationships, in particular when operating with the Army."[5]

The fleet was joined at times by the *Langley*, but the carrier was treated as a curious appendage. To gain enough airflow across the deck to launch airplanes, the carrier had to turn into the wind. Since the fleet was almost always on a different course, the *Langley* would be somewhere off to the side while launching and retrieving airplanes, accompanied by two destroyers, not for defense, but to pluck unlucky aviators from the water.

Nimitz convinced Robison that there had to be a better way. He argued that the *Langley* should be fully integrated and train with the Battle Fleet. Robison passed the suggestion to the Navy Department, but the Bureau of Aeronautics believed that the *Langley*, which was still an experiment, needed a great deal of development and testing before it would be ready. Robison kept pushing, and the *Langley* joined the Battle Fleet in November 1924. The next time the fleet went to sea, Nimitz set up a circular formation with the *Langley* at the center: it was an immediate success. When time came to launch, the whole formation would turn into the wind, keeping antisubmarine and antiaircraft defenses intact.

In 1925 the fleet tested the defenses of the Hawaiian Islands in the first U.S. Navy maneuvers ever held in the Pacific. Admiral Robison's Battle Fleet, with 11 battleships, 6 light cruisers, 56 destroyers, and the *Langley*, played the enemy, designated as "Black." They managed to reach Hawaiian waters undetected. The home team—dubbed "Blue"—had reconnaissance aircraft, but their range was limited and the weather was poor.

After the exercise, some 800 officers met in a large Navy recreation hall for a five-day critique. The consensus: Hawaiian defenses were weak, facilities for aircraft and fleet alike were limited, and the islands were "inadequate to meet the strain of war."[6]

There was another (and predictable) dimension to the exercise. As headlined in the *Washington Post,* "Japanese See War Threat by America in Fleet Maneuver."[7] According to the *New York Times,* Japanese newspapers called the exercise "a menace" and the "secret training of American seamen for an attack on Japan."[8]

Next, the Battle Fleet made a three-month round of visits to Samoa, Australia, New Zealand, and Tasmania. This was not a casual effort; it involved 11 battleships, 4 light cruisers, more than 30 destroyers, 13 supply ships, and some 27,000 sailors and Marines. The fleet conducted tactical exercises with local forces, demonstrating U.S. capabilities, and the visits generated a great deal of goodwill while at the same time alarming officials in Japan. When pressed for their reason for concern, they cited no specifics, noting only that the visits were "suspicious."[9]

In October 1925, Robison (with Nimitz in tow) shifted his flag to the heavy cruiser *Seattle* as he moved up to a one-year tour as commander in chief of the United States Fleet (CINCUS), a post that combined both the Battle Fleet and the Scouting Fleet. When that tour ended, Robison and Nimitz were both off to shore duty. Without their strong support, the integration of the carrier and the circular formation fell into disuse, although it was resurrected somewhat in 1930 through the efforts of Lieutenant Commander Forrest P. Sherman. The "battleship navy" simply didn't understand. It was not until after the Japanese attack on Pearl Harbor, December 7, 1941—which took out the heart of the battleship force but left the carriers untouched—that the old guard realized that the game had changed, forever.

CHAPTER SEVEN

THE PROFESSOR

The Great War had shown that the U.S. Navy couldn't meet the demands for officers during a rapid expansion of the force; an experiment with a three-month cram course called the "Midshipman School" was not very effective. The force needed a cadre of trained and experienced officers, larger than could be produced by the Naval Academy alone, ready to go but held in reserve.

Therefore, the Navy moved to emulate the successful college-level Army Reserve Officers Training Program (ROTC)—which provided classroom and some field military training roughly equivalent to, although not as intense as, that offered at West Point. The Navy set up six Naval ROTC units, at Northwestern, Yale, Harvard, Georgia Tech, the University of Washington, and the University of California (UC) at Berkeley. The program began in the fall semester of 1926, with Nimitz as the first professor of naval science at Berkeley. He was assisted by Lieutenant Commander Ernest Gunther and four chief petty officers.

There was a bit of irony in this assignment, and some personal discomfort. Here he was, a 41-year-old Navy commander, who not only lacked a college degree (not granted at Annapolis until the class of 1933) but hadn't even graduated high school. Now he was ranked as a full professor and dean of his department in an environment where advanced degrees and earned status counted for everything.

There were some touchy moments. At a staff meeting, the head of the department of astronomy learned that Nimitz planned to teach a class on nautical astronomy, a key element in the education and training of any naval officer. He complained—loudly—that this was an invasion of his professional domain. Nimitz quietly asked if the professor might be willing—as he was far more qualified—to take over this course? The professor agreed.[1] Thus, the Department of Naval Science was able to shift a small responsibility off to another department, freeing up time to address other subjects. Over time, jealousies evaporated as Nimitz slowly gained the confidence of the rest of the faculty and was invited to serve on the university's faculty promotion board and new-faculty search committee.

The NROTC program was in two parts of two years each. The first two years—the basic course—offered three hours a week of instruction in navigation, ordnance, and seamanship. The advanced course added a fourth hour for engineering. At drills, students wore uniforms like those at the Naval Academy but were called "naval reserve students," rather than "midshipmen." There was no scholarship or other monetary compensation in the basic course, but students in the advanced course received a $210 subsistence allowance. There were also three summer cruises of fifteen days each for which the students were paid seventy cents a day, but only the cruise during the advanced course was mandatory. Graduates of the full four-year program would be eligible for commissions as ensigns in the Naval Reserve, have the opportunity to attend drills with annual compensation of two months active duty pay, and be on call in the event of war.

The first real problem at UC Berkeley: No students signed up for this brand-new program. Nimitz and Gunther posted announcements around campus and set up a table in a high-traffic area, where they cajoled passersby. Nimitz, looking very official in his dress whites, cruised the campus and buttonholed likely prospects. One young man asked if it made any difference that his father was a colonel in the Army; Nimitz assured him that it did not. The student, James D. Archer, gladly came aboard, perhaps relieved that he might thus be freed from subtle familial pressure to "Go Army." And, he induced his roommate, Tracy D. Cuttle, to enroll also.

Eventually—to his embarrassment—Nimitz attracted more candidates than the program could accommodate. Eighty showed up for the first muster, and twenty had to be told, "Gentlemen, I'm very sorry . . . I will call out twenty names. They will have to go."[2] In the confusion, Nimitz enrolled one student from Finland who was not a United States citizen. This was not an underhanded ploy by the student; he was just never asked. Onnie P. Lattu corrected that oversight and became a citizen before graduation.

Nimitz, obviously, had not been trained as a teacher but had hands-on experience with the subject matter and sufficient experience as a student to establish a program. He adapted some aspects of the Naval Academy practice: The instructors assigned material for study at the end of each class and held a quiz at the beginning of the next. However, while the Naval Academy quizzed students by sending them to the blackboard to be critiqued by the instructor, Nimitz elected for something easier to evaluate, because it created a paper trail that could be saved and reviewed. On entering the classroom, the students drew slips of paper on which were one or more questions related to the day's assignment. The students had twenty minutes to write their answers, and then the instructors would conduct a thirty-minute teaching and discussion session. This certainly was more rigorous than in many of the other classes at the university where students might drift along from week to week, hitting the books only when confronted by a major exam.

The NROTC final exam for the first semester was a three-hour comprehensive open-book review. This was significantly longer than the university standard of one hour, and the students rebelled en masse, turning in blank exam books in protest. When they showed up to register for the next semester of the program, each was handed a note requesting his presence in the office of the dean of men. They learned that by failing to meet the requirements for the last class, they were blocked from enrolling in the next. As the emotional dust was settling, Nimitz walked into the room. "Gentlemen," he said, "I'm going to abide by the rules of the university and I expect you to do so also. I understand that you only have to have one hour for a final exam. So that's what you will have, but you have to take it this afternoon."

Of course, he gave them the original three-hour exam, on which no one did very well. As they turned in their answers at the end of the hour, he said, "I hope this will make better sailors out of you."[3] Was this overly harsh, the mark of a narrow-minded martinet? Not if you allow for the consideration he gave one freshman, poorly prepared in math in high school, to take as much time as he needed—more than six hours—to complete an important exam in navigation. The student passed, albeit barely, but earned high praise for determination.

Nimitz was always attuned to the interests of his students. Joseph Chase was interested in aviation, so Nimitz arranged a series of orientation flights with some basic instruction from the Naval Reserve air unit in Oakland. Chase went on to Navy flight training, became a pilot for Pan American Airways, and during the war assisted Nimitz in mapping air supply and escape routes across the Pacific.

Commander and Mrs. Nimitz believed that socializing with the students was an important part of the job, and on Saturdays they would usually have several to their home for lunch. The students formed a Quarterdeck Club and often invited the pair to their functions, most of which involved dancing. The commander would gamely waltz a coed or two, and Mrs. Nimitz would assay a few steps with one of the students.

At one point, Onnie Lattu invited Nimitz and Gunther to a lunch at his fraternity house. They arrived in their dress white uniforms just as a few of the fraternity brothers were engaged in some extracurricular hijinks. As he was getting out of the car, Nimitz got hit full-on with a bag of water thrown down from an upstairs window. He was not the intended target but was the only one hit. Drenched and dripping, he went on in, chatted amiably with his hosts, sat down to lunch, and never said a word.

After one year in the job, Nimitz was promoted to captain. As enrollment increased, so did the size of the staff. When Nimitz's three-year tour was over, in June 1929, the program had about 150 students and the staff included six commissioned officers and six petty officers. His relief as CO of the unit was Captain Bruce Canaga, his partner in patrolling the Philippines back in 1907.

Nimitz believed that his teaching philosophy, a hybrid of the Naval Academy style and contemporary civilian practice, was an improvement over both. As at the Naval Academy, it was a focused regimen that required the student to dig out things for himself. To that, Nimitz added the daily tracking and a broader civilian-style lecture and discussion period. In 1928, his mentor Admiral Robison—with whom Nimitz had been sharing his pedagogical thoughts—became superintendent of the Naval Academy and introduced the Nimitz method. It did not quite catch on. There was—surprise!—some resentment among the faculty at having the half-brained ideas of an amateur thrust upon them. However, Robison and several of his successors managed to impose a few Nimitz-inspired changes, especially his method of daily testing and grading.

Long-term, the U.S. Naval Academy drifted toward a university system that put less demand on both students and instructors.

In a 1928 article for the Naval Institute *Proceedings,* Nimitz mused, "Has the government made a wise investment in the establishment of the Naval ROTC? We think that in the passage of time this question will be answered in the affirmative."[4] For the record, the NROTC flourished. By the end of World War II, the program was offered at fifty-two colleges and universities. The students were now called "midshipmen" and provided full tuition, books, and a monthly stipend of $50. By the 1950s, some graduates received regular (rather than reserve) commissions in the U.S. Navy, to serve on par with their Naval Academy contemporaries.

The long-range track record for the first UC Berkeley class was a bit spotty. Of the sixty students, only twenty-one made it through to graduation. The others had not failed the NROTC, but most had dropped out of school altogether, especially following the financial shocks of the stock market crash of 1929. Among the graduates of the Class of June 1930: Onnie Lattu went on to a career in the Supply Corps, retiring as a rear admiral; he was one of the first NROTC graduates of any school to make flag rank. Archer became a lawyer and effectively dropped out of participation in the reserves until the war, when, embarrassed that he had abandoned the opportunity to be involved, he managed to get his commission reinstated (with assistance from Admiral Nimitz). He served on a cruiser in the Pacific. After the war, Archer became president of the UC Alumni Association, a regent of the university, and a key player in the successful effort to establish a branch of UC in San Diego. Archer tried to get Nimitz to accept the gift of a house in San Diego, to be purchased with funds contributed by local admirers, but the admiral said "No." The San Francisco Bay Area was his home of choice. Archer's roommate Tracy Cuttle went on to medical school, became a Navy doctor, and, during Nimitz's final years, Captain Cuttle was one of his attending physicians at Oak Knoll Naval Hospital.

Submarine Division 20, Nimitz's next command, was based in San Diego and clustered around a support ship, the submarine tender *Holland.* The squadron was small, only four boats, but they were all V-class, the latest and largest in the Navy, a class that grew out of the deliberations of the Submarine Board of Design back when Nimitz served as a member. The V-class were at least twice as long as the R boats, with a cruising range up to 10,000 miles at 11 knots (five times that of the E-1).

The boats of Submarine Division 20 were occupied with battle problems, to practice, test, and improve operations with the fleet. The officers of the fleet who ran the battle problems were not all that interested in working with submarines. Even after the German success in the war, the majority of naval officers—yes, the battleship navy—simply did not understand. The V-boats were designed to sustain 45-day unsupported patrols, but they were being used as short-range scouts. Nimitz, who had changed his mind since his 1912 War College presentation, thought they should be sent out on independent operations, free to attack the enemy whenever and wherever.

In June 1931 Chester Nimitz entered the most unusual assignment of his career: a two-year stint as commander of a "squadron" of some thirty-five out-of-commission destroyers parked at the San Diego destroyer base. The major responsibility of the commander and his team of carpenters, welders, and electrician's mates was to keep the ships from sinking.

The destroyers, a legacy of the World War I building program, were being held in reserve, and the flagship for this unit was the destroyer tender *Rigel*. It also became the living quarters for the Nimitz family. These were not the spartan spaces you might expect, but were fairly elegant—thanks to the wife of the last squadron commander who had hired an interior decorator—and the Nimitz family was served by a cook, a steward, and two messboys.

The Ritz-Carlton ambience was somewhat spoiled by the rats, which managed to sneak aboard despite the protection of rat-guards on all mooring lines. The family had a cat, but one cat was no match for the rats; periodically the ship had to be fumigated—an action that, of course, left dead rats scattered about, usually in inaccessible spaces. The cat's greatest contribution was to deliver a litter of seven kittens—under the table, right in the middle of a dinner party.

The move aboard was a bit complicated: a new member of the family, Mary, was born the day before. Living on a ship was a challenge for the mother of an infant in diapers—even more so when she became a toddler—but great sport for the teenagers Chet and Nancy. The nested destroyers provided a novel setting for entertaining their friends. Late in 1931 Chet headed off to prep school in Annapolis to bone up on math, and the following summer he passed the entrance exams and entered the Naval Academy.

Kate was enrolled at UC Berkeley and would come home during school vacations. One such visit was especially memorable, when her father was exposed as a fallible human being. In preparation for the annual Naval District formal ball, Nimitz had pulled his midshipman's full-dress kit out of storage and had the gold-braid updated to match his exalted rank. Dressed for the ball and immensely proud of his trim, athletic figure, he boasted to Kate, "I want you to know," he said, "I don't think there are many captains who could get into their midshipman's full-dress uniform."[5] The doyenne of the ball was Mrs. Thomas Jones Senn, wife of the district commandant, a lady of austere dignity and imperial presence, "the personification of the admiral's wife," as Catherine Nimitz was heard to say.[6] At one point during the evening, Mrs. Senn dropped her lorgnette and Chester graciously bent down to pick it up—and split his trousers, right up the rear. He spent the rest of the ball standing against a wall.

Other than socializing—which included long walks with his friend Captain Raymond Spruance, chief of staff to the commander of a San Diego–based active destroyer force—there wasn't much to do. To imply that Captain Nimitz was bored with this boring job might be too strong, but he himself said that it was difficult "to become as deeply immersed and as interested" as might have been possible.[7]

CHAPTER EIGHT

THE *AUGUSTA*

After two years of boredom aboard the *Rigel,* Nimitz was given a true career-enhancing assignment as commanding officer of the two-year-old heavy cruiser *Augusta,* due to replace the *Houston* as flagship of the Asiatic Fleet. He reported aboard October 16, 1933, just as the *Augusta* was finishing a brief predeployment shipyard overhaul in Bremerton, Washington.

There were some issues. There had been an almost 100 percent turnover of the crew while the *Augusta* was in the shipyard, so the level of experience was spotty. Almost all of the continuity came from five ensigns, who had been on board for at least a year. On the other hand, the new crew of some 760 sailors had been screened to ensure that at least two years remained on their enlistments, and most of the 64 officers had agreed to a minimum three-year tour, to provide terrific unit cohesion. The families of married officers could join them in the Far East as could the families of the more senior enlisted men, but few in the rest of the crew were married, so family-separation issues would be minimal.

Also, because of a tight schedule, the *Augusta* was forced out of the shipyard a month early, with the major work accomplished, but not the cleanup. To add insult to injury, much of the 21-day passage from Bremerton to Shanghai was beset by winter storms, and the *Augusta* presented a sad and sorry image in contrast to the gleaming, spit-and-polish *Houston* she was to replace.

Indeed, the *Houston* looked like a dream, a fantasy; even the copper piping *under* the engine room deck plating was polished to perfection. The secret was quickly revealed: Following a time-honored custom, Chinese laborers, in exchange for all of the ship's trash and garbage—a great treasure—worked diligently every day the ship was in port. When the workers ran out of things to polish, they started over. Soon they got to work on the *Augusta,* and as the residue of the shipyard was cleared away, with bulkheads freshly painted and copper piping gleaming, the ship could sail with pride.

The cruiser was based in Tsingtao in the summer and Manila in the winter, and spent a lot of time in Shanghai in between. Nimitz expected his officers to make formal calls at his home; his daughters teased the junior officers, accusing them of being too obsequious, too interested in pushing their careers. Nimitz knew that few of the officers had ever spent much time in China, so he organized a series of seminars. One was conducted by the American consul general (who had lived in the country for thirty years) who told them what he *thought* might be happening in China; another was by the intelligence officer of the Shanghai Marine detachment who told them what he *knew* was happening in China. Other speakers included the commercial attaché who explained the status of imports and exports, and the Chinese government ministers of education and finance, who had difficulty explaining why Shanghai money was no good in Tsingtao or why Amoy money was not good even a couple of miles outside of town.[1]

The ship seldom spent a night at sea unless en route to some exotic location. Weather permitting, movies were shown topside every night—an inducement for some of the crew to stay aboard, have a good meal, and save money. However, some ports of call had inducements of their own, of more interest than the third rerun of a Gloria Swanson movie. Prime among them was Shanghai, which offered an exciting nightlife with, well, "special friends," and overnight liberty was permitted. But sailor-town Shanghai operated on the late side. At first, *Augusta* liberty hours ran from 4 P.M. to 8 A.M., but at 4 P.M. there was nothing for the sailors to do but drink, and 8 A.M. was too early for some to rouse up and return to the ship. It didn't take more than a couple of sailors climbing aboard, late and embarrassed, for the enlightened commanding officer to approve a small shift in the schedule. Thenceforth, in Shanghai, liberty started at 5 P.M., but since that was almost dinner time, most of the sailors would eat aboard, save a buck or two, and not hit the beach until well after 6. And liberty ended at a more civilized, Shanghai time—9 A.M. Everybody won.

On the surface, the Asiatic Fleet was a largely ceremonial affair, a couple of dozen ships, with the flagship often moving alone around the Far East, making port calls from Australia to Japan, showing the flag, and socializing with representatives of other naval forces in the area. In fact, fleet commander Frank B. Upham had the temporary four-star rank of admiral so that he would not be at a disadvantage with his foreign counterparts.[2]

A ceremonial function—but with an edge: China had long been in turmoil, caught in a struggle between Communists and the government and prey to roaming bandits and pirates. While *Augusta* was usually off showing the flag, a squadron of Asiatic Fleet gunboats (the Yangtze River patrol), some destroyers, and a permanent party of U.S. Marines (almost 2,000 in Shanghai, 600 in Beijing) more directly protected American interests.

Port visits involved, of course, reciprocal entertaining, but while most of the *Augusta* was open to visitors, including the Japanese, very little of any Japanese warship was open to visitors from the *Augusta*. Guests invited aboard a Japanese ship for dinner were confined to a limited area, and topside weapons and machinery were covered. When sailors went ashore in Yokohama or Kobe, it was clear that English-speaking cab drivers had been positioned to be at their service—a nice touch—but also, perhaps, to listen in on the unguarded conversations of their passengers.[3] Likewise, the Japanese-American Club in Tokyo hosted golf and tennis outings for the officers, followed by dinner parties with wealthy Japanese families and very attractive young women, who were introduced as their daughters. Perhaps they were, as many seem to have been to school in America. In any event, all spoke excellent English.

The ship's company was not the only target of the snoops. Mrs. Nimitz and her daughters were, for a time, living in the Japanese resort city of Unzen, and they were pretty sure that their mail was being opened and read. They were absolutely sure the day they found a letter from Italy that had been sealed in an envelope from Germany, and vice versa.

On June 5, 1934, Admiral Upham and the *Augusta* represented the United States at the Tokyo funeral of Admiral Togo; every nation that had a ship in Asiatic waters was represented. All ships followed standard naval protocol: Upon entering a foreign port, you would fire off a gun salute and "break" the flag of the host nation—a time-honored process in which the flag was tied in a bundle and hoisted aloft, in readiness. Upon signal, a jerk on the line released the flag

to catch the breeze. The *Augusta* sailed smartly into harbor, started the salute—
and broke the flag of China.

Not a great move, especially considering the tense relationship between
China and Japan. The *Augusta* finished the salute and hastily gave another, this
time with the correct flag. Admiral Upham and Captain Nimitz, embarrassed to
the core, quickly suited up in full dress and went off to apologize.

As it turned out, there had been a mistake at the flag factory and the label
on the recently redesigned Chinese ensign read "Japan." That may have been an
ameliorating factor, but clearly, no one had looked at the flag before it was sent
aloft because it was impossible to confuse the new flag of China (with a large
white twelve-pointed sun centered on a blue field) with the red-and-white rising sun of Japan. Upon his return from groveling, Nimitz summoned the officer
of the deck and the offending signalman and told them through gritted teeth,
"If I wasn't so mad, I'd kill both of you right now," and ordered them never
again to set foot on the bridge.[4]

Each navy represented at the funeral sent an honor guard, a platoon of
sailors. Nimitz picked a platoon made up of the tallest sailors aboard, led
by the tallest young officer. Perhaps this was a bit of one-upmanship, i.e.,
"We may have screwed up with the flags but we're bigger than you." Nimitz
himself attended both the formal state funeral and a later, smaller ceremony
at Togo's home.

This visit to Japan had special significance for Nimitz's daughter Kate.
When the *Augusta* made a port call at Kobe a few days after the funeral, she met
her future husband, Ensign James T. "Junior" Lay. They were married in 1945.

After leaving Japan, the *Augusta* headed south to participate in the October
1934 centenary celebration of Melbourne, Australia, and the city, despite being
as much damaged by the worldwide depression as any, threw quite the party.
The *Augusta* was in port for two weeks, giving all hands an opportunity to enjoy
the legendary Australian hospitality.

On December 23, at the end of this 12,000-mile voyage, the *Augusta* arrived
in Manila to face the annual Admiral's Inspection. This was the first round in a
continuing examination of every ship in the U.S. Navy, each competing within
their own type (cruiser, battleship, destroyer) and force (Asiatic Fleet, Scouting Force, etc.). The Admiral's Inspection was a detailed scrutiny of everything
that went into operating and maintaining the ship. A team of highly skeptical

inspectors, drawn from other ships in the fleet, came aboard to inspect the crew (grooming, uniforms, general all-around smartness), to go over personnel records, pay records, medical records, maintenance schedules, training schedules, and evaluate cleanliness and emergency preparedness ("When did you last hold a man-overboard drill?"). The inspection had to be completed before the end of the year, so it was scheduled to begin just after Christmas. With only two days to clean up after many months at sea, the *Augusta* nonetheless earned the almost unheard-of rating of "Outstanding."

There were other areas of competition. While in winter quarters at Manila, the *Augusta* spent much of the time at the Subic Bay support base at Olongapo—where Ensign Nimitz had taken the *Decatur* into dry dock so many years before. Subic was several hours from Manila but only ten minutes from the open ocean and provided towed targets for surface and aerial gunnery exercises in which, because of scheduling conflicts, the *Augusta* was well out of practice.

The rules were pretty basic. The standard main-battery gunnery target was a 140-foot-long, 40-foot-high screen of wooden battens mounted on a heavy timber raft towed by a fleet tug. The exercising ship would pass by and fire the 8-inch guns controlled by the forward fire-control station, then reverse course and make another run with the after fire-control station in charge. The next pass was time for the 5-inch battery to perform. Scoring was done by counting the holes in the screen. The practice shells were marked with paint, which would leave a trace as they passed through, so that it was easier to tell which battery made the hit.

In daylight, none of this presented much of a challenge but, in those days before radar, nighttime targets had to be illuminated. At the start of the exercise, the target would briefly be revealed by something, perhaps a flash of light from the tug. Then, the exercising ship would use a variety of tools to make the target visible, each spelled out by the rules—perhaps launch a phosphorous shell hanging from a parachute for the first pass and use searchlights to paint the target on the next.

Nimitz was of the opinion that few ships would ever again engage in daylight battles; modern gunnery was just too lethal. But a weaker adversary might seek an advantage by training for and attacking at night. Therefore, he put extra emphasis on night firing, and it paid off. The *Augusta's* score for one nighttime exercise was higher than the sum of the scores of the next three cruisers put together. At the end of the first full competitive year under Nimitz, the *Augusta* beat out the rest of the Navy to win the cruiser battle efficiency trophy.

Because of the physically passive nature of the duty and the generally enervating climate, units of the Asiatic Fleet were required to have well-organized and energetic athletic programs. Participation was mandatory; if the fleet was going to have a baseball tournament, you fielded a baseball team. For whaleboat races, you organized a team to man the oars. Rugby was something that no one on the *Augusta* had ever played, but, as the British were always looking for some competition, the ship came up with a team.

To emphasize the importance of sports, ships were not allowed to cut into liberty time for practice but were required to schedule practice during normal working hours. This certainly fit into Nimitz's great interest in physical fitness. He jumped in with a will, and the crew responded with vigor. A volleyball court was set up on the fantail, with the net set fore-and-aft on the centerline, the back court bounded by some fishing nets strung up to catch errant balls, and the balls themselves somewhat deflated to reduce bounce. The ship held swim call when conditions permitted. Some officers played golf (although this was not the captain's favorite sport—too slow), and there was a very active tennis program. Anytime the ship was in port, the junior officers were strongly encouraged to get in some tennis any and every afternoon they were free to go ashore. Some of the junior officers suspected that this was a ploy by their "father protector" to delay socializing at the officer's club bar.

Before long, the *Augusta* had captured every Asiatic Fleet athletic trophy, including rugby, and soon carried away the cruiser force's "Iron Man" trophy.

Nimitz used sports, especially tennis, as a generator of goodwill with the British and Japanese. The players on the *Augusta* tennis team had been ranked through a series of matches; the executive officer, Commander R. E. M. Whiting, was at number one, Ensign Samuel P. Moncure, number two, and poor Captain Nimitz, number three. This was a position he was certain he did not deserve—he had played the deciding set with a wrenched knee—so he challenged Moncure to a rematch. In another bit of sly humor, the challenge was delivered early one morning after Moncure had just returned from a very late night on the beach, and the match was to be played immediately. Nimitz won.

By this time in his career, Nimitz had developed his basic philosophy of management: Push duties and responsibilities as far down the line as possible, freeing people in higher positions, especially the boss, to worry about the really important things. In a relatively minor but nonetheless instructive example, he firmly believed that ship-handling—as in getting underway, straight-and-steady steaming or maneuvering, bringing to anchor or tying up at a pier—was a job for that most junior of officers, the ensign. Well, at least for any ensign with some training, common sense, and experience. Training largely came from the Naval Academy or NROTC and the ship handler's bible, *Knight's Modern Seamanship.* Common sense was a birthright, quickly discovered or the lack thereof exposed. And, it was up to the commanding officer to ensure that his junior officers gained the necessary experience under carefully controlled conditions. Aboard the *Augusta,* at any time, one of the ensigns might hear his name called forth over the loudspeaker to report to the bridge, where he would discover that he had just been selected to get the ship underway or bring her to anchor. The ensign would gather all necessary information from the quartermaster and navigator, the engine room, the line handlers or anchor detail, take a deep breath, and begin the evolution. Throughout, Nimitz would be watching.

Some years later, one of those ensigns (then a rear admiral) recounted his experience in anchoring. He had checked the chart, verified that the anchor detail was ready, and at what he thought was the right moment, gave the order "Let go the anchor." The ship, however, was moving much too fast and kept going. Ensign O. D. "Muddy" Waters ordered all engines back full and finally got the ship under control, but not until he ran out ninety fathoms of chain and came close to ripping what remained clean out of the ship. Then, slowly, he took in chain until the *Augusta* was where it was supposed to be.

All the while, Nimitz just stood there and said nothing. When the excitement had ended, he asked, "Waters, you know what you did wrong, don't you?"

"Yes sir, I certainly do. I came in too fast."

Nimitz said, "That's fine." And that was the end of the lesson.[5]

Nimitz's habit of trusting his officers was infectious. One very dark night, while getting underway from Manila, Nimitz turned to Junior Lay, who was on the bridge observing, and said, "Take her out through the breakwater." Lay never forgot the heart of the lesson. When he later had a command of his own, he passed it along. His destroyer was coming in to port, and the officer of the deck was getting nervous, shifting his feet, and finally asked, "Captain, are you going to take over?" Junior Lay said, "No." The ensign asked, "Well, sir, what do you want me to do?" and Junior Lay said, "I want you to tie the ship up to that buoy."[6]

Another Nimitz tactic: Approaching an anchorage in small harbor in the Philippines, just before the ship was in position and without advance notice, Nimitz invited the first division officer (the man in charge of the anchor detail) to leave his station and come to the bridge. He wanted to see if the assistant division officer, an ensign, could handle the anchor team without supervision. This was, of course, a double test—had the division officer been training the ensign and was the ensign up to the challenge? Both passed but word spread quickly throughout the ship: "Be ready."

An officer who failed either test more than once or who simply didn't try— whether as teacher or student—might soon be transferred off the ship with a very modest rating of fitness, along the lines: a typically fine and dependable naval officer who easily meets the minimum standards of his rank. The officer in question might think this high praise. The detailers who handled assignments would know exactly what it meant: This was someone who might want to consider a career change.

A division officer could be held responsible, within reasonable limits, for the behavior of his men. For many lieutenants (senior or junior grade), serving as a division officer provided their first opportunity to be officially observed in a command role, albeit a limited one. A division officer might be excused for his inability to control or cure the sociopaths, petty thieves, or criminals who joined the Navy one step ahead of the law. But no excuse was tolerated for a failure to do his job, which, at base, was to weed out the weak from the strong, send the miscreants and malcontents off to some other pursuit, and ensure that his division was at all times fully ready to perform duties assigned, in war or peace.

As a general rule, sailors caught in (or strongly suspected of) some minor breach of good order and discipline would be brought up before a "captain's mast," a hearing, conducted by the commanding officer for lesser offenses than would typically be referred to court-martial. The captain would hear the charges, the sailor would give his side of the story, and his division officer (acting as a character witness) would have an opportunity to offer something in mitigation. Typically, a division officer (who, after all, wanted to maintain the loyalty and cooperation of each of the fifty or so men in his division) would say something like, "Captain, this man has always done a good job. Sometimes he gets into trouble ashore, but he is a good man and a credit to the ship . . . etcetera etcetera."

At captain's mast, Nimitz was fair and his findings were usually correct, but we may offer one example where he was more than fair but judicially in error. He couldn't help himself. While the ship was in port at Tsingtao, a petty officer on shore patrol was caught in a state of undress in the room of a cabaret girl and charged with dereliction of duty and being out of uniform. The available records are silent on how he was caught, but we may assume that his shore patrol officer saw him leaving his post and entering a building, perhaps accompanied by the young woman. Thus, caught he was, out of uniform and not on patrol.

Nimitz asked, "Now, young man, what do you have to say for yourself?" And the young man replied, "Well, captain, it was this way. I know that when you're on shore patrol you're supposed to be in proper uniform, and I had snagged my uniform getting out of the boat that brought us ashore, and I knew this girl who lived nearby and she offered, if I would come up to her room, to sew up the snag and that is why I was in her room with my jumper off." Nimitz could barely keep from laughing out loud and later said it was the best story he'd ever heard. The petty officer did indeed get high marks from his division officer, and the case was dismissed.[7]

By contrast, another case had a different outcome. A Marine was charged with being asleep on watch. The evidence was presented, the young man was contrite, and Nimitz asked the officer in charge of the Marine Guard, Lieutenant Lewis Puller, if he had anything to say. Puller replied, much to the astonishment of all present, "I certainly do, Captain. Get rid of the SOB. He's not a Marine if he goes to sleep on watch. I never want to see him again." The man was remanded to court-martial. (Puller was the third Marine assigned as officer in charge of the Marine Guard; Nimitz had fired the first two for incompetence. Puller was a keeper.) Puller, who was at some point tagged with the nickname "Chesty," retired in 1955 as a lieutenant general, having earned, among other awards, five Navy Crosses in World War II and Korea.[8]

In 1935 Nimitz was headed for the next station in his career, assistant chief of the Bureau of Navigation in Washington, D.C. The change of command ceremony (with the *Augusta* anchored in the Huangpu River, Shanghai) was a full-dress affair. The flagship of the Asiatic Fleet did a lot of things in full dress, even Sunday services. Full dress in the 1930s dated from the Civil War—frock coat, gold-striped trousers, epaulets, fore-and-aft hats—a kit that did not survive World War II. Immediately following the ceremony, Nimitz was to be shifted a few hundred yards upriver to the commercial liner *President Lincoln,* where his family was waiting for the voyage home. To his honest surprise, he found that the "shifting" was to be courtesy of twelve volunteer junior officers manning the oars of a whaleboat. In an imaginative gesture of respect, they appointed the captain "honorary coxswain" and made him steer; on arrival at the *Lincoln* he made them secure the boat and follow him aboard for a ceremonial drink.

It must have been a coincidence that the upriver portion of the oarsman's effort was with the incoming tide, and at the return, the tide had turned. It was not a coincidence that five of those Nimitz-trained junior officers, 40 percent, made flag rank. The norm, in war or peace, was nearer 2 percent.

CHAPTER NINE

IN TRAINING

Nimitz's new office, the Bureau of Navigation, was in a building known as Main Navy, on Constitution Avenue at 18th Street, NW, which housed the major administrative offices of the Navy, from the secretary on down. The chief of the bureau was Rear Admiral Adolphus Andrews, who was often out of town on business, and Nimitz would fill in as acting chief. At times, Nimitz was also acting secretary of the Navy because the incumbent, Claude Swanson, was frequently ill. Doing three jobs at once could make for long workdays, but dealing with aspects of the Navy Department that were not part of his regular job provided invaluable experience.

The Bureau of Navigation (BUNAV) was a major component of the Navy Department; the title was a carryover from earlier times but did not reflect the work of the bureau, which handled recruiting, education and training, manning levels of ships and shore stations, promotion, career planning, and other personnel matters.[1] The Navy, unlike most large organizations, could not hire senior management from outside; the leaders had to be hired at entry level and nurtured, and it was BUNAV's job to make it all work.

When Nimitz reported aboard in the spring of 1935, the Great Depression was in full swing and the U.S. Navy—like the nation—was bumping along a rough path, trying to hang on. The fleet was undermanned—not even up to the limits allowed by the 1922 Washington Treaty—and the size and shape of the fleet kept changing. Toward the end of *his* tour, 1931–32, President Herbert Hoover, desperate to save money, put more ships in reserve and canceled funding for annual USNR training.[2] Hoover also suspended ongoing ship construction; incoming President Franklin D. Roosevelt (FDR) offered a fresh shipbuilding program as a stimulus package to put people to work. As Secretary of the Navy Swanson announced, "Every state will benefit" since more than 125 trades and multiple suppliers were involved.[3] New battleships and heavy cruisers were blocked by the treaty, but the Navy could build a few light cruisers and aircraft carriers and a large number of destroyers to replace aging ships. Roosevelt's National Industrial Recovery Act (NIRA) provided $237 million for thirty ships. In 1934, Congress upped the ante with the Vinson-Trammel Act: About 100 ships would be started over the next three years, all to be completed by 1942. BUNAV had plenty of work to do, from developing crew requirements for the new ships (how many gunner's mates, or boiler tenders, or ensigns) to recruiting and training the men to fill the jobs—and dealing with several long-running issues.

For one, there were problems with officer promotions: Up to the rank of lieutenant commander, officers were promoted by seniority, not competence, and too many of the officers from the World War I buildup had remained on active duty. In 1934 there were 250 officers on the list for promotion to lieutenant commander but only 80 vacancies. BUNAV dumped the seniority system and instituted selection boards for lieutenant and lieutenant commander, not so much as a method to reward performance but as a scalpel to thin the herd.

Aviation was another issue. Naval air was proving its worth in fleet exercises but had not grabbed the attention of the bulk of naval officers. Aviators were treated as a separate breed, not quite naval, with limited opportunities for advancement. BUNAV understood that aviators should be line officers, just like submariners, and eligible to fill line officer billets, at sea and ashore, provided they were qualified. However, by the mid-1930s, few aviators had any experience doing anything except flying airplanes. And few aviators of whatever level of experience were senior enough for major command when Congress decreed that commanding officers of carriers, seaplane tenders, and aviation shore facilities must be aviators. A solution of sorts was created when senior line officers were invited to attend a truncated version of flight training and be designated "aviation observers," thus meeting the "aviator" requirement. Over time, perhaps thirty-six volunteers completed the program, although some of them elected to take the full course and be designated "pilots." Among those were a pair of 52-year-olds, Bill Halsey in 1935 and John S. McCain (Nimitz's assistant on the *Panay*) in 1936. By their own admission, they were not very good pilots, but qualified nonetheless.

Trouble was brewing throughout much of the world. Japan invaded China in the summer of 1937 and, among other atrocities, sank the 1927 China-built U.S. gunboat *Panay*—namesake of Nimitz's first command. The Japanese "apologized" (Sorry, didn't see the American flags) and under pressure paid an indemnity of just over $2 million. Japan's moves on China were aided by a steady stream of imported American oil and steel scrap. Japan was more dependent upon imports, in war or peace, than either Great Britain or Germany, and meeting their needs was good business for American companies.

In March 1938, Germany annexed Austria. Congress authorized a new billion-dollar shipbuilding program including a couple of battleships ($50 million each, 85 percent of which would be for labor; another job-creation program).

Nimitz and Andrews worked together at BUNAV until 1938, when both were promoted. Vice Admiral Andrews went on to be commander of the Scouting Fleet in the Atlantic. Rear Admiral Nimitz was given command of a cruiser division in San Diego—but he lost the assignment after suffering a hernia serious enough to require surgery. This turned out to be a bit of good luck because his next job was even better: commander of Battleship Division One aboard the flagship *Arizona*, based in Long Beach, California. He assumed that post in September, with Lieutenant Preston V. Mercer—whom he selected from a list of four candidates—as his flag secretary. Nimitz, Mercer, and *Arizona* skipper Captain Isaac Kidd had apartments within a few doors of each other and walked to the pier together almost every morning.

A few months later, most of the Battle Fleet headed to the Caribbean—the first time it had left the Pacific since 1934—to train against a possible invasion by Germany. Nimitz remained behind, now the senior naval officer on the West Coast and commanding Task Force Seven—*Arizona, Saratoga*, a cruiser, several destroyers and auxiliaries, and an oiler. Task Force Seven had two missions, one subtle and one specific. Subtle: as a signal to Japan that the U.S. Navy had not abandoned the Pacific. Specific: to refine the method of underway refueling and to train for amphibious landings by putting Marines on the beach of San Clemente Island, off the coast of Southern California.

The refueling methods developed by *Maumee* and improved in the Battle Fleet exercises of 1924 were now fine-tuned. Nimitz found that, with a bit of practice and a steady hand on the wheel of both ships, oiler and customer, they did not have to be tethered by stout mooring lines but could steam safely at a separation of about fifty feet, with the only connections between them being the fueling hose and a telephone line. Also, for the first time, a carrier was refueled at sea.

The amphibious exercises proved that the Navy was not equipped for landing Marines on a hostile shore. Standard-issue ship's boats, the traditional transport of choice, were totally unsuited. Whaleboats, pointed at both ends, handled well in the surf but couldn't carry many troops. The larger motor launches had squared-off sterns that could be swung around by an incoming wave, turning them parallel to the beach and unable to back off. Marines scrambling over the side of any boats were highly vulnerable to enemy fire, and depending on the slope or configuration of the bottom, even with the bow resting on the beach, a fully loaded Marine could drop in water over his head.

With inspired timing, commercial boat builder Andrew Higgins had just proposed a flat-bottom landing-craft design based on one of his models used in the Everglades. With some improvements, especially a drop-down bow ramp for a quicker, safer exit, he, and the Navy, had a winner. It was known variously as the "Higgins boat" (named for the manufacturer) or the "Landing Craft, Vehicle, Personnel," LCVP (named by some bureaucrat).

In June 1939—after only eight months away—Nimitz was ordered back to BUNAV, this time as chief of the bureau. He relieved Rear Admiral James O. Richardson, who was headed out as commander of the Battle Fleet—soon to be renamed the Pacific Fleet.

Nimitz rented an apartment in the same Q Street building that housed daughters Kate and Nancy. It was just the right distance from Main Navy for a brisk daily walk, both ways weather permitting. He brought one of the *Augusta* ensigns, Lieutenant J. Wilson "Bill" Leverton, in as his aide. He asked Mercer if he would come along as flag secretary. Mercer was flattered but said he needed more sea-time in grade to be eligible for promotion. "I don't think I ought to go ashore right now . . . I'd rather go and command a destroyer."[4] Nimitz agreed, and issued the orders.

Just as Nimitz was taking over BUNAV, pioneer aviator Rear Admiral John Towers (the third naval officer to earn his wings) came on board as chief of the Bureau of Aeronautics, BUAER. Towers—a hard-nosed sort who had a knack for raising controversy rather than settling issues—claimed that his job gave him the responsibility for recruiting and training pilots. However, by law and regulation, "recruiting and training" of personnel was the job of BUNAV. This created some friction, but Nimitz managed to find suitable compromises. Along the way, Nimitz and Towers toured aviation training facilities together, and nearly died together when a student pilot at Jacksonville cut in front of Towers's plane, barely missing a collision.[5]

In September 1939—about three months after Nimitz took over BUNAV—Germany invaded Poland. England and France declared war on Germany and President Roosevelt declared a state of limited national emergency; reservists were encouraged to volunteer for active duty. In November, in his first annual report, Nimitz warned the president that the fleet was only 85 percent manned and that the Navy was short more than 1,000 officers. BUNAV was making adjustments; for example, sailors were replaced by civilian workers in such shore services as laundries, barbers, and tailor shops. FDR authorized an increase in enlisted strength by 35,000 sailors. It was not enough.

In May 1940, Germany followed the conquest of Poland by invading Belgium, the Netherlands, and France, and within seven weeks all three had surrendered. FDR's limited national emergency became full-blown with recalls across the board: reservists, graduates of the Naval Academy, NROTC, and Midshipman Schools who had left the service. Retired officers were recalled to active duty to help administer the shore establishment, thus freeing a number of younger officers for sea duty.

In June, Nimitz announced the V-7 program, an accelerated Midshipman School for unmarried recent college graduates—one month at sea, followed by a qualifying exam, followed by three months training ashore and a commission as ensign in the Volunteer Naval Reserve. This program was a particular favorite of the president, as it was a variation of a scheme FDR had sponsored in 1917 (he served as assistant secretary of the Navy from 1913 to 1920).

The administration proposed a massive shipbuilding program, which moved speedily through Congress as the "Two-Ocean Navy" Vinson-Walsh Act of July 19, 1940. This would increase the size of the Navy by 257 ships and 13,000 aircraft. Recruiting and training became the top priority.

Also in July, FDR recruited newspaper publisher Frank Knox—the 1936 Republican candidate for vice president—to serve as his secretary of the Navy. The 1940 election was coming up and the president was courting Republican support.

The Japanese saw the fall of France and the Netherlands as a golden opportunity, leaving resource-rich French Indochina and the Dutch East Indies ripe for plunder. At the end of September, Japan moved into Vietnam and used it as a base for bombing southern China. In reaction, the United States stopped the sale of scrap metal to Japan—a mild and somewhat silly rebuke because we kept sending them oil, a gesture the administration thought might keep Japan out of the oil-rich Indies. At the same time, Japan signed a treaty with Germany and Italy that obligated any and all to go to the defense of any of the three that might find itself at war with some other nation. Unspoken, the "other nation" was the United States.

By October a newly created Selective Service System was open for business and began "selecting" (drafting) men for service in any or all of the armed forces, wherever there was a need. The draftees were dubbed "trainees." The Navy did not plan to use any but did not reject the idea out of hand. In fact, Nimitz symbolically participated in drawing numbers for the second draft lottery.

In November, FDR was elected to a third term as president. Nimitz issued his annual report for the year 1940; he noted that officer levels had increased by only 200 since 1939, and there had been a scant and meaningless increase of fleet manning level to 87.2 percent of the peacetime complement. This was barely enough men to operate the ships in normal times and far below the recommended wartime complement of 115 percent. Wartime required additional men to handle the increased tempo of operations and cover combat casualties.

CHAPTER TEN

PREPARING FOR WAR

BUNAV stepped up recruiting advertising and planted newspaper stories about the joys of Navy life.[1] There was a revised recruiting goal, and a big thermometer poster was frequently updated to show progress. Thanks to the Depression, waning but still a factor, many good men were signing up. As J. Wilson Leverton later recalled, it was clear there was going to be a war, and if it was to be a choice between joining the Army or the Navy, the Navy seemed to have the edge: You could sleep in a clean bunk every night instead of a muddy foxhole, and "if you got in a fight with the enemy, they wouldn't be shooting at you, they were shooting at the ship. In the Army, they were shooting at you."[2] In truth, recruiting was going well: The Marine Corps had all quotas filled and the U.S. Navy was close behind.

Of course, not every applicant could be accepted—one young man failed the Navy enlistment physical, but his mother didn't understand and wrote an angry letter to the secretary of the Navy: "We're a fine and God-fearing American family and some derned foreigner named Nimitz won't let my son in the Navy."[3]

To speed the time it took to move an enlistee from recruiting office to first duty station, Nimitz enlarged recruit training stations and cut basic training from eight weeks to six. He increased enrollment at the Naval Academy and reduced the course from four years to three. Just as his own class had graduated early to meet the needs of the fleet, commencement of the class of 1941 was moved up to February, and, as Nimitz told the Senate Appropriations Committee, the class of

1942 would graduate in February of that year and the class of 1943 would graduate in June 1942, a full year ahead of schedule. The number of NROTC units was increased to twenty-seven and NROTC graduates were allowed to transfer from the reserves to the regular Navy.

Meanwhile, the president wanted to make Pearl Harbor the home port of the Pacific Fleet, which up to that time was based on the West Coast. FDR thought this might deter Japanese expansion in the Far East. Fleet commander Admiral James O. Richardson thought that trying to maintain the fleet at Pearl Harbor was short-sighted and impractical. Support services were inadequate. There was only one way in or out of the harbor, a narrow channel that only one large ship at a time could use; Richardson called it "a God-damned mouse-trap."[4] He complained loudly to anyone who would listen, including directly to the president. Several times. In January 1941, after one complaint too many, he was fired.

Roosevelt took a great personal interest in the Navy. If he wanted to "talk personnel," especially flag selection and senior officer assignments, he would invite Nimitz to drop by. FDR had his favorites and Nimitz was one of them, and thus he was offered the job as commander in chief of the Pacific Fleet to replace Richardson. But Nimitz declined; he thought he was far too junior, and there were many more qualified senior flag officers, some of them already stationed at Pearl Harbor. He also knew that being seen as teacher's pet would not be an asset.

Rear Admiral Husband E. Kimmel, also well known to the president—having been FDR's aide back in his days as assistant secretary of the Navy—got the post on February 1, 1941, and was promoted to admiral. He was only one year senior to Nimitz. He soon found himself in the wrong place at the wrong time.

Back in November, when Nimitz addressed the first group of 264 V-7 graduates, he assured them, "You are joining a fast-moving, hard-hitting team, and you will make the grade upon your efforts and not because you came from a certain school." No distinction, he said, would be made between them and Annapolis graduates.[5] By March 1941 the V-7 program had delivered a symbolic 1,776 graduates and some 1,200 men were in training.

Nimitz told the House Naval Affairs Committee, "Probably many of the admirals of the future" he said, "will never have been to Annapolis." *Time* reported that members of the committee "found this wild prophecy just funny" and noted that since 1914 there had not been a single flag officer who was not a graduate of the Naval Academy.[6] But Nimitz made his case: Annapolis, then graduating about 700 ensigns a year (almost triple the rate some six years earlier), could never meet the requirements of a two-ocean navy. Looking ahead five years, the Navy would need 36,000 officers to man ships and stations and another 15,000 to fly its airplanes. The previous summer the total on board had been only 10,817.[7]

Nimitz refused to create a special class of enlisted women to perform clerical duties, as the Navy had done during World War I (the class was called "Yeoman F"). He felt that the Civil Service handled these duties well and at much lower overall cost. In two years, the number of Civil Service clerks at BUNAV rose from 280 to 950. He did, however, have some quibbles: Not all of these employees were "imbued with the spirit of defense work," some perhaps less willing than others to provide "voluntary overtime" to meet the growing workload. But he did not waver.[8] Nimitz was long gone from the bureau when Congress authorized the creation of a female-branch of the Navy, the Women Accepted for Voluntary Emergency Service (WAVES).

When Leverton's tour was up, Nimitz went shopping for another aide. He found one, working close by: Naval Reserve Lieutenant H. Arthur Lamar was on the congressional desk at the Navy Department, where he spent most of his time writing letters for Admiral Nimitz's signature. Lamar had been doing a good job, so when his boss told him he was invited to dinner with Admiral and Mrs. Nimitz at their apartment, he assumed it was a reward. The dress was black tie, so Lamar also assumed it was a party—but soon discovered that he was the only guest. He was being given a tryout. The admiral was gleefully pouring martinis and soon enough Lamar realized that Nimitz was trying to get him drunk, so he stopped drinking. Nimitz questioned him on many topics. Monday morning Lamar's boss said, "You've made the grade. You've just been appointed as aide to the chief of the bureau."[9]

Nimitz sent out a dispatch to all flag officers that he had taken a reserve officer as his personal aide, and he urged all to do the same in the shortest possible time, letting their Naval Academy graduates go to sea.

Nimitz didn't play the Washington game, courting members of Congress and looking for legislative favors, but his job put him in front of a string of congressional committees to offer his opinion on various pieces of proposed legislation. He became quite friendly with Georgia Democrat Carl Vinson, chairman of the House Naval Affairs Committee. Vinson, who served more than fifty years in Congress, was the single most effective champion of the U.S. Navy. Nimitz did have a passing acquaintance with some other members, especially the Texas delegation, but that was kinship, not politics. His dinner parties were for friends, especially those interested in music or art. Almost everyone in his family played a musical instrument, and since his two daughters lived down the hall, evenings would at times degenerate into impromptu concerts. The admiral did not play. He did not direct the orchestra. He may have tapped his foot to keep time.

By 1941 Main Navy was too confining, there was not enough space to accommodate staff expansion, and BUNAV was being relocated to a new building. Known as the Navy Annex (officially Federal Office Building 2), it would also house the headquarters of the Marine Corps. The Annex was just up the hill from the site of the soon-to-be-finished Pentagon and was almost ready; most BUNAV functions had been shifted but not the immediate offices of the chief of the bureau. Nimitz spent much of his day just shuttling back and forth, twenty minutes, more or less, each way.

One of the still-open work orders was to accommodate a Nimitz request that a toilet be installed in what would be his personal office. This was not some nonegalitarian, class nonsense but very sensible. When scheduled to meet an endless series of visitors, supplicants, or malefactors seeking redress, it was not seemly for the head of the bureau to have to walk through the waiting room ("Hi! How are you? Be with you in a moment!") or sneak out a side door and head down the hall to the men's room where he might run into some of those same supplicants.

The chief of a Navy bureau deals with a steady stream of visitors—from angry losers to true heroes. Part of his job is to sort it all out. For instance, back in 1933 when there weren't enough active duty slots for all Naval Academy graduates, only about half were commissioned. One of those dropped was Draper Kauffman, because, he was told, he failed the eye exam (he likely would have been cut anyway because of his low class standing). He got a job with a steamship company, and after the fall of France he joined the Royal Navy Volunteer Reserve (RNVR) in England, where, at great personal peril, the man who failed the eye exam became an expert in deactivating unexploded German bombs. In October 1941 Lieutenant Kauffman resigned from the RNVR and came home to take a USNR commission. He wanted to put his recent experience to work for the nation and assumed he would not be eligible for a U.S. Navy appointment. His father, a naval officer, asked Nimitz to bring Draper into the regular Navy without prejudice. Nimitz agreed and had him transferred with the same rank he had held in the RNVR. Lieutenant Kauffman won the Navy Cross on his first assignment, defusing an unexploded Japanese bomb at Pearl Harbor. He went on to help create the Navy's Underwater Demolition Teams (UDT), the frogmen who cleared enemy harbors and beaches just ahead of the invasion force. After only nineteen years as a U.S. naval officer, the man who was initially denied a commission was promoted to rear admiral. His flag officer assignments included a tour as superintendent of the Naval Academy, a poetic touch, as if righting an ancient wrong.[10]

Another incident revealed the flip side of Nimitz's sense of justice and reason when he made a potentially career-limiting decision. The brand-new undersecretary of the Navy, James V. Forrestal, asked Nimitz for a favor. He wanted a friend to have a commission as a lieutenant commander. However, the friend was a convicted felon, and U.S. Navy policy was clear: no commissions to men with a record. Nimitz said "No." Forrestal asked him to reconsider. Nimitz wouldn't budge. It was not a good start for a working relationship that would last until 1947.[11]

At the end of June, Nimitz asked the Senate Naval Affairs Committee for authority to retain men in service after their six-year enlistments had expired, "as long as the national interest is imperiled." He suggested that this would conform with similar authority granted in the Selective Service Act, whereby the one-year terms of trainees could be extended by Congress. Senator Hiram Johnson (Republican from California) called this an "infringement" upon personal rights; the Navy, he said, had no right to compel men to serve beyond the terms they had accepted when they enlisted. Nimitz countered, "Where the interests of the individual and the government come into conflict, the government's interest must prevail."

Also, trying to set the record straight, Nimitz told the committee that published reports of a "near riot" staged by unhappy sailors of the battleship *Pennsylvania* at Honolulu were "absolutely false and unfounded." He also shot down another rumor, that the carrier *Yorktown* could not get underway because the crew was "absent" after shore leave in Norfolk. Nimitz said these rumors were being circulated by "subversive elements" to weaken public confidence in the Navy. "We are approaching the time," he said, "when even if stories are true and are inimical to public interest, they should be weighed carefully before being printed."[12]

The next day, his assault on the sanctity of contracts was rebuked by the committee, which denied his request to extend the service of current enlistees. However, in a burst of logic, the committee did allow the Navy to put future volunteers on notice that, upon congressional action, they could be held in service after their enlistment expired.

On October 31, 1941, a German U-boat sank the destroyer *Reuben James*, the first U.S. Navy ship sunk by hostile action in World War II. Navy enlistments immediately fell off by 15 percent. Nimitz told a press conference that the drop was almost exclusively due to the withdrawal of parental consent for minors. Nimitz admitted that, overall, enlistments were now running about 9,000 a month against a target of 13,000. Nonetheless, the Navy was avoiding draftees—volunteers would be more motivated. Advertising was bumped up in twenty-eight states. Physical standards for reserve officers were relaxed, especially for correctable conditions involving teeth and eyesight.

Throughout this period, America was focused on the full-scale war in Europe, ancestral homeland of most citizens, and activities in the Far East, while troubling, were not compelling. But relations with Japan continued to deteriorate, and the United States finally stopped all trade with Japan. The Japanese tried negotiating; they really needed the oil. The negotiations failed. On November 26, the United States formally demanded that Japan get out of China. Japan declined the invitation.

On November 27, the CNO sent a "war warning" message to the Commander-in-Chief, Pacific Fleet (CINCPAC). Some aggressive Japanese action was expected, possibly against the Philippines, Borneo, or Malaysia. There had been reports of Japanese forces moving south.

CHAPTER ELEVEN

WAR

It was a cold but sunny day in December in the nation's capital. At home in their apartment on Q Street, Catherine, the admiral, and their daughters had settled down to listen to the Sunday afternoon broadcast of the New York Philharmonic Orchestra when an announcer broke in: The Naval Base at Pearl Harbor, Hawaii, was under attack by the air and naval forces of Japan.

The news was a shock to the nation but not a total surprise to the government. In the past few days there had been troubling exchanges with the Japanese. (This information had not been shared with Nimitz, whose job did not involve diplomacy, military operations, or war plans.) There had been hints that an increasingly bellicose Japan might take action—perhaps attack Singapore. A Japanese naval force had been spotted heading south along the east coast of Vietnam, and the British had moved a small defensive force into the area, just in case.

But when the target proved to be a territory of the United States hit by an undetected naval force operating far to the north, the world was thrown into turmoil. President Roosevelt said it best: Sunday December 7, 1941, was "a date which will live in infamy."[1]

Nimitz called Lamar and told him to get in uniform and get to the office, then grabbed his overcoat and told Catherine, "I won't be back till God knows when."[2] By the time he reached the office, some of the staff was already there and he got a quick update, though sketchy because the attack was still underway. Over at the secretary of the Navy's office he got more details—Frank Knox had been on the telephone with a senior officer in Hawaii who reported what he could see from his office window, and updates were flooding in by radio. The final tally: twenty-one ships sunk or damaged, almost two hundred airplanes destroyed, a thousand men wounded and more than two thousand killed (half of them aboard one ship, the *Arizona*, when a bomb penetrated the forward ammunition magazine). With approval of the president and before any formal declaration of war, Chief of Naval Operations Admiral Harold Stark sent a flash message to all Navy commanders in the Pacific: "Execute against Japan unrestricted air and submarine warfare." The World War I criticism of Germany for attacking without warning was put aside in the realities of the moment. However, unlike the German declaration of February 1917, the United States did not establish war zones in which all traffic was in jeopardy, but just assumed that all Japanese merchant shipping, anywhere in the world, was operating in service of the military.[3]

There were false sightings of Japanese warplanes, especially up and down the West Coast. New York's Mayor Fiorello LaGuardia ordered guards posted at all tunnel and bridge crossings, and anxious citizens rushed to stock up on food, booze, and gasoline. Japanese restaurants closed early and turned out the lights—some of them forever.

Nimitz got home around midnight, grabbed a few hours sleep, and was back in the office early in the morning. By long-standing custom, military officers in the Washington area wore civilian clothes to work; uniforms were worn only for occasions of high ceremony. That changed overnight; someone put out the word that all officers would report for duty Monday morning in uniform. Some officers—whose job descriptions did not include participation in high ceremonies—had trouble finding a full uniform. One flag officer showed up with a sporty tweed overcoat over his dress blues. Others reported to work with the wrong shoes and some were unable to fasten the buttons of uniforms they had not worn for several years of sedentary shore duty. Such minor embarrassments may have provoked the only smiles of a bleak and troubled day, the day the president called on the Congress to declare war on Japan. In response, Germany exercised their treaty commitment to Japan and declared war on the United States on December 11. Italy followed soon after.

In the meantime, the Japanese force that had been spotted heading south began the invasion of Malaya. They easily took out the British defensive force by sinking the one-year-old battleship *Prince of Wales* and World War I–vintage heavy cruiser *Repulse*. In doing so, they signaled a new era of naval warfare. The ships, for which a hopelessly naive admiral had denied air cover, were sunk—along with the admiral—by swarms of Japanese airplanes.

Other Japanese forces attacked the Philippines, Hong Kong, Guam, Midway, and Wake Island. In the entire operation, they lost no naval ships larger than a destroyer.[4]

Nimitz and his staff attacked myriad personnel issues. There were families of the dead and wounded to be notified, funerals and hospitalizations to be arranged, crew requirements of the damaged ships to be evaluated, and sailors to be reassigned. There was a rush of new recruits in the wake of the disaster, but one thousand were turned away in New York City on Monday because there weren't enough doctors to process their physicals. The commanding officer of the Great Lakes training base ordered emergency construction of thirty-two new barracks buildings. The population at Great Lakes skyrocketed from 8,500 to 68,000 men in six months, and the six-week training course was compressed into three.

Secretary Knox had to deal with a personnel matter of his own: What should he do with Admiral Kimmel? Knox flew out for a quick inspection on December 11, and was so appalled at the destruction in Hawaii that he had trouble listening to briefings by the admiral and his staff. They tried to assure Knox that they had been ready. They told him about a fleet exercise in November that assumed a Japanese air attack on Oahu. They told him that on December 7, the carriers were all out at sea, patrolling, and there had been ammunition topside by the guns and ready for use on all of the ships in the harbor. And the attackers had been taken under fire.

It all fell on deaf ears. Frank Knox, as a former newspaper editor and part-owner of the *Chicago Daily News,* understood the power of public opinion. Blame must be laid on someone for allowing such a large enemy combatant force to approach undetected. Under the circumstances, however, there was no time to resolve questions of misfeasance, culpability, or just plain bad luck. This was an issue that could be addressed only by the president. Kimmel, Army commander Lieutenant General Walter Short, and Army Air Forces commander Major General Frederick L. Martin were relieved of duty. The president ordered a board of inquiry headed by Supreme Court Justice Owen J. Roberts; it was a politically charged hearing, focused on retribution, not redemption. The public and the Congress, although neither would admit it, were primed for a hanging.

Vice Admiral W. S. Pye, commander of the now-defunct Hawaii-based battleships, was named as interim replacement for Kimmel. For a permanent relief, there was only one candidate: Nimitz. Or, as FDR put it to Secretary Knox, "Tell Nimitz to get the hell out to Pearl and stay there till the war is won."[5] On December 16, the day after Knox returned from his trip to Pearl Harbor, he called Nimitz over to his office and without preamble said, "How soon can you be ready to travel?"

Nimitz, frazzled from working eighteen-hour days, was in no mood for conundrums. "It depends on where I'm going and how long I'm going to be away."

"You're going to take command of the Pacific Fleet, and I think you'll be gone for a long time."[6]

Nimitz once again tried to back off, suggesting that the more senior Pye should have the command as CINCPAC; he was already on the scene, familiar with the playing field and the players. Knox said "No." He gave Nimitz one bit of good news, a carrier task force was heading out from Pearl Harbor for the relief of a beleaguered Marine garrison at Wake Island, a bright spot of hope in a dark and dismal time.

Not long after Nimitz returned to his office to sort things out, the phone rang; it was a man asking for "Chester." Lamar was a bit put out by the tone of familiarity from someone whose voice he didn't recognize until the voice continued, "This is the president. Put him on the phone." The admiral took the call, listened, muttered a few words, hung up, and asked for his car to be brought around. "I've got to go to the White House," he said. The president wanted to discuss his new assignment.[7]

There were housekeeping chores—making sure that Catherine and their daughters were secure financially and domestically during his absence (not a problem, they were used to looking out for themselves) and packing for the trip. When Catherine noticed that her husband was in full automatic mode, packing his tuxedo because he always packed his tuxedo, she told him to sit down and took over the chore. Nimitz also arranged for a replacement to take his job at BUNAV. He told Knox that there was only one option, his deputy Captain Randall Jacobs. Knox said, "You can't have him, FDR doesn't like him." Nimitz replied, "God damn it, he's the only man who can do the job!"[8] Knox backed off. Nimitz gave Jacobs the news that both of them were being reassigned and told him to have someone cut the orders. With or without FDR's blessing, newly promoted Rear Admiral Jacobs was to head the Bureau of Navigation (soon renamed the Bureau of Naval Personnel, BUPERS) for the rest of the war.

Nimitz knew that he would have to make a public statement about his new assignment. He didn't want to be caught off guard, so when he was back home, he scratched something out on a small pad of paper, which one member of the family quickly tore off as a souvenir. So he wrote it out again. Someone else grabbed that copy. Finally, he ran out of family members and was able to keep a copy for himself, "It is a great responsibility, and I will do my utmost to meet it."[9]

His appointment was announced to the press on December 18, and Nimitz delivered his brief statement (slightly modified) to waiting newsmen: "All I can say is I am very sensible of the fact that I am being entrusted with a very great responsibility which I intend to discharge to the utmost of my ability."[10] Press reaction was favorable. *Time* gave him a proper warrior image: "a calm, frosty-faced, steel-blue-eyed Texan."[11]

Knox had a plane standing ready to take Nimitz to the West Coast, but the admiral begged off. He said he would rather go that part of the journey by train, so that he could catch up on his sleep and collect his thoughts. Thus, his departure was delayed a day, which allowed him to attend his daughter Mary's performance in a school event. Nimitz and traveling companion, his aide Lamar, pulled out of Washington's Union Station headed west on Friday afternoon, December 19.

On orders from the White House, Nimitz and Lamar were to travel in civilian clothes and were booked as "Mr. Freeman" (Catherine's maiden name) and "Mr. Wainwright" (a hero of the Spanish-American War). They were advised not to acknowledge any friends they might run into along the way. So, of course, the very first night out a college professor whom Nimitz had met at a conference two months before addressed the admiral by rank and name. He was given an awkward cold shoulder, but later Lamar overheard the professor pointing out "the admiral" to another traveler. During a change of trains in Chicago, Nimitz took a taxi to the naval training center on Navy Pier and got a haircut—so much for traveling incognito.

The trip was not without a minor adventure. Just before one stop, Nimitz went into the toilet. The porter, doing his job to keep passengers from flushing while in the station (the flush did not go into any kind of holding tank but was dumped out on the tracks), and not realizing someone was already inside, locked the door. Nimitz tried to get out, could not, and was trapped until the train was once again underway and the porter unlocked the door. An unhappy Nimitz confronted the man, and the porter, certainly puzzled, replied, "The door can be opened from the inside," and Nimitz said, "Show me," and locked the porter in the bathroom. And the porter could not get out. To Nimitz the educator, it was a fine teaching moment.[12]

Nonetheless, the trip was just what Nimitz needed, a chance to decompress, work on his own schedule for a few days, and read classified reports on the action and damage at Pearl Harbor that Lamar was carrying in a nondescript canvas bag. The information was devastating, much worse than what he already knew. But at the same time, he could see the role that chance had played in destroying Kimmel's career; as he told Lamar, "It could happen to anyone." He knew, in truth, that it could have happened to him in much the same fashion had he taken the fleet job a year earlier.

On arrival on the West Coast, Lamar returned to Washington and Nimitz arranged for a Navy seaplane flight to Hawaii that departed on Christmas Eve. Nimitz, among the most gracious of men, apologized to the aircrew for taking them away from their families at Christmas. The weather was poor, and after a bumpy ride they arrived over Oahu just past dawn in the middle of a rainstorm. As the seaplane banked to line up for a water landing, Nimitz got a visual snapshot of rain bouncing off the surface of an oil-covered harbor, with devastation everywhere. After landing, a waiting whaleboat with a welcoming committee of one rear admiral and two captains came alongside. Nimitz asked for news of the relief of Wake Island.

There was an awkward moment: The news was bad. Kimmel had organized the expedition to go to the aid of Wake Island, but when his successor Pye learned that the Japanese had moved a stronger force against Wake, the relief was canceled, the garrison surrendered to the Japanese, and Pye began pulling the Pacific Fleet into a defensive shell.

The whaleboat was so covered with oil, inside and out, that the passengers stood up for the ride to the pier. Nimitz, stunned by the loss of Wake and dazed by the reality of what he had just seen, noted several small boats out in the harbor. He asked what were they doing out in the rain? Recovering bodies, he was told, which were still rising to the surface. He made the rest of the ride in silence.

Pearl Harbor had long been an industrial enclave surrounded by pineapple farms. First-time visitors always commented about the sweet, fragrant smell of ripening fruit. On Christmas Day 1941 the smells were far from sweet—burned oil, burned wood, burned paint, and those burned and bloated bodies still being pulled from the waters of the harbor.

There was work to be done, and little time to do it, but Nimitz needed a few days to get on top of things before he felt he could step in and take over. He spent the time getting briefed on force levels and readiness, and meeting key members of the staff.

There were two staff divisions that dealt with issues far removed from any in Nimitz's previous experience—public relations and intelligence—that soon would occupy a great deal of his time and attention. The public relations office was headed by a reserve officer—a former reporter with the *Los Angeles Times*—Lieutenant Commander Waldo Drake, who joined the CINCPAC staff early in 1941. His highest priority was making sure that no information escaped that might be of any use to the enemy. Otherwise, he was making it up as he went along; there were no established rules or guidelines for dealing with reporters.

The intelligence officer was Lieutenant Commander Edwin T. Layton, a Japanese language and culture expert, who would become one of only two CINCPAC staff officers who remained through the end of the war; the other was Nimitz.

Layton worked closely with Station Hypo, a Pearl Harbor–based Japanese-language code-breaking unit that monitored naval traffic, picked up through a network of radio intercept (RI) stations. Hypo shared efforts with two similar units: one in Melbourne, and Op–20–G, which was part of the naval communications office in Washington, DC. Hypo was headed by Commander Joseph Rochefort, an experienced cryptographer and also a Japanese specialist. He and Layton had spent three years together in Japan (1929–32), studying language and customs. When Nimitz took over, the Hypo staff was just having some success with a new version of the Japanese naval code, JN-25.

All of Hypo's efforts were in direct support of CINCPAC, but it was administratively attached to the commander of the 14th Naval District (COM 14), which handled support services. The district commandant was Rear Admiral Claude Bloch, who back in 1940 had worn four stars as the fleet commander but reverted to his permanent rank when Admiral Richardson came in and he changed jobs. As Nimitz would quickly learn, Bloch still thought of himself—in a friendly sort of way—as the man in charge.

Nimitz came to realize that the Pearl Harbor disaster was not nearly as bad as it seemed, and infinitely better than it might have been had Admiral Kimmel received warning in time to send the fleet to confront the attackers. The Japanese ships were faster, fully primed for action, and their six carriers would have been well nigh invincible. In a postwar letter to then chief of naval operations Admiral David L. McDonald, Nimitz wrote, "it was God's divine will that Kimmel did not have his fleet at sea to intercept the Japanese Carrier Task Force."[13] The fleet would have lost, he estimated, all of the ships, sunk in water too deep for rescue or salvage and 20,000 men would have been killed.

It turned out that most of the physical damage was temporary. Six of the eight battleships would return to duty. The cruisers—eight at Pearl, two untouched, five with light damage, one with heavy damage—would all be repaired. (Three of the battleships and two of the damaged cruisers were back in service by February 1942.) Of the twenty-nine destroyers at Pearl, two were destroyed and two were damaged. The four submarines were untouched. Most of the tenders, minelayers, minesweepers, fleet tugs, and other auxiliaries were untouched. In fact, of the 101 ships at Pearl Harbor, only about 20 percent were affected, and most of those not for long.

No carriers were hit because the three Pacific Fleet carriers *Lexington, Saratoga,* and *Enterprise* had been at sea with their fast cruiser, destroyer, and oiler escorts; they soon would be joined by the *Yorktown,* en route from the Atlantic. In one bit of great good luck, the *Enterprise* and her escorts had been scheduled to enter Pearl Harbor at exactly the time of the first wave of attack, but they had been delayed by weather and were still two hundred miles to the west. Eighteen *Enterprise* planes were sent off in advance, a normal practice, to get the planes off the decks and safely ashore before the carrier docked. Those unarmed planes arrived in the middle of the attack; five were shot down, most likely by defenders, the others managed to land.

The Japanese did not hit Fleet Headquarters, which housed the vital communications and cryptography center, the machine shops, much of the shipyard, the sub base, and, most important, the tank farm with 4,500,000 barrels of fuel oil. Had the Japanese left the ships alone and only destroyed the tank farm, they would have met the primary objective of the attack, which was to impact the fleet's ability to conduct effective operations against Japanese expansion. The fleet would have been forced to pull back 2,500 miles to the West Coast. With the fuel farm intact, the undamaged elements of the fleet, especially the carriers, were ready to do battle.

Was this an oversight? Possibly, but the Japanese fleet commander, cautious to a fault, feared counterstrikes from the American carriers, location unknown. He believed he had achieved the prime objective as his pilots reported that the battle fleet was in ruins. Further, his aircraft needed resupply, which meant that if he launched another wave, the next mission might not be finished until after dark—and his pilots had not been trained for nighttime landings. So the Japanese fleet, triumphant, headed for home.

There were two significant, and certainly unintended, consequences of the Japanese attack. First, by taking out the battleships, the Japanese forced an end to the ingrained, time-honored fascination with the so-called queen of the seas. Of necessity, the burden was shifted to those heretofore naval stepchildren of the twentieth century: the submarine and the aircraft carrier. In the near term, all of the Pacific Fleet battleships—including those repaired after the attack—were shifted to ports on the West Coast. Nimitz quickly realized that these World War I–vintage ships were too slow to keep up with the carriers and unable to defend themselves against air or submarine attack without strong escorts, which were not, at that time, available. Second, the attack coalesced American public opinion as never before. Appeasement, denial, isolationism—which had been a major part of the public and political opposition to any involvement in the troubles in Europe—were gone. "Remember Pearl Harbor!" became the rallying cry. In a few hours on December 7, 1941, Japan planted the seeds of its own defeat.

On December 31, in dress white uniform and wearing a new set of four-star shoulder boards that had been presented to him by the staff of the submarine base, Chester Nimitz, 56, took command of the U.S. Pacific Fleet. He was standing on the deck of the submarine *Grayling*. The symbolism—the lowly submariner taking over from the battleship admirals—was not lost on the observers. Nimitz gave a quick speech: "We have taken a tremendous wallop . . . but I have no doubt of the ultimate outcome," and he offered his advice for the near-term with a bit of Hawaiian slang, "Hoomanawanui" (patience). When asked for a translation, he improvised, "Bide your time, keep your powder dry, and take advantage of the opportunity when it's offered."[14]

His remarks were as much for the members of the press as for anyone else. Robert Casey, a habitually skeptical journalist from the Knox paper, *Chicago Daily News,* complained that Nimitz "was reasonably frank about saying nothing."[15]

Next on the agenda was a meeting with the staff, not eagerly awaited by those officers who had worked for and supported Admiral Kimmel. They were certain they would quickly be reassigned, as did other staff officers who worked with Vice Admiral Pye and had been bombed out of a job. All were tainted by failure, and it was natural for the new admiral to bring in his own trusted team.

Thus, they were ready when Nimitz began a predictable little speech, thanking them for their loyal and valiant service, complimenting them on their professionalism. But they weren't ready for what came next—he wanted all of them to stay on to work with him.

CHAPTER TWELVE

OPENING GAMBIT

Nimitz had been picked for the CINCPAC job by President Franklin Delano Roosevelt without the concurrence of either the chief of naval operations (CNO), Admiral Harold Stark, or the newly appointed commander in chief of the U.S. Fleet (COMINCH), Admiral Ernest J. King.[1] Stark favored Nimitz's academy classmate Royall Ingersoll, and King thought of Nimitz as a "political admiral" who had gained his influence through repeated tours in Washington, not as a war-fighter. For a time, until King came to realize that Nimitz was up to the job, their working relationship was strained. King—with a well-deserved reputation as a brilliant but hard-nosed martinet—treated Nimitz more as an errand boy ("do this, change that") than a fleet commander.[2]

In fact, a mission was already underway under the long-distance control of King when Nimitz took command. The *Yorktown*, just coming into the Pacific from duty in the Atlantic, would escort a Marine brigade from San Diego to Samoa (the only American base in the central Pacific) and then go on to make largely symbolic strikes against Japanese bases in the Gilbert and Marshall Islands. Those raids would not have much impact on the war, but at the least they would show the Japanese—and, more important, the American public—that the Pacific Fleet was still in business.

Nimitz resented being told what to do with his forces before he even really knew what he had to work with, but he knew the rules. However—no matter that it was hatched by King, there was a major flaw in the plan. It was reasonable to assume that the Japanese knew something about the mission and might try to stop it, thus putting the carrier at risk, because the five ships that would carry the Marines and their supplies had been loading out in San Diego, in plain sight of any loitering Japanese agents. The shipping crates, piled high on the dock, were prominently marked, "Supply Officer, Naval Station, Tutuila, Samoa."[3]

Vice Admiral W. S. Pye, who was sitting in on staff meetings while awaiting orders, recommended that Nimitz add a second carrier to the mix, and Nimitz easily agreed; the *Enterprise* was assigned. The two carrier groups would both protect the mission and then use their combined strength to carry out King's directive to hit the Marshalls and Gilberts. The Marine brigade left San Diego on January 6, escorted by the *Yorktown;* Vice Admiral Bill Halsey and the *Enterprise* would be waiting near Samoa, along with a bombardment force headed by Rear Admiral Raymond Spruance.

Just at this time—in his first week as CINCPAC and while still trying to navigate through the King thicket—Nimitz had to deal with complaining newsmen. He was alerted by a rather snippy dispatch from Secretary of the Navy Frank Knox that Robert Casey, the reporter for his newspaper, the *Chicago Daily News,* was griping about censorship. Knox told Nimitz that Casey, "will call on you. Please listen to him on Navy censorship question. . . . Hope you can correct present conditions that are complained of."[4]

Nimitz was not interested in giving Casey the honor of a private forum; he called in all of the newsmen working the CINCPAC beat and got right to the point: "All right, men," he said, "let's hear your gripes." First and foremost, they said, they needed news. Nimitz told them that so far the only news was bad news, and he was not about to let the Japanese know how well *they* were doing. Next came the complaint about censorship. The process was complicated—stories had to be reviewed by censors at both the naval district COM 14 and CINCPAC—and seemed capricious and arbitrary, and, most irritating, the reporters were not even allowed to see what changes had been made to their copy. Nimitz cut out the COM 14 censors and told Waldo Drake to ensure that each correspondent would see the censored material.

He also gave Casey and a few other complainers permission to board the *Enterprise,* just about to get underway for Samoa. They might just run into some "news."

On January 11, 1942, Japan declared war on the Netherlands and began moving to take control of the oil, rubber, and tin-rich islands of the Dutch East

Indies. On the same day, the *Saratoga* was torpedoed and put out of action for five months.

And, meeting in Washington, D.C., FDR and British Prime Minister Winston Churchill agreed on a "Europe First" strategy. Britain, which had been fighting the war for three years, was in imminent danger of capture or collapse. Therefore, in the allocation of resources, defeating Germany and freeing Europe would have priority. In the near term, efforts against Japan would be limited to slowing Japanese expansion, with more aggressive moves to be undertaken if and when increased resources allowed. Fortunately—for Nimitz—the European war had become largely a land war with naval forces focused on transport and anti-submarine efforts. There was little need for carriers and fast battleships. The United States already had some 11 carriers, 15 battleships, 54 cruisers, 191 destroyers, and 73 submarines under construction. As the war went on and more and more new warships entered service, most would be allocated to the Pacific. In the meantime, Nimitz had to make do with what he had.

On January 15 an impatient King called for more speed in moving against the Marshalls and Gilberts and ordered a follow-on attack on Wake Island by the *Lexington* force. Nimitz couldn't do much about the pace of operations— the Marines wouldn't even arrive at Samoa for another week. He did task Vice Admiral Wilson Brown and his *Lexington* group with an assault on Wake and sent the oiler *Neches* out in support, but when the oiler was sunk by a submarine, Nimitz canceled the mission.

On January 29 Nimitz held his first formal press conference, not to announce the ongoing operations but to explain Army-Navy command relationships in the Pacific, a topic that would be of continuing concern throughout the war. He was, he said, in overall command for the coordination of military operations but had no involvement in Army internal administrative matters. He would decide the objectives to be attained and the military forces and tasks needed to achieve them. Command responsibility then passed to whoever was in charge of the forces assigned.

When asked for some "reassuring word for the people back home," Nimitz said, "We have every expectation" of holding the Hawaiian Islands.[5] This probably didn't reassure anyone, but what else could he say?

On February 1 the *Yorktown* and *Enterprise* groups hit their targets in the Marshalls and Gilberts. On this, the first-ever combat operation under his command, some of the King style of management seems to have overtaken Nimitz's normal hands-off leadership. He sent *thoughtful* directives to Halsey, as in "It is essential the attacks be driven home. . . . Exploit this situation by expanding operations, utilizing both task forces in such repeated air attacks and ship bombardments as developments and logistics make feasible. If practicable, extend offensive action beyond one day."[6] Halsey was insulted; he had been commanding aircraft carriers since 1935 and knew very well how to allocate and employ his resources.

One thing Halsey had not yet learned, however, was how to evaluate the after-action reports of his aviators. In his early reports to Nimitz, results were greatly exaggerated—eight ships sunk (including two submarines, a light cruiser, and a small carrier), many others damaged, and many shore facilities destroyed. A follow-up dispatch corrected the score: three ships sunk (a transport and two smaller vessels), nine damaged, and a few fires set ashore. At this stage in the war, the Navy men who flew airplanes were not trained in ship identification and damage assessment. In the heat of the moment, when they were themselves under attack, they didn't go back for a closer look. (This was to be an even more frustrating issue with Army pilots, many of whom had never even seen a ship of *any* kind until reporting for duty in the Pacific.)

The low score was irrelevant (and not fully reported to the press); the U.S. Navy had gone on the offensive. Newspaper coverage was joyous: "U.S. Pacific Fleet Batters Japanese Bases." This was "an answer," said the *New York Times*, "to the question long raised and repeated frequently by critics: 'Where is our Navy?'"[7] The next day Nimitz told the press assembled at Pearl Harbor, "I know that a question uppermost in the minds of the American people has been, 'Where is the fleet?' This question was answered yesterday by the splendid achievements of our ships and planes in the attacks on enemy concentrations in the Marshall and Gilbert Islands."[8]

The *Enterprise* returned to Pearl Harbor on February 5 to a grand reception. Halsey, the "hero of the moment," played it up for the press. Soon enough, the newspapers crowned him with the sobriquet "Bull." The origin of "Bull" is a bit murky—possibly a typographical error for "Bill," but in any case it stuck.[9]

Next, King ordered Nimitz to send the *Lexington*, a heavy cruiser, and two destroyers, and all of the patrol planes and Army bombers he felt he could spare down to Australia, fast, where Japanese strength was growing. He also told Nimitz to bring out the battleships parked on the West Coast and take "prompt action to check enemy advance."[10]

On February 8, in his own exasperation, Nimitz fired back:

> Pacific Fleet markedly inferior in all types to enemy. Cannot conduct aggressive action Pacific except raids of hit-and-run character which are unlikely to relieve pressure Southwest Pacific. Logistic problems far surpass peacetime conception and always precarious due to fueling at sea and dependence upon weather.[11]

It would be pointless, he wrote, to deploy the battleships because they were of World War I vintage, too slow to keep up with the carriers, and too exposed in other applications without air and antisubmarine coverage, which simply was not available. As for "prompt action to check enemy advance," Nimitz advised King, "Unless this fleet is strengthened by strong additions, particularly in aircraft, light forces, carriers, and fast fleet tankers, its effectiveness for offensive action is limited." In keeping with King's earlier order to protect Hawaii and the line of communications, he would keep one of his two available carrier groups at Pearl Harbor and send the other toward Samoa.[12]

On February 9, King returned fire:

> Pacific Fleet not, repeat not, markedly inferior in all types to forces enemy can bring to bear within operating radius of Hawaii while he is committed to extensive operations in Southwest Pacific. Your forces will however be markedly inferior from Australia to Alaska when the enemy has gained objective in Southwest Pacific unless every effort is continuously made to damage his ships and bases.[13]

King suggested that any action toward the southwest will "protect Midway-Hawaii line" while affording badly needed "relief of pressure in Southwest Pacific." He told Nimitz to "review situation" and "consider active operations."

Frustrated with King's failure to grasp the logistic realities of operations in the vast Pacific Ocean, Nimitz sent Pye—one of King's few close friends—flying off to Washington to brief King on some simple facts of life. It took, for example, three oilers to support the *Lexington* group operating so far from home—three times as many, that is, as would be required to support a carrier group in King's former area of command, the Atlantic. Nimitz didn't have the resources to undertake much more than was already underway.

King backed off. He would be satisfied, for now, with occasional raids on the Japanese island bases.

Pye also carried a personal message from Nimitz to King. The helpful suggestions of COM 14's Admiral Bloch had become a distraction; Bloch was eager to share his wisdom with Nimitz, to pass on his advice on how to run the war. Nimitz hoped that King might find another assignment for Bloch, where his advice might be appreciated. King understood; Bloch was appointed to the General Board, the group of "wise men" who proposed overall naval policy.

But Nimitz was not about to ignore King's pleading for more victories, however symbolic. Nimitz knew that any action he might undertake with the forces currently at hand would have little impact on the Japanese juggernaut, but another series of raids among the islands—say, Wake and Marcus—could add another boost to morale at home and, more important, give the fleet more experience. He gave the job to Halsey.

There was a glitch: Bold warrior Halsey was superstitious. His group had been designated Task Force 13 and it was scheduled to sail on Friday, February 13. An easy fix, as noted in the CINCPAC command diary entry for the day, "deference was paid to possible superstitious persons." Nimitz changed the Task Force number to 16 and the sailing date to Valentine's Day, February 14.[14]

Singapore surrendered to the Japanese on February 15 and 80,000 allied troops became prisoners of war. On February 19 a Japanese attack devastated the harbor at Darwin, Australia. Morale in the states was dipping lower.

Halsey raided Wake on February 24 and Marcus on March 4, sinking one small patrol craft and setting a few buildings on fire. As Nimitz predicted, this had nil effect on the Japanese. On February 28 the Japanese began the invasion of Java—an island with a population as large as that of England—and by March 9 had secured it.

There was a small victory for the Americans on March 10—a combined *Lexington-Yorktown* assault on Japanese forces delayed a planned landing in New Guinea. The task force commander Vice Admiral Wilson Brown, aboard the *Lexington*, then headed back to Pearl Harbor, leaving the *Yorktown* to cruise around the Coral Sea. When Brown reached port on March 26, he and the *Lexington* had been at sea for fifty-four days, and the New Guinea raid had been the only action.

Brown told Nimitz that attacking heavily fortified bases from poorly charted waters was too risky for carriers. Having operated in those same areas—and having suffered from poorly charted waters—Nimitz was satisfied with that explanation, but King was not. He thought Brown wasn't aggressive enough and had to go. Nimitz assigned Brown to a new command, the Amphibious Force, headquartered at San Diego, whose mission was to train for future amphibious operations against enemy-held islands. It was hardly a demotion, and in fact was a good job for Brown, a former superintendent at the Naval Academy and an experienced trainer and educator. This was a perfect example of Nimitz's skill at putting the best-qualified men in the most important jobs.

On March 11, 1942, President Roosevelt ordered the most experienced officer in all of the armed forces, General Douglas MacArthur, to leave the doomed Philippines and head for Australia. MacArthur, a former Army chief of staff who had lived in the Philippines since 1935, was spirited away to Mindanao (along with his family and aides) under cover of darkness aboard four PT boats. The rest of the journey, from Mindanao to Australia, was by air. MacArthur announced, "The President of the United States ordered me to break through the Japanese lines and proceed . . . to Australia for the purpose, as I understand it, of organizing the American offensive against Japan, a primary object of which is the relief of the Philippines. I came through and I shall return."[15]

On March 30, the lines of command in the greater Pacific were drawn by the Joint Chiefs of Staff (JCS). MacArthur was not to be the sole organizer of the offensive but had to share responsibility with Nimitz. MacArthur was named supreme commander, Allied Forces in the Southwest Pacific Area, which included Australia, the Solomons, New Guinea, the Bismarcks (a collection of islands just north of New Guinea with a key base at Rabaul), and the Philippines. Nimitz was commander in chief of the Pacific Ocean Areas (CINCPOA)—which was pretty much everything else—and all of the forces therein. The Pacific Ocean Areas was divided into North, Central, and South regions. The South was the hot zone and merited a subordinate commander of its own. Nimitz wanted to appoint Vice Admiral Pye to that post. King had his own candidate, Vice Admiral Robert L. Ghormley, who got the job.

Meanwhile, the *Hornet* was being transferred from the Atlantic and due to arrive in San Diego on March 20. Nimitz was looking forward to having four active carriers in his fleet. He decided to give his old shipmate John McCain command of a new task force built around the *Hornet,* but when he proposed that assignment to King on March 12, he was told to hold off. King had other plans. Nimitz drafted a proposed schedule of operations for his enlarged carrier fleet, which he shared with King on March 14. King again said hold off and sent a staff officer to brief Nimitz on a mission that had been in the works since January. A two-carrier task force, the *Hornet* and the *Enterprise,* with Halsey in charge, was to carry a force of Army Air Force B-25 bombers into position to make a mid-April air raid on Tokyo, Yokohama, Yokosuka, Nagoya, and Kobe. This certainly was the most daring—and could have been the dumbest—act of the Pacific war.

Nimitz might be forgiven for thinking that King had lost his mind, risking two carriers on a grandstand play that could have no appreciable effect on the conflict. However, as recorded in the CINCPAC command diary, "This was not a proposal made for [Nimitz] to consider but a plan to be carried out by him."[16]

About the same time, Nimitz was hit by a bit of distressing news that was not shared with him officially but of which he most certainly became aware. In February, Knox had convened a secret selection board of nine admirals, active and retired—led by Stark and King—to identify the "most competent" flag officers in the Navy. Knox sent the results to the president on March 9. The winners included, among others, Halsey, Ghormley, Jacobs, McCain . . . and King. Nimitz was not on the list.

Nimitz kept his personal feelings hidden from his associates, but left a clue in one of the surviving letters to his wife. Not only was King trying to run the show in the Pacific, but Nimitz had heard not a word about anything from Knox since the "Hope you can correct present conditions" note back in January. On March 22, Nimitz confided to Catherine: "I'm afraid [Knox] is not so keen for me now as he was when I left—but that is only natural. Ever so many people were enthusiastic for me at the start but when things do not move fast enough—they sour on me. I will be lucky to last six months. The public may demand action and results faster than I can produce."[17]

Nimitz could take comfort, however, in one solid fact: He had been named CINCPOA several weeks after FDR saw the list, so his standing with the boss did not seem to have been affected.[18]

On April 18, 1942, sixteen B-25 bombers were launched from *Hornet* in what had to be one of the greater ironies of the day: Army bombers with the official nickname "Mitchell" (as in, Brigadier General "Billy," the 1920s denigrator of the Navy) flying from the deck of a Navy carrier. The planes had been loaded aboard *Hornet* at the Alameda Naval Air Station on San Francisco Bay; once en route to the target, the *Hornet* was escorted by the *Enterprise* and four destroyers, all under the command of Halsey. The air crews, all volunteers, were led by Army Lieutenant Colonel James H. Doolittle.

The B-25 pilots had been trained to take off, fully loaded, from a short runway, about the length of a carrier deck, but had never practiced on an actual carrier. They would head off for their targets when the carrier was about 500 miles from Japan; after dropping their bombs, the planes would continue on to land on friendly airfields in China. The force was sighted by Japanese picket ships while still 650 miles out, but Doolittle elected to go anyway. Surprisingly, in spite of the alert, there was little opposition to the raid—most likely because the Japanese knew that the ships were well outside the striking range of any typical carrier aircraft, and thus not much of a threat. All of the bombers made it safely past Japan, but because of the extra 150 miles added to the mission, fifteen didn't quite make it to those Chinese airfields, ran out of fuel, and either crash-landed or were abandoned by their crews, who parachuted to safety. The sixteenth plane landed in Vladivostok, where it was impounded by the Russians (not then at war with Japan, they were playing a neutrality game). Eighty-one men went on the mission, seventy-one survived.

The raid was wildly celebrated in the United States, though it inflicted little physical or psychological damage in Japan—the overwhelming majority of Japanese didn't even know it had happened. However, combined with the earlier interference with the New Guinea invasion force and the hit-and-run raids on the islands, it was a wake-up call for the Japanese government. Something had to be done about the American carriers.

In the meantime, day-to-day Japanese operations continued unabated. Collating radio intercepts from around the circuit, Joe Rochefort and Station Hypo determined that a force of transports and three aircraft carriers were headed for the Coral Sea, at the eastern end of New Guinea, to attack the capital, Port Moresby. After consultation with MacArthur—this was in his area but he didn't have the forces—Nimitz did what he could. Unfortunately, thanks in large part to Admiral King's "initiatives," CINCPAC's assets were limited. The *Saratoga* was still being repaired and the *Hornet* and the *Enterprise* would not return from the Doolittle raid until April 25, too late to get them ready and into the southwest Pacific. The mission fell to the *Yorktown* and the *Lexington*.

The action began on May 7 with a string of mistaken identities. In making a report, American scouts miscoded a sighting of two cruisers and two destroyers as two carriers and four heavy cruisers. The Japanese mistook an oiler for a more lethal carrier. Two Australian cruisers were mistaken for carriers, which were attacked (without result) by Japanese planes, and a short time later, the same ships were assumed to be Japanese and attacked (without result) by a flight of B–26s from Australia. And, in one of those true events that seem like the stuff of fantasy, confused Japanese pilots joined the landing circle of the *Yorktown* until one of them was shot down and the others got the message.

But the *Lexington* group sank the smallest of the Japanese carriers and American pilots shot down a number of Japanese planes, which brought the opposing forces to remarkably even terms: each now had two heavy carriers, the Americans had 121 planes, the Japanese 122, ready for action.

On May 8, after ducking in and out of rain squalls, the scouting planes of the forces detected each other at almost the same moment. There was an exchange of air strikes in what became history's first naval battle in which the opposing ships never sighted each other.

This Battle of the Coral Sea was something of a draw: The *Yorktown* and *Lexington* were both damaged (*Lexington's* damage soon proved fatal), and the oiler and a destroyer were sunk, but the Japanese lost more planes (and experienced pilots) and were forced once again to cancel the invasion of New Guinea. Of greater importance, the damage to one of the Japanese carriers and the losses to the other carrier's air group kept both ships out of the next major action of the war: an attack engineered by Admiral Isoroku Yamamoto, who had planned the Pearl Harbor raid, to draw the American aircraft carriers into a trap.

CHAPTER THIRTEEN

THE CODE-BREAKERS

Much of military code-breaking consists of searching for probable words—names of senior commanders, components of the force, possible targets—and looking for patterns. In the most basic of code systems, one letter is substituted for another. For example, if the message has been written in English, the most common letter in the alphabet, "e," might be replaced with the letter "z." If you see "sdzzh" you might suspect, in context, "fleet"—which, if correct, gives you the substitutes for three more letters. As more target words begin to appear, you can test, and retest, your assumptions, a painstaking operation. At the other end of the cryptologic scale are the machine-based systems, such as the German Enigma, by which each letter in the original message would be encrypted multiple times before transmission. That is, an e might become z and z would change to t and t to g. The message could only be read at the receiving end with another Enigma machine operating at exactly the same settings as the sender's—settings that could be changed daily, with the "key lists" usually communicated by courier.

The Japanese naval code, JN-25, was not machine-based, but was so complex that the Japanese assumed it to be secure. A group of five numbers representing a word were chosen from a code book with a list of some 30,000 words—all, of course, in Japanese. Each five-number group was then replaced by another five-number group, taken from a similar list of numbers that was literally laid alongside the first. To add to the confusion for the code-breakers, there was no fixed point at which the second list of numbers was paired with the first. On any given day, the matches might start at any point; the sending and receiving stations shared the key. For example, the key might instruct, "Start the substitutions on this date at the 400th number on the list." Thus, 00510 could mean "kantai" (fleet), but it might be transmitted as 13012 today and perhaps as 27332 when a new scheme kicked in on a future date. Even if you had captured a copy of the code book with all 30,000 words and had the list of substitute numbers, you could not line up the numbers and read the message without the key. If you had neither the code book or the key, you would be just where the cryptanalysts started out. Code-breaking was exhausting, tedious, and mind-challenging work.

In early May, the code-breakers at Station Hypo began to see hints of a very large forthcoming operation. After weeks of unimaginable effort, the team could describe the composition of the Japanese force: more than 200 ships including 8 carriers, 11 battleships, 22 cruisers, 65 destroyers, 21 submarines, and approximately 700 aircraft, along with transports carrying some 5,000 troops. It looked like something was going to be invaded, but where—and when—was still an unknown. Working on the same problem, Op-20-G, the code and signals group in Washington, believed the ships were headed to California. Joseph Rochefort and his team in Hawaii thought that was unlikely—as a practical matter, 5,000 troops were not nearly enough for a major invasion, and it made no sense for the Japanese to put their ships in range of all of the land-based aircraft on the West Coast while leaving the dreaded American carriers free to block any withdrawal. But some in Washington were so sure that the target might be San Francisco that a senior Army Air Forces officer limited the number of aircraft reinforcements he sent to Nimitz because he had to be prepared to defend that fine city.

Japanese message traffic hinted at a possible location—AF. But no one was sure exactly what AF meant. In the Japanese system, A usually stood for something American and the code-breakers knew, for instance, that AH stood for Hawaii and AK for Pearl Harbor. But AF remained a mystery until one Japanese dispatch mentioned that the U.S. operated extensive air searches from AF, thus AF must have either an airfield or a seaplane base, or both. There was only one place within several thousand miles west of Hawaii that met that description. Midway.

By coincidence, Nimitz and King had just discussed the vulnerability of that island, some 1,300 miles to the west of Pearl Harbor. Early in May Nimitz and a few staffers flew over to Midway for a look around. They climbed in and out of gun positions and the underground command center, getting a refresher on the layout and defenses. The real purpose of the visit was to show the troops—Navy pilots and a couple of thousand Marines—that they had not been forgotten. In a nice touch, Nimitz promoted the base commander and the Marine unit commander to captain and colonel, respectively.

As days passed, the code-breakers' store of knowledge grew by bits and pieces. A Japanese ship asked for copies of a series of charts for waters west of Hawaii. One message requested weather reports from station ships north of Midway to cover three days of air operations; the dates, however, were enciphered in a separate, as yet unreadable, code. Another message mentioned that planes would be launched fifty miles northwest of AF.

Nimitz quickly added to the forces stationed at Midway, bringing the totals to 99 Navy and Marine aircraft, about evenly divided between dive bombers, fighters, and patrol planes, along with 19 Army B-17 and 4 B-26 bombers. He stationed a seaplane tender with destroyer escort at French Frigate Shoals, halfway between Midway and Oahu, to provide fuel and support to American patrol planes and block the location's use by Japanese seaplanes operating as long-range scouts. Nimitz also called Commander John Ford—Academy Award–winning movie director who had been in the Naval Reserve since 1934—and told him to "throw a bag together and get out here."[1] He sent Ford to Midway to film the forthcoming attack.

Station Hypo determined that the Japanese ships were organized in several groups, with at least an invasion force, a striking force, and a much smaller force apparently headed toward Dutch Harbor, Alaska. This might be an effort to draw American ships 1,600 miles away from Midway, or as cover for a separate invasion. There was nothing definitive one way or another. Nimitz sent five cruisers and four destroyers to Alaska.

The capture of Midway would give the Japanese a base from which their long-range, land-based aircraft could control a wide swath of the Pacific. Unknown to the Americans, however, the real purpose of the attack was to draw the U.S. Navy into a trap, an epic battle with the Japanese fleet, and finish what had been started at Pearl Harbor. The striking force was the bait; the much larger main force would be lurking 200 miles to the west, waiting. Timing was critical: The Japanese knew that the United States had several hundred warships under construction, many of which would soon be headed to the Pacific. If the Pacific Fleet could be annihilated, the Japanese could then pick off the new arrivals one at a time and get on with their plans to control the resources of the western Pacific.

Some officers in Hawaii and Washington could not let go of their fantasies. Why was Nimitz so certain that Midway was the target? To them, AF could mean anything or nothing. The naysayers' favorite target, no matter how illogical, remained the West Coast of the United States.

The clincher grew out of a casual conversation among Hypo staffers. The subject was Midway, and one code-breaker mentioned that Midway once had some seawater desalinization problems. Another staffer half-joked that if they had a problem with their equipment and sent a radio message to Pearl, you can bet a Japanese radio intercept station would be telling their world.[2]

Bingo!

Midway and Pearl Harbor were linked by underwater cable, which could not be tapped and was thus secure. On a regular basis, innocuous messages were exchanged by radio in order not to alert the Japanese to the hidden asset. A message was sent to Midway via cable, requesting that they send a plain-language radio message to COM 14 at Pearl, complaining of a shortage of drinking water.

Sure enough, on May 22, the station in Melbourne intercepted a dispatch from Japanese naval intelligence: "The AF air unit sent following radio message . . . 'at the present time we have only enough water for two weeks. Please supply us immediately.'" And the Japanese naval command ordered that water desalination equipment be included with the invasion force.[3] At the same time, Hypo broke the cipher the Japanese were using for dates and predicted the attack would begin on June 4. Nimitz tried to maintain a controlled persona but, according to one staffer, was "radiating excitement."[4]

Nimitz was convinced, but not Army commander Lieutenant General Delos C. Emmons. He believed that the real target was Oahu. To assuage the general, Nimitz assigned a senior officer to try to blow holes in all of the Hypo assertions and shared some of the most sensitive intelligence information with the general. Emmons wasn't persuaded and warned Nimitz that he was placing too much reliance on reports of Japanese intentions. He advised Nimitz to base his plans instead on Japanese capabilities—as taught at all of the War Colleges. Nimitz countered that any American force sent forth on the assumption that

Midway was the target would be positioned between the enemy and Oahu, so the Hawaiian Islands were covered.

The Americans indulged in one brilliant bit of deception, attributed to General Douglas MacArthur. A few ships and shore stations in the Coral Sea area exchanged radio traffic that would be consistent with carrier operations; Japanese communications analysts reported to Admiral Yamamoto that he wouldn't have to worry about one American carrier task force as the *Yorktown* was still operating in the faraway Coral Sea.

As it developed, the Midway striking force consisted of 4 carriers, 2 battle-ships, and a mix of 15 cruisers and destroyers. The Americans had mustered 8 cruisers, 20 destroyers, 3 oilers, 19 submarines, 5 auxiliaries, and 3 carriers: the *Enterprise, Hornet,* and *Yorktown,* which had just barely been repaired in time for the attack. She had limped home from the Coral Sea on May 27 and was immediately sent into dry dock, where a rubber-booted Nimitz led a team of repair experts to inspect the damage just as the last of the water was being pumped out. Assessments were quick; patch this, shore-up that. Nimitz said, 72 hours, no more, and the ship must be underway. It was—with repair crews still aboard, patching.

There was a last-minute shift in American commanders: Halsey reported in sick, suffering from a painful and debilitating case of shingles. He was in the hospital and out of action (and would be until September). Ray Spruance took over Halsey's force. Rear Admiral Frank Jack Fletcher, aboard the *Yorktown,* assumed overall command of the Midway operation.

Japanese radio intercept stations noted a jump in Pearl Harbor–area air-ground radio chatter and urgent messages, suggesting a carrier force must be putting to sea. Incredibly, this information was not passed on to the Midway striking force; Yamamoto had commanded strict radio silence, and strict radio silence he got. The first few days in June, as the Japanese and American forces were rushing headlong to a game-changing collision, only one side—the American—knew about the other.

On June 3 one of the Midway patrol planes spotted the Japanese transport force and the battle was on. Six Army B-17s were sent out to attack the transports, without result. Later in the day, a Navy patrol plane put a torpedo into an enemy oiler; the damage was not significant. Then, early June 4, another Midway scout spotted the striking force carriers and reported attackers headed in. This gave Midway about thirty minutes warning. The patrol planes flew off to safety at French Frigate Shoals, an attack force went out to find the enemy ships, and the defending fighter planes took off about twenty minutes before the enemy arrived. The base commander, whose battle station was in the underground bunker, gave Commander Ford a nonphotographic assignment: Take station on top of the power plant, the highest point on the island, and report by telephone, moment by moment and in detail, whatever he saw. "We are going to be attacked," he told Ford. "Forget the pictures as much as you can . . . I want a good accurate account of the bombing."[5] Ford managed to do both—keep the CO informed and get good pictures, the most memorable of which shows an exploding bomb sending a large chunk of concrete directly at the camera. The impact earned Ford a Purple Heart. His documentary film of the attack on Midway earned him another Academy Award.

The Japanese attacked the island with more than a hundred planes. They shot down 17 defending Marine Corps fighters but lost a third of their force, largely to antiaircraft fire. They did not succeed in closing down the airfield; to observers, it seemed they were carefully preserving the runways for their own use. The counterattacking Navy, Marine Corps, and Army Air Force planes from Midway caused minimal damage to the Japanese carrier force, and many were shot down by the vastly superior Japanese fighter aircraft and antiaircraft fire. A flight of 16 Midway B-17s came in very high above the clouds and dropped 128 500-pound bombs. There is no evidence that they scored any hits.

Just as this wave of American attacks was ending and the Japanese planes were returning to their carriers, a patrol spotted the American carriers fast approaching. This news triggered a quick change in plans. The Japanese had a number of planes in reserve, which they expected to send off on a second attack on Midway. Now, they had to swap out already-loaded contact-detonation bombs (used against land targets) with antiship weapons—torpedoes and armor-piercing bombs. It was in this interval, around 9:30 in the morning, with the hangar decks full of loaded and ready-to-go bombers and piles of removed bombs that had not yet been returned to their magazines, that torpedo planes from the American carriers made their first attacks. They scored no hits and most of these planes were lost. However, since the torpedo planes flew just above the wave-tops, they drew the Japanese combat air patrol down to attack. This cleared the way aloft for three squadrons of American dive bombers, each targeting a different Japanese carrier. Within a matter of minutes those targets had been fatally damaged. The fourth carrier was sunk later in the day.

The *Yorktown* was put out of action around noon. Fletcher moved his staff to the cruiser *Astoria*, which wasn't equipped to serve as a command post in the middle of a battle, and by evening he passed tactical control to Spruance aboard the *Enterprise*. Later, the *Yorktown* appeared to be stabilized, and efforts were made to tow her to Pearl Harbor—until a Japanese submarine interrupted the operation, putting torpedoes into both the carrier and an assisting destroyer. The destroyer sank immediately, the *Yorktown* the next day.

Battle reports from Midway Island, including John Ford's telephone relay to the base commander forwarded on to Pearl by way of the underwater cable, were immediate; those coming in by radio arrived at CINCPAC headquarters in fragments, often as excited comments from pilots reporting what they thought they saw, and Nimitz didn't know what to believe. Layton later said that Nimitz was "Frantic, as frantic as I've ever seen him."[6] When a submarine reported that three carriers were burning, there was finally room for optimism. That evening Nimitz sent a "well done" message to his force: "You who have participated in the Battle of Midway today have written a glorious page in our history. I am proud to be associated with you. I estimate that another day of all out effort on your part will complete defeat of the enemy."[7]

Action continued on June 5 and an enemy cruiser was sunk. On June 6, another flight of B-17s dropped their load on a target—an American submarine—which quickly submerged, but not before one bomber took pictures, offered as proof that they had sunk a cruiser. On closer examination the photo spoke for itself. In one of those strange juxtapositions of history, the submarine was the *Grayling*—aboard which Nimitz had assumed his command.

It was soon clear that the Japanese move on Dutch Harbor was a cover for the occupation of two of the outermost islands of the Aleutian chain, Kiska and Attu, carried out while the Midway battle was raging. The enemy did drop a few bombs on Dutch Harbor but were unopposed as they occupied the islands, some 1,000 miles to the west. The islands were of little import, to either the Americans or the Japanese.

The Japanese Combined Fleet had sailed off to do battle on May 27—the anniversary of the Battle of Tsushima, a battle in which Admiral Yamamoto himself had been badly wounded. As a talisman of victory, Yamamoto had To-go's battle-flag flying from one of the carriers. It didn't help.

The still-potent remnants of the striking force withdrew to the west. The Americans followed for a time, but Spruance elected to break off the pursuit and return to Pearl Harbor. He was running low on fuel, he was soon to be in range of Japanese bombers based on Wake Island, and he worried about being caught in a night engagement—the carrier pilots were not experienced at night landings. Spruance was criticized in some quarters, but turning back turned out to be the best move. Although no one knew it at the time, he likely would have run smack into Yamamoto's much stronger main battle force. However, Yamamoto soon realized that his mission was over; too much of his own force had been destroyed, and at about the same time he took his fleet home.

In the end, the Japanese lost 4 carriers, 1 cruiser, 322 aircraft, and perhaps 3,000 men. The U.S. lost 1 carrier, 1 destroyer, 147 aircraft, and 347 men.

Not knowing whether or not the enemy would return, or even how many undamaged carriers they might have in reserve, Nimitz asked the Army to send some Oahu-based B-17s to enhance and extend the patrol at Midway. The Army was concerned that this could leave Oahu without adequate air cover—so Nimitz made a deal: the carrier *Saratoga* was due in from San Diego at any moment with a load of planes, and if the Army would dispatch the B-17s, he would turn over control of the *Saratoga*'s planes as long as the ship was in port. The Army agreed, and soon enough the B-17s were on the way. A short time later, one of the Army officers asked, "Did you say that *Saratoga* was due at Pearl today?" Nimitz said, "Yes, she should be in any moment now."

"How long," asked the officer, "may we expect *Saratoga* to be here?

"Long enough to fuel and then she will proceed to sea."[8]

By way of apology for his unbelief about the Japanese intentions, General Emmons showed up at Nimitz's office bearing a blue-and-gold ribbon-bedecked jeroboam of champagne. Nimitz sent a car to fetch Rochefort to join the party, but in the time it took him to change into a dress uniform and get to CINCPAC headquarters, the bottle had been drained dry. Nonetheless, Nimitz welcomed Rochefort to the celebration by telling the assembled staff, "This officer deserves a major share of the credit for the victory at Midway."[9]

CHAPTER FOURTEEN

FALLOUT

W hile the battle of Midway was underway, Nimitz issued very brief statements to the press, confirming that a fight was on and offering reassurance that the United States remained in control of the area. On the last day of the battle, June 6, 1942, he reported some details: "one of our carriers was hit" but two or three Japanese carriers had been destroyed and one or two other carriers had been damaged. "Pearl Harbor has now been partially avenged," he announced. "Vengeance will not be complete until Japanese sea power has been reduced to impotence." And he added, "Perhaps we will be forgiven if we claim we are about midway to our objective."[1] The Associated Press reported, "There are no limits to Nimitz."[2]

Robert Casey, the *Chicago Daily News* reporter who had complained to Secretary of the Navy Frank Knox back in January—and was embarked on one of the ships during the battle—now offered praise. "The most outstanding surprise of this war," he wrote, "has been the discovery that the Navy is really as good as we used to think it was on, say, December 6." He explained, "We saw the Navy . . . setting out to do whatever could be done with what materials happened to lie at hand, going ahead with ever-increasing momentum, gathering up material and men as it moved and fought, outguessing Admiral Yamamoto . . . with something of the traditional American brilliance."[3]

During his June 26, 1941, congressional testimony, Nimitz had predicted, "We are approaching the time, when even if stories are true and are inimical to public interest they should be weighed carefully before being printed."[4] Well, that time had arrived. On Sunday, June 7, the *Chicago Tribune* celebrated the victory at Midway and in a page-one sidebar with a Washington dateline headlined "Navy Had Word of Jap Plan to Strike at Sea" said:

> The strength of the Japanese forces with which the American Navy is battling somewhere west of Midway Island, in what is believed to be the greatest naval battle of the war, was well known in American naval circles several days before the battle began, reliable sources in the naval intelligence disclosed.

In other words, the Navy had broken the Japanese code. This may have been the only serious violation of security by a major news organization during the Pacific war. The article detailed the order of battle, the organization of the Japanese forces, and a ship-by-ship breakdown of the main units.

Tribune reporter Stanley Johnston had picked up this bit of intelligence not in Washington but out in the Pacific. He was one of the few reporters who had embarked with the fleet—aboard the *Lexington*—during the Battle of the Coral Sea. When the carrier was fatally damaged, he was transferred to another ship and shared a stateroom with the *Lexington*'s executive officer, Commander Morton Seligman. On May 31 Nimitz sent a classified dispatch to his major combatant commanders outlining the presumed Japanese order of battle in the forthcoming Midway operation. A copy was passed to Seligman, who shared the contents with his roommate.

Some thought that Johnston and the *Chicago Tribune* should be charged with espionage, but both were protected by the First Amendment guarantee of press freedom (the reporter was not a spy but had been handed the story by a naval officer) and a political reality: *Chicago Tribune* publisher Robert R. McCormick was a rabid anti-Roosevelt critic and prosecution would have been viewed as an act of political revenge.

Whether or not the Japanese noticed the article is not known, but they soon changed the code.[5]

In all of his communiqués, Nimitz gave equal credit to Army, Navy, and Marine Corps pilots. However, Brigadier General Willis H. Hale, commander of Army Air Force bombers in the Hawaii area, told a reporter that his planes were primarily responsible for the victory. On June 12, the *New York Times* reported: "Officers of the United Sates Army Air Forces disclosed today some of the carnage spread by their high altitude bombers." The pilots "who actually dropped the bombs" reported hits on three carriers, one cruiser, one destroyer, one large transport, and one other "large vessel that may have been either a cruiser or a battleship." It was also clear, the paper reported, "that the Japanese fighter planes were not anxious to tangle with these aerial dreadnoughts."[6] Lieutenant Colonel Walter C. Sweeney, leader of the attacking force, told the *New York Times,* "I am sold on the effectiveness of high-level bombing. If we can get enough planes for attacks like these, nothing can escape us, since we can lay bombs in patterns which no ships can avoid."[7]

Any report of B-17-induced damage, however, was a wild exaggeration. A rough count shows that in all of their attacks—some 55 sorties—B-17s dropped 314 bombs, from which they themselves reported only twelve hits, hardly enough to be "responsible for the victory." A postwar comparison with Japanese accounts cut that number to three hits—at the most. Some of the B-17s took photos, all of which show bombs dropping near but not on *any* of the targets. Perhaps Colonel Sweeney was not aware of the results of the earlier American and British bombing tests against maneuvering ships. One prewar study showed that even from relatively low altitudes, 12,000 to 14,000 feet, at least eighteen to twenty planes would be required to ensure 7 percent hits on a single maneuvering surface craft.

The CINCPAC assistant gunnery officer, Lieutenant Commander E. M. Eller, was tasked with writing the battle report for Midway. This was not part of his job, but Eller had just won the annual U.S. Naval Institute "prize essay" contest and had developed a reputation as a burgeoning writer. In assembling the report, Eller had an advantage not given to many battle-report writers: Within a matter of days, almost every single American participant came to Pearl Harbor, and Eller could interview any of them.

Vitally interested in the report, Undersecretary of the Navy James Forrestal flew out from Washington. He wanted to get it right out, to let the public know about this great victory. Nimitz, however, wanted it to be right and not give too much information to the enemy. Perhaps, for example, they didn't know about the loss of the *Yorktown,* or the destruction of so many of the Midway-based aircraft. Nimitz authorized the release of a summary report on July 14 that noted the *Yorktown* had been "put out of action."⁸ The loss was not made public until the middle of September.

COM 14 nominated Joseph Rochefort for a Distinguished Service Medal (DSM), which Nimitz wholeheartedly endorsed as he sent the nomination along to King. The award was denied on the grounds that Rochefort "has merely efficiently used the tools previously prepared for his use" and that "equal credit is due to the COMINCH Planning Section for the correct evaluation of enemy intentions." Except, no one on the COMINCH staff had made the correct evaluation. That did not stop Captain Joseph R. Redman, director of naval communications, from telling anyone who would listen that the victory at Midway was the result of Op-20-G's efforts in Washington, and that Station Hypo had merely provided assistance. In this construct, Station Hypo missed the boat, but Op-20-G—which, we must note, was headed by Captain Redman's brother, Commander John Redman—saved the day.⁹

Captain Redman wanted to reorganize Pacific-area code-breaking and bring all heavy cryptographic work into, and under the control of, Op-20-G. Station Hypo would be demoted to traffic analysis. Rochefort objected. Both of the Redman brothers wanted Station Hypo to report directly to Op-20-G and not deal with CINCPAC; Op-20-G would be responsible for communicating any fresh information with Nimitz. Rochefort objected to this power-grab. He worked for Nimitz.

Rochefort was something of an outsider. He was not a graduate of the Naval Academy but had earned his commission through a Midshipman's School during World War I. He was a difficult man to work with, not the ideal team player. And Op-20-G wanted him out of his job, to be replaced by someone who understood how they played the game. In a truly Machiavellian plot, the Redman brothers managed to get the master cryptographer Rochefort removed from Hawaii and sent into naval officer limbo as the commanding officer of a floating dry dock.

Nimitz objected, but King told him that this reassignment was the wish of the Vice Chief of Naval Operations (VCNO) and therefore would not be changed. The VCNO, who had never met Rochefort and had no idea about his qualifications, had been told by Captain Redman that Rochefort was only a Japanese language student and the job needed someone trained in communications and radio intelligence. Actually, Rochefort had been well trained in those specialties some years earlier—in fact, he had more such training than his detractors. Commander Redman told the VCNO that "experience has indicated that units in combat areas cannot be relied upon to accomplish more than the business of merely reading enemy messages and performing routine work necessary to keep abreast of minor changes in the cryptographic systems involved."[10] This, two weeks after the smashing success Station Hypo had delivered on Midway.

The VCNO was a busy man. He didn't bother to check with either Rochefort or Nimitz. Nimitz was quite upset that Rochefort had been replaced without his knowledge or concurrence, but at this point, he believed any action he might take would be fruitless. Edwin Layton asked Nimitz to reintroduce the Rochefort DSM recommendation. Nimitz said, "Layton, if you know anything about Admiral King, you know that when his mind is made up, it is made up. I've got enough to do to fight this war right now." And with that, he dropped out of the argument.[11] Understandable, perhaps, but this was not the finest hour for any of the key players.

Rochefort overcame the assault on his reputation as head of a postwar special studies group assessing the impact of communications intelligence on strategic warfare. He was awarded the DSM for his efforts at Midway (along with the Presidential Medal of Freedom) in 1986—ten years after his death.

Above Rochefort's desk at Pearl Harbor hung a notice that read: "We can accomplish anything provided no one cares who gets the credit."[12]

CHAPTER FIFTEEN

THE NIMITZ STYLE

By the end of June 1942, Nimitz began swapping out members of Kimmel's and Pye's personal staffs—because they were overwhelmed by the job or they needed to get to sea to be qualified for promotion. He brought in Rear Admiral Ray Spruance as his chief of staff and Captain Forrest Sherman, recently a carrier commanding officer, as operations officer. Preston V. Mercer, his flag secretary back at Battleship Division One, came aboard as flag secretary, and Nimitz brought Hal Lamar out as flag lieutenant. Lamar would stay with Nimitz through the rest of the war.

Nimitz resisted, to a fault, expanding his staff. As he told Mercer, staff officers too often tried to justify their jobs by passing a lot of papers to each other. Still, the work load at Pearl was immense, and growing. Mercer would read, assess, and refer for action some 400 letters a day, in addition to whatever else he had to handle. Over time, the 1942 CINCPAC immediate staff of some 45 officers would grow to 245.

Nimitz also resisted pressure to have Navy Department women, officers or enlisted, on his staff. On the two occasions during the war that Nimitz traveled to Washington, he was assigned a working space staffed by very efficient, very attractive Navy and Marine Corps women. The officers who managed the women-in-the-Navy programs wanted to convince the admiral that he should allow military women to be assigned to his command. Nimitz, old-fashioned to the core, could not get accustomed to women standing up when *he* entered the room. WAVES would eventually serve on the CINCPAC staff, but only after Nimitz had moved his own office to Guam, later in the war.[1]

The CINCPAC daily schedule was fairly routine, no matter how important the activities of the day. At 8 A.M. the bugler would blow "To the Colors," and all hands would stand to attention for the daily raising of the flag. Nimitz would then convene a closed intelligence briefing for senior officers. At 9 A.M., the meeting was open to staff and visiting commanders. Visitors might be invited to make comments, then Nimitz would outline what should happen in the next four or five weeks—an operation about to be launched, new ships joining the fleet—ask for more comments, and that was it. He did not discuss operational specifics or tactics in the broad staff meetings.

By this time, Nimitz, who back in the days when he ran the submarine base would greet all incoming ships in person, was feeling isolated from the fleet. He announced that arriving commanding officers should make the standard call on the senior officer present—meaning him—as specified in Navy Regulations. Calling hour was 11A.M., and the sessions were set for a manageable (but flexible) 15 minutes when each caller, one or a dozen, would introduce himself and offer a comment or two. For skippers of new ships headed out for the first time, Nimitz would talk with them as if they were his own sons, pump them up with pride, and send them forth to do battle. From skippers returning from the war zone, he was looking for insights, assessments, and suggestions as to what could be done better.

Some sessions he treated as teaching moments. To a group of supply officers just being transferred in from the European theater, he offered meaningful comparisons: It took four ships, for example, to supply men in the forward areas of the Pacific although one could do the job in Europe. "Don't quote me," he said, "but if there is anything in the world that's bigger than the state of Texas, it's the Pacific Ocean."[2] To his former NROTC student Onnie Lattu, now in the Supply Corps and headed west, he urged, "Take care of the small boys," by which he meant the crews of minesweepers and fleet tugboats, which did not enjoy the comfort of the larger ships. "Get them ice cream, fresh cigarettes."[3]

Officers waiting to see the admiral had a chance to review "Nimitz Three Questions" posted on the wall:

1. Is the proposed operation likely to succeed?
2. What might be the consequences of failure?

3. Is it in the realm of practicability of materials and supplies?

Under the glass top on his desk, the admiral had his own checklist of things to think about: "Objective, Offensive, Surprise, Superiority of Force at Point of Contact, Simplicity, Security, Movement, Economy of Force, Cooperation."[4]

Nimitz was quick to form opinions, based on observed poise, self-confidence, and level of knowledge and sophistication appropriate to rank and level of experience. He would often make a mental note "Got to watch that man. We'll use him somewhere."[5] One visiting submarine skipper, Commander Eugene Fluckey, offered to plant antiship mines in a particular body of water that had become a regular passageway for Japanese merchant ships. The idea was sound, but, as Nimitz explained, the timing was not. The operation would be in conflict with a forthcoming campaign of which Fluckey was unaware. But Fluckey's name went into the Nimitz mental filing cabinet.

If a visitor had made his point but kept rambling on, Nimitz would start playing with the pencils on his desk. Word got around: If the hands started moving pencils, time to wrap it up and leave. If a visitor of some influence or importance didn't get the hint, Nimitz might lead him over to the chief of staff's office, suggesting he might continue the conversation with Spruance. Visitors did not hang around the chief of staff's office for long. Spruance worked at a stand-up desk and there were no chairs in the room.

Nimitz was sensitive to the feelings of others and would see nearly anyone who came to call. Once when the *Enterprise* arrived for resupply, a petty officer from the ship, a rather daring Texas boy, came to pay his respects. The caller was, well, unusual, but it had been a rough couple of days at headquarters so Lamar thought a quick diversion might be in order. He told Nimitz about the petty officer, and the admiral said, "Send him in."

It was only a few minutes until the young man broke down and confessed, that in a moment of folly he had bragged to his shipmates that since he was from Texas he could get in to see the fleet commander, and they put up a rather substantial pool of money (several thousand dollars at today's valuation) betting that he could not. Now he was ashamed, but Nimitz said, well, in order to collect your money you will need evidence—and sent for the staff photographer. A quick photo followed by quick processing and the audacious petty officer was on the way back to the *Enterprise* to claim his fortune.[6]

Nimitz gave a hearing to a steady stream of well-meaning (usually politically well-connected) visitors bearing bright ideas. Some were a bit off. One, for example, suggested that the Navy should establish a fishing industry in some newly occupied island and teach the locals (who had lived there all of their lives) to farm and fish, so that the U.S. government wouldn't have to feed them. Nimitz should have burst out laughing, but restrained himself and told the visitor that he would be sure to pass this idea along to the staff for consideration.

A visiting flag officer offered what seemed like a logical proposal: Use a series of radio broadcasts to convince the Japanese people that their cause was hopeless, an American version of the Japanese propaganda efforts of the woman known as Tokyo Rose. Ordinary Japanese citizens, however, were not allowed to own radios unless they had a special license from the police, which was quite difficult to obtain.

One man mailed in a suggestion, Japan could be defeated by diverting the Kuroshio—the warm, tropical Japanese current that flows north along the Asiatic mainland—thus freezing the country into quick surrender. Nimitz sent a kind note back to the author, explaining that the only way he could think of to move the current was to assign the job to the Seabees, but as they were fully occupied building new bases, he couldn't spare them for the task.

On the other hand, some suggestions were of great value. The Pacific Fleet submarine force wanted a fueling and minor repair station at Midway, which would be 1,300 statute miles closer to the enemy than Pearl Harbor and increase operational range of the boats. This would require dredging the harbor, and necessary resources were tied up with other projects. After several presentations by submarine commander Vice Admiral Charles Lockwood had been turned down by Spruance, Lockwood asked if he could make one last pitch directly to Nimitz. Spruance shrugged his shoulders, said, "OK, if you want to butt your head against a brick wall, go right ahead; he's free, go on in." Lockwood spent about fifteen minutes going through the proposal. Nimitz took it all aboard, thought about it for less than a minute, and approved the project to start immediately.[7] The Midway submarine base became not just a fuel depot, but a handover point where a relief crew—a team of maintenance specialists—would go aboard for a couple of weeks while the regular crew flew off to Hawaii for two weeks R&R. The relief crews would handle upgrades, repairs, and other work. When the regular crew returned, they would take over, and go back out on patrol.

When Nimitz was confronted by reports of commanders who displayed poor judgment, didn't follow through on an order, or who let their tempers get out of hand, his "Sampson-Schley" vow to avoid infighting in the Navy was often put to the test, but never violated. In a private conversation with his son, he did let slip how he really felt about someone with whom he was really frustrated. "Chester," he said, "this guy is stupid. I can put up with a stupid person as long as they are of goodwill, but when he is stupid and obstinate that is a dangerous character." Chester knew of two people his father put in that box. True to his father's code, he would not reveal, even to his own death, their names.[8] Nimitz also advised Chester not to make frontal attacks on people who may be getting in the way, especially people who had built up "certain supports," champions who could step in and make things difficult. "The correct way," he said, "to handle a person who is flatly obstructing your proper accomplishment, whatever the purpose, is to continue to be extraordinarily polite and don't reveal to him your purpose, and at all times be slowly removing the rug from under him."[9]

Nimitz would not tolerate poor performance. Coming back from dinner rather late one night, he spotted a drunken sailor staggering along the highway and told his driver to stop and pick him up. The young man, a Seabee, had no idea who had extended this helping hand and was very talkative and full of complaints—his commanding officer was no good, the food was terrible, his hut was dirty—and he rambled on until they let him out at his unit. The next morning, Nimitz called Lamar and said, "At 11 o'clock, we will inspect that Seabee battalion." The surprise visit revealed the truth of much of what the young sailor had said. The battalion CO was relieved of duty.[10]

Nimitz likewise wouldn't tolerate bad manners. One time, driving through Honolulu in his official car, in uniform, with flags flying, Nimitz was greatly annoyed when no one he passed bothered to salute. He therefore asked COM 14 to send out a sting, to assign a couple of officers to walk down the street shadowed by a Navy bus and a shore patrol team. Any enlisted man who did not salute was picked up, put on the bus, and taken back to his unit with that day's liberty forfeited. Word spread quickly, and saluting once again became the norm in Honolulu: a simple tactic to solve a simple problem.

But, Nimitz's approach to good order and discipline was at times positively schizophrenic. At one point, early in 1944, he decided to throw a picnic for all Texans in uniform on Oahu, a beer-fueled event with 40,000 soldiers, sailors, and Marines, some of whom had surely never been to Texas in their life. They turned a city park into a happy wasteland, and the Texas Picnic became the stuff of legend. Sometime later, a retired Army brigadier general put Nimitz, "the Tall Texan among them all," right in the middle of the action. When he arrived at the park, General S.L.A. Marshall wrote, "As one man, the soldiers in this melee quit whatever they were doing to form behind Admiral Nimitz and march the length of the park, forward and then back again, whooping it up like a pack of Comanches. . . . Amid the vast disorder, Nimitz was . . . enjoying himself hugely."[11]

Like many naval officers, Nimitz had a lifelong fetish for punctuality. If the ship was due to sail at 8 A.M., the lines were cast off and the whistle sounded precisely at 8—which confirms to every other ship and command for miles around the exact time of your movement. But the whistle also confirms that the ship had completed a series of likewise scheduled events right on time: port authorities notified; last minute supplies loaded; boilers brought up to steam and brought on line; the crew assembled for muster; special sea detail on station; visitors and tradesmen all ashore. Reputations could be made, or lost, by things that may seem trivial to a layman. In the Navy—as symbolic of the management and skills of the commanding officer and his crew—punctuality was far from trivial. Over the years, Nimitz's obsession with punctuality grew and was carried over to social matters. For a man who managed to disguise his feelings and his emotions in the most difficult of situations, he would become visibly agitated when guests did not arrive on time or if he was running late for an appointment.

The admiral's personal schedule was fragmented. His normal bedtime was 10, as it had been for most of his life, and his youthful practice of early rising to study was modified but slightly: He would wake up at 3 and read until 5, then go back to sleep for an hour. However, Hawaii was right in the time-zone saddle, five hours earlier than Washington and six hours later than, say, the Philippines. In times of great activity, Nimitz would go down to his headquarters at his early-morning waking-time to catch the first dispatches from Washington, then go back to bed. He would check messages again after dinner. Once he saw a message before it had been read by any of the staff; the submarine *Darter* wanted to shift operations to another area where it might find better hunting. Rather than wait for the staff to respond, Nimitz could not resist and handled it directly: "Yes, my darling *Darter,* you shouldn't oughter, but since you wanter, approved. Nimitz."[12]

At some point Nimitz developed a tremor, which was diagnosed as nervous tension, and his doctor suggested that he take up target shooting with a pistol. Putting a focus on pulling the trigger was a form of distraction, if only for a moment. A pistol range was set up just outside his office, with a sand berm behind the target and a flagpole on which the red "Baker" signal flag would be displayed—a standard Navy alert—when the range was in use. The weapon of choice was a .45 caliber automatic converted to handle .22 caliber ammunition. While hitting the bull's-eye was the usual goal, another was to balance a half dollar above the barrel and slowly squeeze the trigger without tipping the coin off. Whenever Nimitz felt particularly pushed—as when awaiting reports from an ongoing action, or distressed because of reports just received—he would go out to the range and squeeze off a few rounds. When things were especially tense—waiting for reports from an action just begun—he might invite a journalist or two to join him, either on the target range or pitching horseshoes—another of his favorite hobbies. He was not being sociable. He was trying to create an image of great calm at headquarters. If the admiral could take time off for some target shooting, all must be right with the world.

Eventually the tremor disappeared, but Nimitz continued target practice throughout the war.

His passion for physical fitness was unabated. He played tennis when he could, but the main event was a weekly four-mile walk on the beach, followed by one-mile swim back and a walk for the other three. Round trip, eight miles. Nimitz usually had some senior staffers as companions but truly believed that these outings would be a great opportunity for the junior officers. Every once in a while, the junior members of the staff might get a visit from Lamar. "Would you like," he would ask, "to go across the island for a little swim this afternoon?"[13]

This is not a joke: After only one such adventure, some junior members of the staff would actually hide in a closet when they saw Lamar coming.

And here is something that Nimitz might have wished *was* a joke. One day while the admiral and visiting Undersecretary Forrestal were out for a swim, they spotted a landing craft coming toward the beach. Nimitz-the-teacher went to some length to describe the process: The Higgins boat would pull alongside a troopship, the Marines would climb down a rope netting, the boat would head for the beach with the Marines hunkered down, only the coxswain visible. The boat would touch the sand, the bow ramp would drop, and a platoon of Marines would rush forth to do battle. The evolution seemed to be going along as described, until the boat touched sand and the bow ramp dropped, and out popped a bevy of nurses in bathing suits. Forrestal's reaction was not recorded.

Nimitz shared living quarters with his chief of staff and the fleet surgeon. Each had their own work schedule, but dinner was usually communal, and it was a rare night that they didn't have guests. When Spruance was chief of staff, he mixed cocktails—two drinks per guest, no more, just enough to put them at ease. Because of the limited variety of available booze, a guest usually had the option of an Old Fashioned or a Nimitz concoction known as the CINCPAC Punch—rum, bourbon, ice, and vanilla. Spruance himself did not drink except for a sip or two to appear sociable.

Nimitz had two other tactics to put his guests as ease. One: he took such satisfaction in target practice that he set up an indoor range in the hallway of his quarters, using an air-powered pellet gun, pitting his dinner guests in friendly competition.

The other: He was a lifelong collector of jokes, which he would tell with polished skill. He may have entered the joke-telling business as a confidence-building ploy—just as an insecure schoolboy might become the class clown—to help him fit in with his naval peers who came from backgrounds much more sophisticated than his. As years went by and he gained in rank and authority, he found that a timely joke could do a lot to defuse contentious meetings—a tactic also employed by Abraham Lincoln. Much later, when he had to handle the often probing questions of reporters, Nimitz might dodge a touchy subject with a disarming, "That reminds me of a story. Did you hear the one about . . . ?"[14]

The dinner guest list might include fellow staffers, or commanders passing through Pearl Harbor, or visiting politicians, industrialists, and "best friends" of all of the above. Nimitz as always was a good host, but had a simple stratagem for ending the party without being rude. When the meal was properly finished, he would beg off, say he had to go down to headquarters and read the evening dispatches. It was, indeed, part of his daily routine, but he knew that the party would naturally break up when the host departed. Then he could sneak back to his quarters whenever and not have to worry about leftover guests eager to offer one more suggestion about winning the war.

Nimitz's personal relations with newsmen were cordial. Whenever possible, he would meet with newly arrived correspondents, just as he met with the incoming commanding officers. He would, from time to time, have a senior or exalted newsman over for dinner. But he did not like to do interviews and wasn't interested in being photographed. For one thing, he was a modest fellow; he did not want to put himself forward or take credit for the accomplishments of others. And for another, he didn't like being told what to do, as when photographers invariably shouted out orders: "Move to your left," or "Shake hands and smile," or "Look over here!"

There was, perhaps, one time when Nimitz was able to appreciate photographers. Admiral Ernest King, COMINCH, had introduced a gray uniform with black stripes, gray cap cover with black chinstrap, which he wanted to replace both dress blues and khakis. This might save money and save gold braid, but was highly unpopular. Nimitz resisted King's effort to get the Pacific Fleet in grays by offering the more-or-less reasonable explanation that the tropical operating conditions and the limited laundry services made khaki more suitable. At one of their wartime meetings in San Francisco, leaving their hotel for lunch on a rainy day, Nimitz and King were both wearing black raincoats which bore no sign of the wearer's rank. Nimitz, his cap glowing with gold, looked like an admiral. King, with his black and gray cap scheme, looked like a chief petty officer. This was verified when one of the waiting photographers said, "get out of the way chief, I want to get a picture of Admiral Nimitz." Admiral King was not amused.[15]

Mindful of continuing complaints from newsmen, Nimitz shifted censorship duties from Waldo Drake, who was often away on other business, and gave them to Eller, who had written the Midway battle report. After all, an accomplished author should be good at reviewing the work of the journalists. But Eller did not understand how the media worked. He would let the dispatches pile up for a few hours or a few days at a time while he handled his primary job. There were enough complaints that Eller was taken off censorship duty.

Even in the middle of the war, Nimitz continued to remember and celebrate birthdays and anniversaries of people who had worked with him. When former shipmates were passing through Pearl Harbor and dropped by headquarters to make a call, Nimitz might start the conversation, "How are Emily and the children? Where are they now?" before getting down to the business of the day. If one of the men from any part of his career was wounded or sick, he was likely to show up at the hospital with a bunch of flowers. When Tracy Cuttle of the UC NROTC unit, now a Navy doctor, had been wounded in action and was recovering, Nimitz sent a car and invited him to dinner. It wasn't clear to onlookers how he knew that Cuttle had been wounded, but he seemed to have a special sense. This applied not just to shipmates, but even to former neighbors. Edward V. Brewer Jr., who as a child had lived across the street from the Nimitz family in Berkeley, was now a naval officer, recovering from an operation in Pearl Harbor. He was lying in his bed when the nurses started scurrying around, removing empty glasses, plumping the pillows, arranging the chairs, and in popped the fleet commander, carrying a copy of a San Francisco newspaper.

Over time, Nimitz got a lot of mail—much of it from parents of dead Marines and sailors; bitter letters saying, "You killed my son." Mercer sent these to Lamar for action, and he answered all—calling on the skills he learned in answering contentious congressional correspondence—but after the first deluge, he didn't let Nimitz see most of them.

But there were pleasant letters, too, including one from a woman who asked what could she do for the sailors? Nimitz answered, perhaps send playing cards and paperback books. And she did, more than once. A mother sent him a bag of dirt saying her Marine son would be happy if only he could get his feet in Mississippi soil. Nimitz found out where the boy was stationed and forwarded the bag to the commanding officer, with instructions to put the dirt around the flagpole and have all the Mississippi boys come remove their shoes and socks and walk through it. A young girl in Iowa began writing with no other purpose than to tell him about life on the farm. Nimitz kept in touch, and some years later when he was giving a talk about the United Nations in her hometown, he invited her, along with her parents and brother, to join him as he rode into town to address an audience of some 40,000 Iowans.

One letter began, "Dear Chester," and continued, "Eleanor has decided she's got to come to the Pacific. I don't approve of the visit. If you want to turn her down, go ahead and do so." Whether or not Nimitz truly wanted to entertain President Roosevelt's wife, he made sure she was welcome. Eleanor was traveling as a representative of the Red Cross, to visit and encourage sick and wounded servicemen throughout the South Pacific. She was most conscientious. She not only stopped to chat with each patient but wrote down the names and addresses of each so she could send letters along to their families.[16]

Nimitz's daughters Kate and Nancy—still living on Q Street in Washington—wanted to send a Father's Day greeting, and they thought, great, we'll send a telegram. They wrote out a warm but longish screed . . . and were told it would be thirty cents a word. They didn't have the money. The clerk, sympathetic, said, "If you send it by 'cable deferred,' it's only 15 cents per word—but, it won't arrive until Sunday." Perfect! Sunday was Father's Day. So they rewrote their telegram to fit their budget:

> We love you father
> by cable deferred
> even at 15 cents a word.

In return, via air mail from their father, they received:

> Father's Day message
> by cable deferred
> caused my spirits to soar
> like the wings of a bird!
> Was ever a father
> so happily blessed
> with such splendid daughters
> who rank with the best!

He added, "Not my best, but I'm a little busy right now."[17]

CHAPTER SIXTEEN

ON THE OFFENSIVE

On June 30, 1942, with Midway behind them, Nimitz and some staffers flew to San Francisco for a second planning session with COMINCH Admiral Ernest King. The trip did not start out well. When landing in San Francisco Bay, the chief pilot, perhaps groggy from the fifteen-hour flight, did not make a proper prelanding pass to make sure the area was clear of obstructions. The seaplane hit a piling that had broken loose from a pier and was bobbing in the water; the plane flipped over. The passengers and crew scrambled out through a freight hatch, gathered on the underside of the wing, and waited for rescue by a crash boat carrying two doctors, several corpsmen, and blankets for the wet and shivering survivors. Most of the passengers and crew were pretty banged-up—bruises galore, a few broken bones—and one of the pilots had been killed.

Nimitz refused to leave—the symbolic captain of the sinking ship—until he was certain that everyone had been rescued. But he was getting in the way, and finally one of the sailors, who had no idea who he was, yelled, "Commander, if you would only get the hell out of the way, maybe we could get something done around here." Nimitz got the message and got in the boat. Then, wrapped in a blanket, he stood in the stern to watch the continuing rescue and got yelled at by another sailor, "Sit down, you!" He did, the blanket fell aside, and the sailor saw more gold on one sleeve than he had ever seen in his life. As the young man was trying to apologize, Nimitz said, "Stick to your guns, sailor. You were quite right."[1]

The purpose of the meeting, once underway, was to schedule forthcoming operations in the Pacific. There were many options, each championed by one or another senior commander, and the planners had to review a recent series of long-distance exchanges between MacArthur, Nimitz, General George C. Marshall, and King. MacArthur wanted to capture the heavily fortified Japanese base at Rabaul. Nimitz wanted to take Tulagi in the Solomons first, to provide land-based aircraft support to MacArthur. King agreed with Nimitz and mentioned that, of course it would be a Navy operation. MacArthur objected: He told General Marshall the Solomons were within his Southwest Pacific operating area and therefore must be under his command. King suggested that since the Army had the top command in Europe where most of the forces were ground troops, the Navy should have control of action in the Solomons where all of the units would be from the Navy and Marine Corps. MacArthur complained that the Navy was trying to reduce the Army to a subordinate role, "placing its forces at the disposal of and under the command of Navy or Marine officers."[2] It was enough to make anyone's head swim.

Marshall and King came up with a Solomonic compromise: The line of demarcation between Nimitz's South Pacific Ocean Area (SOPAC) and MacArthur's Southwest Pacific Area (SOUTHWESTPAC) would be shifted west a touch, so that about half of the Solomons were clearly under CINCPAC's jurisdiction.

Thus evolved the plan to which everyone at the meeting agreed. Nimitz would take Tulagi, the Santa Cruz Islands, and whatever else in the area was deemed important, by August 1. MacArthur would charge ahead and occupy Japanese bases on the northeast coast of New Guinea and then proceed, with air support assured, to Rabaul.[3] And the Navy would take the next steps in the march toward Japan: Truk, Guam, and Saipan.

However, just as the meeting was ending on July 5, a bit of game-changing news arrived from Hawaii: Station Hypo had broken a Japanese message revealing that Japanese troops and construction crews had just landed on Guadalcanal, an island about the size of Delaware, 19 miles south of Tulagi. They were going to build an airfield from which they could control the Coral Sea between the Solomons and Australia. As a result, the Santa Cruz Islands fell out of the plan and Guadalcanal was substituted, with a launch date of August 7.

Initial estimates put 5,000 Japanese troops on Guadalcanal. After the Marines had landed and established a foothold, the estimates were adjusted—there were only 1,000 troops and 2,000 construction workers, which was great news. But the Japanese quickly decided that Guadalcanal was important and began a series of air raids, ship bombardments, troop reinforcements, and attacks on Allied forces at sea. The night of August 9, two days after the landings, a group of Japanese cruisers surprised an American-Australian force at Savo Sound, sinking four heavy cruisers, and damaging one cruiser and two destroyers. It was called the greatest defeat in battle ever suffered by the U.S. Navy.[4]

There would be more such clashes during the six-month-long struggle to take the island. On August 24, the *Enterprise* was severely damaged by a Japanese carrier attack and headed off to Pearl Harbor for repairs. On August 31, the *Saratoga* was put out of action by a torpedo and also returned to Pearl. Two weeks later, the *Wasp* was torpedoed and sunk; and on October 27, the *Hornet* was lost.

Nimitz was desperate to keep his losses from the enemy. If they knew that one or another task group had been weakened, they would pounce. If they knew there were only one or two fully operational carriers in the Pacific, they would be bold. The one time that Waldo Drake saw his boss truly angry was when he learned that FDR, at a press conference, revealed that the *Hornet* had been sunk.[5] A few months later when the *Chicago* was sunk, Nimitz told Drake, "I'll shoot the man who lets it get out that the *Chicago* has been lost."[6]

Admiral King's public relations policy was more in line with Nimitz's than FDR's. In mid-August, when things were not going well at all, King's PR officer was being badgered by the press; in frustration, he asked King, "What should I tell them?" King replied: "Tell them nothing. When the war is over, tell them who won."[7]

In the midst of these devastating losses, Nimitz and King had another San Francisco session, from September 6 to 9. They discussed the performance of Vice Admiral Robert Ghormley, who was in overall command of the Guadalcanal operation but did not seem to actually be commanding. Nimitz said he would go and take a look. They also discussed some flag officer assignments: King was sending Towers, chief of the Bureau of Aeronautics (BUAER), to join the CINCPAC staff as commander, Air Force, Pacific Fleet with a promotion to vice admiral. It seems that King was just as frustrated with Towers as Nimitz had been back in his BUNAV days. Nimitz was not particularly thrilled, telling his wife in a letter home, "I am to have a new air advisor. Never mind. We will get along fine."[8]

Halsey, who had finally recovered from his debilitating illness, was also at the meeting and was more than ready to go back to work. He returned to Hawaii with Nimitz, to once again assume his roving command with the *Enterprise* as his flagship. Nimitz, scheduled to present awards aboard the ship, took Halsey along and offered the crew a grand surprise: "Boys . . . Bill Halsey's back." The cheering rocked the waterfront, and tough-guy Halsey later admitted that "my eyes filled up."[9]

Army Air Forces (AAF) commander General H. H. "Hap" Arnold arrived at CINCPAC headquarters on September 20, one of a series of visits by senior commanders who wanted a firsthand look at conditions in the Pacific. General D. C. Emmons, who had just returned from a tour of his own, told Arnold that both Ghormley and MacArthur were convinced that Guadalcanal was a loss and could not be held. Nimitz argued otherwise: The Japanese were losing men, ships, and aircraft faster than they could be replaced. The Marines just needed to hold on for a while longer until they could be reinforced.

Nimitz invited General Arnold to go along on his planned visit to the South Pacific. Ghormley's headquarters were at Noumea on the French island of New Caledonia, some 1,000 miles from Guadalcanal. The harbor was in chaos, jammed with cargo ships carrying vital supplies but lacking adequate facilities for unloading. An obviously harassed and visibly haggard Ghormley was living and working in hot, cramped spaces aboard a support ship, the twenty-year-old "miscellaneous auxiliary" *Argonne.* There seemed to be a number of suitable buildings ashore that would have made for better working conditions, but apparently his French hosts had not offered and Ghormley had not asked. He seemed overwhelmed and was clearly trying to handle every detail of every issue, instead of handing things off to his staff.

Nimitz had a few very pointed questions. Why were so many airplanes being held in reserve? Why were Japanese ships allowed free access to bombard the Marines and reinforce Guadalcanal? Why was there a large garrison of idle troops standing by on New Caledonia? There did not seem to be many answers.

The journey continued, with a visit to Espiritu Santo, to be followed by Guadalcanal. There was no suitable, safe-water landing area at Guadalcanal, so the Nimitz seaplane was given a rest, and the party transferred to an AAF B-17, whereupon began a series of aircraft adventures. They started when the pilot, who had no credible charts of the Solomons, got lost. It was only when Lamar produced a *National Geographic* map of the South Pacific that Nimitz's air officer, Commander Ralph A. Ofstie, was able to help the pilot find Guadalcanal.

Once there, Nimitz toured the base, inspected facilities, visited the wounded and sick, and presented some awards. He also conferred with Marine commander Major General Alexander H. Vandegrift and his staff, who were quietly convinced they could hold the island. Twenty-three of those staffers would become general officers, and Vandegrift and two others, Clifton B. Cates and Randolph McCall Pate, would later serve as commandant of the Marine Corps.

The next day it was time to fly out. Nimitz then learned that the airfield was barely qualified to handle the B-17; construction of the airstrip was a work-in-progress. About two-thirds of the length was covered with heavy metal matting, which handled most traffic just fine; however, an unfinished 1,000-foot extension was just dirt and mud. Coming in, the Nimitz B-17 had landed on the matting, but takeoff required a longer runway. Therefore, to reduce take-off weight, the Nimitz party was divided in half, to fly out on two B-17s. When the pilot of the first plane introduced himself, Nimitz's level of confidence, already low, fell even further. The man claimed to be an Army major, but was bearded, barefoot, and wore only a zippered coverall. He outlined his plan: He would start on the matting, and even though he would be headed downwind, he was certain that, at full-throttle, he would gain flying speed before hitting the dirt.

It didn't work out that way. The pilot aborted the takeoff, skidding to a halt just before the plane would have fallen off into a deep ravine. Nimitz said, with more apparent calm than was felt by anyone else in his party. "We'll try this again after lunch."[10]

Next time, the pilot wisely chose to head into the wind and started at the far end of the runaway, in the dirt, and managed to take off. The second B-17 followed about 20 minutes later. Nimitz's plane reached Espiritu Santo just at sunset—a good thing, because the field was unlit and the island was under blackout. But as night descended, it was obvious that the second plane was lost. Nimitz had the anchored seaplane tender Curtiss light off the biggest searchlight and point it straight up in the sky. Someone else arranged for the airstrip crew to set a bunch of drums, filled with oily waste, along the runway. The beacon was spotted by the lost B-17, and when the sound of the approaching bomber was heard, the drums were ignited, bringing a bright ending to this adventure.

At Noumea, Nimitz had a final meeting with Ghormley. Guadalcanal needed more troops and, he told Ghormley, don't worry about reducing the security on some other islands because the Japanese were too focused on Guadalcanal and did not have the resources to take on another assault. Nimitz then headed back to Pearl Harbor; Ghormley sent an Army infantry regiment to Guadalcanal, which arrived on-scene on October 13. That night, two Japanese battleships, followed the next day by bomber raids and a cruiser attack, tore up the Guadalcanal airstrip and took out most of the American planes on the island. On October 15, enough Japanese troops landed to match the beleaguered Americans in number, but they were fresh and ready to fight. Most of the Americans were worn out.

Nimitz, by then back at Pearl Harbor, ordered all available planes in the Central Pacific to be sent south; an Army division on Oahu was put on alert, and the *Enterprise* was rushed back into service. Halsey and his staff flew to Noumea for a situation briefing. They would be ready to pick up the carrier as it passed through.

Nimitz had to deal with the issue of Ghormley. He called a staff meeting. The enemy was not about to give up; was Ghormley the right man for this job at this time? Everyone at the meeting agreed that it was time for Ghormley to be replaced. The consensus on his replacement was unanimous: Halsey.

On October 16, Admiral King approved, and in a carefully worded dispatch, Nimitz gently broke the news to Ghormley:

> After carefully weighing all factors, have decided that talents and previous experience of Halsey can best be applied to the situation by having him take over duties of COMSOPAC as soon as possible. . . . I greatly appreciate your loyal and devoted efforts toward the accomplishment of a most difficult task. I shall order you to report to Halsey for the time being, as I believe he will need your thorough knowledge of situation and your loyal help.[11]

When Halsey's plane coasted to a stop in the harbor at Noumea, it was met by Ghormley's flag lieutenant, who handed a sealed envelope to the admiral.

Nimitz on his first summer cruise, in 1902: from left, Nimitz, G.V. Stewart, and Royal Ingersoll. On the back of the photo, Nimitz wrote: "The only one working—you know who!"

Credit: Nimitz family collection

Passed-Midshipman Chester Nimitz, en route to duty in the Philippines, posing with his family in 1905. From left, stepfather (also uncle) Willie Nimitz, half-brother Otto, half-sister Dora, and mother Anna.

Credit: Nimitz family collection

Ensign Nimitz, about to take his first command, a captured Spanish gunboat.

Credit: U.S. Naval History and Heritage Command Photograph

1908: Nimitz's second command tour: the destroyer Decatur. *It did not end well—the ship ran aground and Ensign Nimitz was court-martialed for "neglect of duty."*

Credit: U.S. Naval History and Heritage Command Photograph

Nimitz's next command was the Plunger *in 1909, the U.S. Navy's second submarine. At a time when the Navy prized battleships over all else, this likely felt like a form of punishment.*

Credit: U.S. Naval History and Heritage Command Photograph

In 1920, Commander Nimitz was given command of a submarine flotilla at Pearl Harbor, Hawaii—but first he had to build the submarine base, using surplus materials and equipment left over from World War I. His headquarters was aboard the aging cruiser, the Chicago, *seen at the left.*

Credit: U.S. Navy photograph, from Nimitz family collection

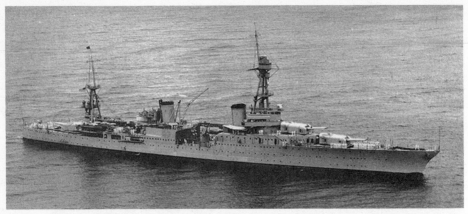

A true, career-enhancing job, commanding officer of the heavy cruiser Augusta. *This was his chance to truly shine and to play the Navy game for all it was worth.*

Credit: Official U.S. Navy Photograph, now in the collections of the National Archives

Nimitz in full-dress uniform. The Navy of the 1930s, never to be seen again.

Credit: U.S. Naval History and Heritage Command Photograph, from the Nimitz family collection

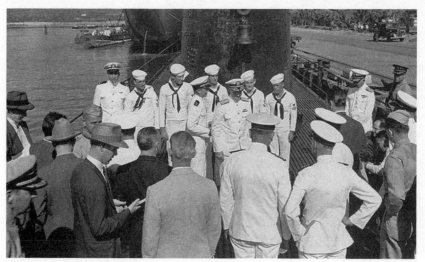

Pioneer submariner Nimitz assumes command of the Pacific Fleet—aboard a submarine in 1941.

Credit: U.S. Naval History and Heritage Command Photograph, from the Nimitz family collection

Nimitz, his wife Catherine, and dog Freckles in California, during one of his periodic visits to the mainland for planning conferences.

Credit: Nimitz family collection

General Douglas MacArthur, President Franklin D. Roosevelt, and Nimitz in 1944. A disdainful MacArthur showed up in very informal garb, while Nimitz had the whole fleet in dress whites in honor of the president.

Credit: Official U.S. Navy photograph, from the Nimitz family collection

Nimitz and William F. "Bull" Halsey.

Credit: Official U.S. Navy Photograph, now in the collections of the National Archives

1945: Nimitz accepting the Japanese surrender on behalf of the United States, aboard the battleship Missouri.

Credit: Official U.S. Navy Photograph, now in the collections of the National Archives

Nimitz, posing with two men with whom he at times had difficult working relationships, Fleet Admiral Ernest J. King and Secretary of the Navy James V. Forrestal, on the day Forrestal announced Nimitz's appointment as chief of naval operations.

Credit: Official U.S. Navy Photograph, now in the collections of the National Archives

The official portrait of Nimitz, as chief of naval operations, the job he wanted and almost didn't get.

Credit: Official U.S. Navy photograph, now in the collections of the National Archives

Nimitz with his first grandson, James Thomas "Jimmy" Lay, Jr.

Credit: Nimitz family collection

Inside was another sealed envelope, marked "Secret" and inside that, a copy of a radio dispatch from CINCPAC: "Immediately upon your arrival at Noumea, you will relieve Vice Admiral Robert L. Ghormley of the duties of Commander South Pacific Area and South Pacific Force."

Halsey's reaction was simply put, "Jesus Christ and General Jackson!" The turnover was friendly but awkward, as was Nimitz's next meeting with Ghormley—who acknowledged that he had not been up to the job. He went to Washington to await a new assignment. A physical exam revealed that he was suffering from an ulcer and a mouth full of rotten teeth. Before long, Nimitz gladly brought a rejuvenated and rehabilitated Ghormley back to Pearl Harbor and assigned him as COM 14.[12]

Back at Noumea, Bull Halsey abandoned the *Argonne* for more suitable accommodations ashore, gaining staff space in a warehouse and living quarters in the abandoned Japanese consulate. And Halsey did something that Ghormley had not—he visited Guadalcanal, met with the troops, cheered the sick and wounded, and rallied his men for the fight against the Japanese. He sent 6,000 fresh troops to Guadalcanal; the Japanese planned to counter with 10,000 troops of their own. This led to a series of inconclusive naval battles from November 12 to 14, 1942, now called the Naval Battle of Guadalcanal, in which the Japanese lost two battleships, one cruiser, three destroyers, and eleven transports, while the U.S. lost two cruisers and seven destroyers. The battles were "inconclusive"—except, most of the 10,000 Japanese troops never made it ashore. Some were drowned, some were rescued and taken away, and those that did make it to shore landed without supplies. There was another action on November 30 at the cost of one American cruiser sunk and three heavily damaged. The Japanese lost one destroyer, but also lost heart. Soon the Tokyo government gave up on the dream of retaking Guadalcanal, and by the end of December the troops were quietly being evacuated; all would be gone by the first week in February. And Halsey won his fourth star.

In January 1943, Secretary of the Navy Frank Knox toured the Pacific theater. After his snippy letter to Nimitz about censorship, Knox had made amends, telling him, "All of us here are very proud of the way you are handling your job."[13] The secretary arrived at Pearl Harbor and, after some meetings, was escorted by Nimitz as tour guide on a visit to Midway and points south, including an almost-subdued Guadalcanal.

Knox, Nimitz, and their party came in for some heavy bombing at every stop on the tour. The Japanese did not need to break our codes to track some operations; often, the sheer volume of traffic that followed any really important person around the Pacific spoke volumes. After one visit, when the party had left, the base communications officer was about to send a routine "Departure" message up the chain of command when one of his staffers urged, "Send it in Japanese, I want 'em to know for sure that the high-price help has left here!"[14]

At Guadalcanal, the travelers were treated to an all-night air raid. Knox and the other visitors headed out for the enhanced protection of a foxhole in the open rather than that offered by a collapsible building. Nimitz, longing for some sleep, refused to leave his bunk. None of the others were injured. Nimitz came down with malaria.

Soon after he returned to Pearl Harbor, the symptoms were clear and Nimitz had to be hospitalized. However, that could have implied he was unable to carry on his duties, which therefore would have been passed down to the next-senior officer in the command, Halsey. While Nimitz avoided saying anything negative about anyone, he was not comfortable with the idea of the impetuous Halsey in charge of the entire Pacific Fleet. He therefore went to some effort to conceal his absence from the office. His four-star flag still was flown over his headquarters—the Navy's time-honored signal that the commander was at his post—and most of the staff were told he was simply unavailable.

During the first week of March 1943, MacArthur's forces stopped an enemy advance in the Battle of the Bismarck Sea. The effort was successful, but not nearly as glorious a triumph as MacArthur would claim—not just then, but forever. He announced that U.S and Australian bombers sank 22 destroyers and transports, killing 15,000 Japanese and downing as many as 100 planes. A couple of days later, MacArthur adjusted the toll: 12 transports, 7 destroyers, and 3 light cruisers. The Associated Press announced, "Congratulatory messages poured in upon General MacArthur (Winston Churchill, FDR, even Admiral King)."[15] A week later, the New York Times opined, "United Nations forces, under the leadership of General Douglas MacArthur, will tarry no longer than is absolutely necessary in striking out to upset Japan's plans."[16] MacArthur held a press conference to affirm that control of the sea "no longer depends solely or even perhaps primarily upon naval power, but upon air power operating from land bases held by ground troops."[17]

Soon, captured documents translated by Commander Layton showed that only eight destroyers and eight transports had participated—and that four destroyers survived. Nimitz passed the documents along to MacArthur, suggesting that AAF claims should be viewed with caution. (As Nimitz told his staff, "if three or four cruisers that I thought were sunk are still afloat, I've got to change my tactics a little bit.")[18] MacArthur accused Nimitz of impugning his integrity, and MacArthur's air chief, Lieutenant General George C. Kenney, said, "The actual number is unimportant and the whole controversy is ridiculous."[19] Nimitz wisely let the matter drop, but MacArthur would not let it go. Two and a half years later, the *New York Times* headlined an interview, "Air War Won in '43, M'Arthur Asserts." The general added, "Some people [i.e., Nimitz] have doubted the figures in that battle, but we have the names of every ship sunk."[20]

For the record, the final, accepted numbers—today—have four destroyers and eight transports sunk, as determined by Layton in the first place, with the loss of about 3,000 (not 15,000) Japanese soldiers and sailors. Fifty or sixty planes were shot down, not 100. Four destroyers were damaged but escaped. Sometimes, you can't keep score without a referee.

On March 15, COMINCH announced a new fleet numbering system, replacing the old Battle Fleet, Scouting Fleet, Asiatic Fleet, etc. Even numbers were assigned to the Atlantic, odd numbers to the Pacific, where so many new ships were arriving that Nimitz could now assemble three numbered fleets: the Third Fleet for the South Pacific area, the Fifth Fleet for the Central Pacific, and the Seventh Fleet for the Southwest Pacific. Halsey would head the Third Fleet, and Nimitz nominated Ray Spruance for promotion to vice admiral and command of the forces in the Central Pacific.

Just after 8 A.M. on the morning of April 14, 1943, Layton handed the latest decoded Japanese intercept to his boss. It began: "The Commander-in-Chief Combined Fleet . . ." That was enough to grab the admiral's attention and the following details brought him up out of his chair. Admiral Yamamoto, Nimitz's nemesis, the man who planned the Pearl Harbor attack and was in command at Midway, was going to visit three small bases four days later, departing by air from Rabaul at 6:00 A.M., two medium bombers with an escort of six Zero fighters. He would arrive at the first stop at 8:00. The entire day's itinerary was laid out, almost minute by minute. Yamamoto, too, was well known to be a stickler for punctuality. If the schedule said "arrive at 8:00," he would be climbing down the ladder at 8:00.

Nimitz walked over to the big wall chart and traced an itinerary that at one point might bring Yamamoto within striking distance of long-range fighters. "What do you say," he asked Layton, "do we try to get him?"

"Aside from the Emperor," Layton replied, "probably no man in Japan is so important to civilian morale. If he's shot down, it would demoralize the navy and stun the nation."

"It's down in Halsey's bailiwick," Nimitz said. "If there's a way, he'll find it," and scratched out a dispatch with the full itinerary and the suggestion, "If forces your command have capability to shoot down Yamamoto and staff, you are hereby authorized to initiate preliminary planning." And, to avoid revealing the code break, Nimitz recommended that the information be attributed to Australian coastwatchers around Rabaul.

The next step was to get permission. A planned assassination of such a prominent person, wartime or not, might have political repercussions, so Nimitz checked with Knox, who checked with the president, who said, "Get Yamamoto." At the same time, word came back from Halsey that the mission was possible; they would use Army P-38 fighters equipped with external drop fuel tanks to make the required thousand-mile round trip. Nimitz sent out the "execute" order, along with a personal note: "Good luck and good hunting."

Sixteen P-38s arrived at the planned rendezvous within one minute of the scheduled arrival of Yamamoto—an amazing feat—and met the Japanese, who were just descending for a landing at the third stop of the day. There was a brief, hot fight, and the two Japanese bombers were shot down. One P-38 was lost, and the Americans failed to take out any of the Japanese fighter escorts, but that didn't matter. Yamamoto would have been aboard one of the bombers.

Then came the waiting. Although the attack took place on April 18, coincidentally the first anniversary of the Doolittle B-25 raid on Tokyo, it wasn't until May 21 that Radio Tokyo announced that Yamamoto, "while directing general strategy on the front-line in April of this year, engaged in combat with the enemy and met gallant death in a war plane."[21]

The mission had been conducted, of course, in total secrecy, and details were not published until the week after the war was over. In his 1964 memoir, MacArthur pulled all credit into his personal orbit. He wrote, "We" made one of the most significant strikes of the war. "Our" Air Force shot down Yamamoto. The Japanese code had been broken, and an intercepted radio message informed "us."

"There was much skepticism that the message was a hoax," he wrote, "but I knew Yamamoto as a front-line fighter who always pressed forward to the decisive points of contact." Never a mention of who broke the code, or where, or of Nimitz who conceived the strike, or Halsey who planned it, or of FDR who approved it.[22]

Nimitz set May 11 as the date to take back the Aleutian island of Attu, captured by the Japanese during the Battle of Midway. In bitter cold, 15,000 American soldiers confronted 2,900 Japanese defenders—who fought to the bitter end, with a banzai suicide charge to and through the American front. This was much to the astonishment of the largely noncombatant soldiers in the rear who became engaged in chaotic hand-to-hand fighting. In sum, 549 Americans were killed and only 29 Japanese survived.

Two months later, Nimitz upped the ante for the recapture of the other Japanese-held Aleutian island, Kiska. He assembled an invasion force of 100 ships and 35,000 U.S. and Canadian troops. The island was bombarded by ships and aircraft ten times between August 2 and 15, including one imaginative but unauthorized attack during which a large number of empty beer bottles were dropped on the island; the crew of that bomber hoped that the whistling sound they made as they fell would demoralize the enemy.

On August 15, when the landing force went ashore, they found that the island had quietly been evacuated before any of the bombardment began.

CHAPTER SEVENTEEN

MIDCOURSE CORRECTION

By November 1943 Nimitz was ready to take on the next major target: Tarawa Atoll in the Gilbert Islands, about 1,000 miles to the northeast of Guadalcanal. As they had planned to do with Guadalcanal, the Japanese were turning Tarawa into an airbase from which they could seriously impact U.S. efforts in the central Pacific. Nimitz's attack force—a true armada—included 12 battleships, 6 fleet carriers, 5 light carriers, 8 escort carriers, 100 other ships, and 18,300 men in the landing force. They were to take out a garrison of some 2,500 combat troops plus the same number of construction workers. It should have been a walk in the park. It was a crawl through bloody hell.

The pre-invasion bombardment was intense and the landings were a failure. Because of an exceptionally low tide, most of the landing craft could not make it over the reef and on to the beach. The troops had to wade ashore under heavy enemy fire, against a determined defense. The bombardment seemed to have had no effect whatsoever.

Eventually, almost all of the Japanese defenders were killed, along with perhaps 1,600 of the invading force. About 2,000 Americans were wounded.

Two days after the island fell, Nimitz headed for a visit to see what went wrong. Spruance, in charge of the operation, tried to dissuade him: There were holdouts hiding in caves; the runway was not ready for any heavy aircraft; most of the dead had not yet been buried. Nimitz went anyway, but his plane had to circle for an hour while the Seabees finished lengthening the airstrip. He landed to the stench of rotting corpses; it was, he told Lamar, "The first time I've ever smelled death."[1]

Nimitz saw that the enemy had been dug in so well that ship and aerial bombardment had been largely ineffectual; the troops were hunkered down in solid concrete bunkers covered with tons of shock-absorbing sand and logs. One of the few Japanese survivors said his commander had boasted a million men could not take the island in a hundred years.[2]

Nimitz had a mockup of the Tarawa defenses constructed on Kahoolawe, a small uninhabited Hawaiian island, and tested the effectiveness of various types of ammunition. Fire control teams, to be landed with the first wave of troops, were trained to spot targets and direct more accurate fire.

One lesson learned at Tarawa: The landing force commander needed solid hydrographic reconnaissance before a mission was even planned. How deep was the water, what was the slope of the bottom, where were the obstructions—natural or manmade—and what could be done to remove them? This directly led to the development of the Navy's Underwater Demolition Teams (UDT), organized by the bomb-disposal expert who Nimitz had encouraged to transfer in from the British Naval Reserve. Commander Draper Kauffman shifted from training Navy bomb disposal teams to disposing of landing-zone obstacles. The work of the UDTs sounded more hazardous than it was, because the men operated underwater and usually under cover of the pre-invasion bombardment, which kept curious defenders from poking around in the surf.

Nimitz had been under some pressure from Washington to improve the flow of news from the Pacific, and Tarawa was the first test of a new approach. For the first time in the war, Navy radio circuits were open to press copy during a major operation. Under the headline, "The Not-So-Silent Service," *Time* saluted the changes: "For nearly two years U.S. newsmen covering the Pacific Fleet had chafed at red tape, slow censorship, slow transmission of dispatches. Now things changed. . . . CINCPAC Chester W. Nimitz issued a directive ordering fleet, force, and unit commanders to extend fullest cooperation to correspondents everywhere." Tarawa was covered by twenty reporters, five photographers, two artists, and a newsreel cameraman. Though some eyewitness dispatches reached U.S. readers after only three days, Navy actions were "not yet being covered as fast or as well as Army operations . . . but Navy coverage was better and faster than it had ever been before."[3]

A major focus of the next King-Nimitz planning session, January 3 and 4, 1944, was personnel. Undersecretary James Forrestal—a World War I naval aviator— was pushing to have more aviators assigned to positions of prominence, but few aviators in the Pacific had sufficient experience with fleet operations to be qualified for top commands. No matter how much pressure Forrestal might exert, Nimitz would not put an aviator in a job for which he simply wasn't ready. As a workaround, King and Nimitz developed some logical ground rules: All major commanders who were nonaviators must have an aviator as chief of staff or second in command, and those commanders who were aviators must have a surface officer in second position.

And, as a particular concession to Forrestal—and to follow the rule they had just created—they decided to make John H. Towers the deputy CINCPAC. It worked out just fine.

Some six months earlier, the Combined Chiefs of Staff (consisting of the U.S. Joint Chiefs of Staff plus their counterparts among the Allies) had agreed on a dual strategy for the Allied advance across the Pacific. MacArthur would move westward, step-by-step, along the north coast of New Guinea, eliminating Japanese bases until he reached a point where he could jump across some 1,200 miles of open ocean and into the southern Philippine island of Mindanao; he would then move north through the Philippines. At the same time, Nimitz would capture, among other targets, the Gilberts (including Tarawa), the Marshalls (notably Kwajalein), and take Saipan, Tinian, and Guam in the southern Marianas, only 1,500 miles from Japan.

MacArthur had no problem with the Gilberts-Marshalls part of the plan, but from the beginning he objected to Nimitz moving on to the Marianas. For one thing, as a military man, he thought it was too hazardous without land-based aircraft support, and for another, a successful effort might eliminate the need for his "return" to the Philippines—in his mind, the most important target in the Pacific.

MacArthur believed that Tarawa had proven the folly of the Combined Chiefs plan—Nimitz should abandon the island-hopping strategy and send all of the forces under his command south to support MacArthur. Indeed, MacArthur asked the Joint Chiefs to order Nimitz to do just that, but they declined. In January MacArthur conveyed his frustration to Secretary of War Henry L. Stimson:

> These frontal attacks by the Navy . . . are tragic and unnecessary massacres of American lives. . . . The Navy fails to understand the strategy of the Pacific. Fails to recognize that the first phase is an Army phase to establish land-based protection so the Navy can move in. . . . Mr. Stimson must speak to [the president], must persuade him. Give me central direction of the war in the Pacific. . . . Don't let the Navy's pride of position continue this great tragedy to our country.[4]

In truth, Nimitz was just as shocked as MacArthur with the results at Tarawa and was coming around to MacArthur's point of view. On January 27 and 28, 1944, he convened a Pearl Harbor conference (which included representatives from MacArthur's staff) to address the issue. Were the Marianas still a viable option? They were on the target list in part because a new long-range bomber, the B-29, would be able to reach Japan from bases on Tinian or Saipan. However, no U.S. fighters had the range to accompany the B-29s, so the bombers would be vulnerable to interception from Japanese fighters based along the route. The consensus: Continue the planned invasion of the Marshalls (scheduled to begin the day after the conference), but skip the Marianas and support MacArthur's advance through New Guinea.

When Admiral King learned the results of the conference, he blew a fuse: Leaving the Japanese in control in the Marianas was inviting disaster. As he reminded Nimitz in a message, the primary reason for taking the Marianas was not "to provide for B-29 bombing attack against the Japanese Empire." That was merely a byproduct. The objective was to clear the line of communications to the northern Philippines area. Touching on MacArthur's favorite scheme, he wrote, "The idea of rolling up the Japanese along the New Guinea coast . . . and up through the Philippines to Luzon . . . to the exclusion of clearing out the Central Pacific, is to me absurd."[5]

When MacArthur heard that the conference supported his plan (he did not know of King's reaction), he was elated. He sent an immediate request to General Marshall to have all Pacific forces placed under his command, including all naval forces. His request was denied. Then, MacArthur reacted angrily to a Nimitz suggestion that the boundary of the South Pacific Area be shifted again, to accommodate development—by Nimitz and his Seabees—of a JCS-approved naval base at Manaus. This was, MacArthur wrote to General Marshall, an insult and an assault on his "personal honor." Marshall wrote back, assuring MacArthur that his "professional integrity and personal honor are in no way questioned," and that no one was trying to take away any part of his command "unless you yourself see fit to turn over control."[6]

On January 31, 1944, on schedule, the Marines landed on Kwajalein in the Marshall Islands. It was the largest coral atoll in the world, encompassing 324 square miles and containing 96 islets and islands, three of which had been fortified. Some CINCPAC staffers were concerned that Kwajalein might be too heavily defended, and that it might be a better move to capture some inconsequential outlying atolls first, and quickly build airstrips to provide support for the assault on Kwajalein. Nimitz called a commanders' conference: Spruance, who would have overall command, Rear Admiral Richmond Kelly Turner for the amphibious operations, and Major General Holland Smith for the Marines. Nimitz asked each in turn for their recommendation. They each named one or another of the fringe islands. Then Nimitz said, "Well that's fine. We'll hit Kwajalein."[7]

Having learned many things from Tarawa, Nimitz greatly increased the size of the attacking force: 374 ships (including 12 carriers, 8 battleships, 6 cruisers, and 36 destroyers), 700 carrier aircraft augmented by 475 shore-based planes, 53,000 assault troops (and another 31,000 to remain behind on garrison duty). After several weeks of raids by the land-based bombers, the three fortified islands were given three days of shore bombardment, each hit by about four times the weight of shells and bombs that impacted Tarawa. The first formal UDT unit in the Pacific led the way to the beach.

There were 8,000 Japanese defenders on the atoll; when the battle had ended, only 265 had survived. U.S. casualties were just under 400 killed and about 1,500 wounded.

Nimitz dropped in for a visit two days after the islands were secure. As he stepped ashore, reporters asked, "What do you think of the island?" "Gentlemen," replied Nimitz, "it's the worst scene of desolation I have ever witnessed—except for the Texas Picnic."[8]

Taking the Marshalls went so well that Nimitz modified his position; the Marianas might well be a good target, but first the Japanese naval base at Truk (billed as "the Gibraltar of the Pacific") should be taken. King was adamantly opposed; he wanted the Marianas front and center. Fair enough, but Nimitz exercised his own initiative and sent the Fifth Fleet to at least assault the Japanese fleet at Truk. They sank 18 naval ships, 20 cargo ships, 5 tankers, and about 200 aircraft. Daughters Kate and Nancy could not resist a celebratory cable:

Like Carrie Nation guzzling booze,
When man runs over Truk, that's news.[9]

Spruance ordered some reconnaissance photos of the Marianas, and during the photo mission his force shot down 168 Japanese aircraft defending Tinian and Saipan.

There were myriad chain-of-command issues within the joint CINCPAC staff. The latest senior Army officer, Lieutenant General Robert C. Richardson, was not happy that Navy or Marine officers were often in command of Army units. He argued, for example, that training soldiers was his job, but Nimitz said it was the responsibility of the officer in charge of ground forces, who happened to be a Marine. Richardson complained directly to General Marshall—who wrote back, this was a matter for Nimitz to decide. When the casualty lists came in from Tarawa, Richardson said it was because the Marines were in charge. He recommended that the Army—under his overall control—be put in charge of amphibious operations in the Pacific. Nimitz ignored the recommendation.

But Richardson would not let go. He believed that senior Marine Corps officers were not competent to command large bodies of troops because they lacked discipline and their training was superficial. Nimitz would not listen, so Richardson headed off to Washington to make his case. On February 18, Nimitz sent a heads-up to King, noting, "I propose to handle these matters locally and bring them to your attention only as a precautionary measure. . . . They are, for the most part, outcroppings from the clash of difficult personalities and will not be removed by changes in organization."[10] The matter was not settled, but simmered on . . .

The first week in March, the Joint Chiefs decided that Nimitz and MacArthur should to come to Washington to work out their differences and develop plans for the future. Nimitz went, but MacArthur declined—he never visited the United States, not once, during the war. He sent his deputy, General Richard Sutherland.

Whatever may have been the problem with the naval base at Manaus, it was resolved. The base would be built, using Nimitz's assets under Nimitz's control, but the line of demarcation between SOPAC and SOUTHWESTPAC would not again be changed.

For the near future, Nimitz and the Joint Chiefs agreed that Truk would be neutralized and bypassed, and the invasion of the Marianas was scheduled for June 15. Other items on the schedule: the Palau Islands (which controlled the sea route from New Guinea to the Philippines) would be taken on September 15, and Nimitz would support MacArthur's invasion of the southernmost Philippine island of Mindanao on November 15. Next would be the invasion of Leyte, set for December 20.

March 11, after the planning sessions had ended, Nimitz and King paid a call on the president. To Nimitz, who hadn't seen FDR in more than two years, the president looked unwell. After lunch, as the meeting was breaking up, he seemed tired and began asking questions irrelevant to the discussion of the day. For instance, after the blazing raid on Truk, he wondered why Nimitz had sent his forces on to attack the Marianas.

Nimitz said, the question reminded him of a story that went something like this: A surgeon at a teaching hospital asked a patient, a man about to have an appendectomy, if it would be all right for a group of students to watch. The patient said, of course. Some hours later, after the patient came out of the anesthesia, the surgeon dropped by to see how he was doing. The patient said, "Oh, all right, my abdomen is pretty sore but I guess that's to be expected. But why do I have such a horrible sore throat?" The surgeon replied, "Well, when I finished with the appendix, the students gave me such a rousing ovation that I took out your tonsils for an encore."

"So you see, Mr. President," Nimitz said in conclusion, "that was the way it was. We just hit Tinian and Saipan for an encore." The president burst out laughing, and the visit ended on a pleasant note.[11]

On March 15, Nimitz arrived back at Pearl Harbor to find a most unusual message from MacArthur:

> I have long had it in my mind to extend to you the hospitality of this area. The close coordination of our respective commands would be greatly furthered I am sure by our personal conference. I would be delighted therefore if when you are able you would come to Brisbane as my guest. I can assure you of a warm welcome.

Nimitz accepted this "very kind invitation which is greatly appreciated" and was on his way within a week.[12] He prepared by selecting a few gifts for Mrs. MacArthur (a small collection of rare orchids contributed by wealthy friends in Oahu) and for their seven-year-old son, Arthur (custom-made silk Hawaiian playsuits and a box of that grand Hawaiian delicacy, the macadamia nut). Upon arrival, the general met Nimitz on the dock—apparently a special honor—and took him to meet his family. Mrs. MacArthur was delighted with the orchids; the nuts made young Arthur violently ill.

But the two men got on famously. Nimitz discovered MacArthur's chief of staff, General Sutherland, had been screening Nimitz message traffic intended for MacArthur, which explained in part why there had been so many misunderstandings. However, there was more to the matter than misplaced messages. The visit was going quite well until Nimitz brought up a directive from the Joint Chiefs that required he and MacArthur prepare alternate plans for moving forward, faster—that is, bypassing the Philippines—if Japanese strength seemed to be waning. In a confidential memo to Admiral King, Nimitz wrote:

> He blew up and made an oration of some length on the impossibility of bypassing the Philippines, his sacred obligations there—redemption of the 17 million people—blood on his soul—deserted by American people—etc., etc.,—and then a criticism of "those gentlemen in Washington, who far from the scene, and never having heard the whistle of pellets, etc., endeavor to set the strategy of the Pacific War."[13]

Nimitz, true to his personal code, never gave public indication of his feelings about MacArthur. He certainly did not want to perpetuate a feud that other folks had created. A friend tried to push him to comment, but after thinking for a moment, Nimitz said only, "He has a great memory."[14] But Nimitz may have planted a clue for future historians. One time at CINCPAC, he let his guard down, when Layton asked why he kept a framed photo of General MacArthur on his desk. Nimitz replied, "That's to remind me not to be a horse's ass and make Jovian pronouncements complete with thunderbolts." Nimitz may have thought the comment would remain private, but to this day it is repeated by staffers in Hawaii when commenting on the Nimitz legacy.[15]

CHAPTER EIGHTEEN

THE MARIANAS

The agenda at the May 5 and 6, 1944, San Francisco planning session included a briefing on next month's cross-channel invasion of Normandy, D-Day, and a discussion on how next to employ Halsey, who was running out of targets in the South Pacific Area. There was an easy solution: Merge the units of Halsey's Third Fleet and Spruance's Fifth Fleet to form one larger force, free to operate throughout the Pacific on a two-platoon system, with two commanders. When Halsey was in charge, it was called the Third Fleet; after a period at sea, the command and the designation would shift, Halsey and his team would go to Pearl Harbor to refresh, regroup, and plan for their next operation, and Spruance and his team would move aboard a redesignated Fifth Fleet flagship. As Halsey later explained: "Instead of the stagecoach systems of keeping the drivers and changing the horses, we changed drivers and kept the horses . . . [it gave the enemy] an exaggerated conception of our seagoing strength."[1]

The two men offered a contrast in style and personality. To the public—indeed, to the sailors—it was "Bull" Halsey but "Admiral" Spruance. Halsey operated with a huge staff (which would have been even larger, but Nimitz set a limit of seventy officers). Spruance fought the whole war with seventeen officers. Halsey would fire off midnight dispatches with the plan for the next day. Spruance would issue a set of plans well in advance. One commanding officer later recalled, "My feeling was one of confidence when Spruance was there and one of concern when Halsey was there . . . he never did things the same way twice."[2] In a charitable moment, Nimitz compared the two to prize horses pulling a loaded wagon. One, head down, straining hard, silently pulling his utmost. The other, head high, tossing manes and tail, was pulling just as hard.[3] As Chester Jr. would later explain, for a job that required flair, publicity, and esprit de corps, his father would send Halsey. For a job that had to be done for which there could be no failure, he would select Spruance.[4]

Nimitz and Halsey had some violent arguments—over public relations! Halsey boasted, more than once, that when the war was over he was "going to ride the emperor's white horse through the streets of Tokyo." He did not seem to understand that the Japanese emperor, revered as a deity, had absolute control over his people and his support would be vital, postwar. Nimitz told him, "If you ever say that again I will relieve you of command. The emperor is the only person who can save our souls after we occupy Japan."[5] Nimitz got caught in a disagreement between Halsey and MacArthur. Halsey wanted to bomb the emperor's summer palace, to "send a message" to the Japanese. MacArthur said, "Don't bomb it—I'll use it as my headquarters." Nimitz, more sensitive to probable postwar issues than either of them, nixed both their ideas. According to Lamar, Nimitz had to get the backing of the Joint Chiefs but won the argument.[6]

Tarawa and Kwajalein had been small specs of land poking up above the ocean; the principal islands of the Marianas—Guam, Tinian, and Saipan—were substantial, variously 10 miles to 25 miles long. It would be impossible to neutralize every square foot with bombing and bombardment, so the Americans prepared for a prolonged campaign. The invasion force vastly exceeded the size of that sent to Tarawa: 535 ships carrying 127,000 troops, over six times the number of men at Tarawa. Two-thirds of those were Marines, but Army units were heavily involved and this was *their* kind of war, with room to maneuver. The Army style of advance was to take the ground, one foot at a time. They would lay down an artillery barrage, wait for the dust to settle, move forward, and clear out the opposition one enemy at a time. By contrast, the Marines—who would be fighting shoulder to shoulder with the Army—believed in moving quickly by leaps and bounds, bypassing pockets of resistance while consolidating their gains. At some point, they would send patrols back to root out the holdouts. And, much to the distress of Army Lieutenant General Robert Richardson, the Marines would be in charge of this operation: Marine Lieutenant General Holland Smith was in overall command, his two deputies next, and then the Army or National Guard commanders who came with the troops.

This provoked some heated discussions; Nimitz used his storytelling skill to cool one down. "This all reminds me," he said, "of the first amphibious operation—conducted by Noah. When they were unloading from the Ark, he saw the pair of cats come out followed by six kittens. 'What's this?' he asked. 'Ha, ha' said the tabby cat, 'and all the time you thought we were fighting.'"[7]

If only it could have been so easy.

Saipan came first. The air attack began on June 11, bombardments were added June 13, and the landings began on June 15. In the meantime, the intelligence teams discovered that the Japanese were assembling a naval force to stop the invasion, so a number of U.S. submarines were sent out to monitor various geographic points through which that fleet would have to pass. On June 13, one submarine spotted six carriers, four battleships, and eight cruisers. Other submarines picked up the trail. Thus forewarned, Spruance was ready, and on June 19 and 20, in the Battle of the Philippine Sea, his fleet sank 2 carriers and destroyed 476 combat aircraft (some 91 percent of those engaged), killing 445 Japanese aviators. The U.S. lost 130 planes and 76 aviators. It was the largest air battle of the Pacific war and was so one-sided that it has gone down in history as "the Great Marianas Turkey Shoot."

The landings on Saipan, however, were not going well. On June 23, Marine Lieutenant General Holland Smith summarily relieved Army Major General Ralph Smith of command of the 27th Division of the National Guard. The Army unit simply wasn't moving fast enough, and it was falling behind the two Marine divisions on either side, leaving them exposed to attack by enemy soldiers whom the Army should have neutralized. Another Army general was given temporary command of the division. He removed some dilatory officers, including a regimental colonel. Spruance gave the move official approval and Ralph Smith was shipped off to Pearl Harbor, where an enraged General Richardson set up an all-Army board of inquiry to determine how in the world a Marine Corps officer could fire an Army officer.

Soon, word got around that Smith had been relieved of duty and newsmen started asking questions. Nimitz refused to say anything and left any announcements up to the War Department; he would do nothing to hurt Ralph Smith. The War Department was silent. Of course, this let the story grow in the press, each telling reflecting the prejudices of the separate tellers. On the one hand, friends of the Army charged that "Howlin' Mad" Smith, dubbed "The butcher of Tarawa," was at it again. On the other hand, Marine Corps partisans said National Guard troops simply refused to fight. The *San Francisco Examiner* demanded that MacArthur be given overall command, a general whose "difficult and hazardous military operations . . . have been successfully carried out with little loss of life in most cases." *Time* magazine upheld the right—nay, the duty—of field commanders to relieve subordinates. If they hesitated to do so "for fear of interservice contention, battles and lives will be needlessly lost."[8]

Richardson stormed out to Saipan and confronted Holland Smith: "You can't push the Army around," he said, and launched into his favorite theme. Marines "are not as well qualified to lead large bodies of troops as general officers of the Army . . . you Marines are nothing but a bunch of beach runners . . . what do you know about land warfare?" Smith—to the amazement of all who heard the story—held his temper.[9] Richardson then got into a screaming match with the amphibious force commander, Richmond Kelly Turner— who did not hold his temper. Turner accused Richardson of insubordination. Richardson said he was in no way accountable to any officer in the Marianas. Turner put Richardson on report for "unwarranted assumption of command authority."

Nimitz thought it was all pretty silly. He received Turner's statement of charges as well as the findings of Richardson's board of inquiry (Ralph Smith was exonerated), but ignored the controversy and deleted all negative references to the 27th Division from Spruance's official report. He also sent an informal alert to King, along with copies of the various complaints. "If I forward them to you officially," he wrote, "it may become necessary for you to take the matter up with the War Department, which might result in unpleasant and unnecessary controversy at a time when we need all our energies to win the war. I am anxious that you should be fully informed on these matters should Marshall ever bring up the subject with you."[10]

General George C. Marshall, the Army chief of staff, did just that, noting that the board of inquiry had exonerated Smith; King said Richardson had no right to create an all-Army board to pass judgment on a Marine Corps officer. Marshall disagreed on the grounds that the board was simply providing advice to Richardson. The silliness soon evaporated. There was a war to be won.

Right in the middle of the Marianas campaign—indeed, just a few days after both Guam and Tinian had been invaded—President Roosevelt hosted a Nimitz-MacArthur planning session at Pearl Harbor to discuss the next major step: Was it logical to take back the Philippines, or go around them and invade Formosa? Nimitz first learned of the impending conference when a Secret Service man flew in to pick a hotel for the president. Nimitz was instructed to invite MacArthur to Hawaii without, for security, including any reference to FDR. The general responded along the lines, "We have nothing to talk about."[11] Next, Admiral King issued the invitation, ostensibly to discuss bringing British forces into the mix. MacArthur was "too busy." Finally, General Marshall *ordered* MacArthur to attend. MacArthur got the message.

FDR traveled from San Francisco aboard the cruiser *Baltimore* the day after the Democratic National Convention had nominated him for a fourth term as president (Senator Harry S. Truman of Missouri was to be his running mate). The two-day planning session convened at Pearl Harbor on July 26, 1944. In attendance: Nimitz and staff, MacArthur and staff, and President Roosevelt (accompanied by Admiral William Leahy but none of the other members of the Joint Chiefs). Nimitz, acting as protocol officer-in-chief, showed his respect to the president by having every sailor at Pearl Harbor in dress-white uniform, manning the rails of all ships and saluting as the *Baltimore* and the president passed by. MacArthur—no fan of the president and in fact a political rival who until just the month before had been angling for the Republican presidential nomination—showed his disdain by arriving late, wearing khakis, a leather jacket, and the cap of a Philippine field marshal.

Next came the formalities. General Richardson arranged for the president to visit some installations and inspect some troops. The president favored open touring cars, so he could wave to cheering throngs. But there were only two such cars on the island: a smallish red one belonging to the fire chief, and a proper open limousine belonging to Honolulu's most notorious madam. Understandably, the small red one won the toss. MacArthur could barely conceal his anger; he resented being used as a prop in a campaign stop, engineered to show the president in charge and advising the Army and Navy on winning the war in the Pacific

However, the meeting, once underway at FDR's hotel, was appropriately cordial. The session lasted well into the evening and continued the next morning. There were some questions passed along from the Joint Chiefs: How many casualties might be sustained in a Philippines operation? Are the Philippines of strategic or just PR importance? Would it be possible to bypass and isolate the Philippines and target Formosa instead?

Formosa? MacArthur was scornful. The population of that island had been under Japanese control for half a century, and it seemed unlikely that people who had known no other government would rise up and shift sides. The Philippines would be a different story: home to friends, ready to cast off the yoke of the oppressor. Further, if the United States were to isolate the Philippines and cut off their supplies, the Japanese would likely withhold rations from our loyal Filipino allies and from the almost 4,000 American POWs they were holding in the islands. Not a happy prospect.

When the president suggested that an attack on Luzon would result in "heavier losses than we can stand," MacArthur scoffed, "My losses would not be heavy. . . . The days of frontal attack are over. Modern infantry weapons are too deadly, and direct assault is no longer feasible. Only mediocre commanders still use it. Your good commanders do not turn in heavy losses."[12]

Nimitz, to his great and grand credit, said nothing.

The general handed the problem to the president. "The national honor," said MacArthur, "is at stake!" Nimitz was willing to give MacArthur the nod as long as he, Nimitz, was satisfied that the strategy was militarily supportable. The president promised to pass the challenge to the Joint Chiefs. And the meeting adjourned, just shy of noon, and everyone headed to lunch.

The day before, at the end of Richardson's guided tour, FDR had turned to Lamar and said, "Lamar, I'm having lunch with you tomorrow, may I have a nice cold martini before?"

Lamar affirmed the possibility—and as the wheelchair-bound president was pushed into the hotel, Lamar and Nimitz looked at each other in what we might call stunned amusement. Lamar said, "I thought we weren't going to have any meals?" The admiral said, "I did too, but now we're in it."

Soon enough a Secret Service man showed up to inspect the admiral's quarters. He began issuing orders: Move those palm trees, lay down a mat over the lawn so the president's car could drive around to the back where he could disembark unseen by passersby and neighbors, enlarge the back door and the bathroom to accommodate the wheelchair.

Enter a team of Seabees, rearranging the lawn, rebuilding parts of the house, drying wet paint with blow torches in a rush to finish.

The president arrived right on time, to be greeted by some hastily invited star-studded guests (literally: Lamar counted a total of 146 stars among the group, which included MacArthur, Leahy, Nimitz, Halsey, and 32 others). The president's "nice cold martini" miraculously expanded into three. A great time was had by all.

After lunch the Seabees came back to repair the lawn and replant the palm trees. Nimitz was a great fan of the Seabees, for whom, seemingly, no challenge was too great. Compared with building a massive supply base in the middle of a nowhere jungle, rearranging palm trees and bathrooms overnight was a small accomplishment. Once, he lamented to Lamar, that he now regretted his prewar support for a Bureau of Medicine and Surgery requirement that anyone recruited to be a Seabee had to have at least "four opposing molars." He noted, in the world at large, "You never see a plumber or carpenter or a painter that has a full set of teeth. How many valuable men," he wondered, "did we lose to the Army Construction Corps because we were so damn persnickety about teeth?"[13]

The Marianas campaign soon ended. Tinian was secured on August 1, and Guam fell on August 8, 1944. Nimitz decided to move his immediate staff to Guam, whenever a new headquarters building could be constructed. He picked the site, and then, after rejecting suggested plans, sketched out the design himself. When finished around the end of the year, the headquarters complex included cottages for senior officers and visitors and some Quonset huts for the junior officers and enlisted men.

This move would put Nimitz 3,500 miles closer to the action and also get him away from the hubbub of Pearl Harbor, the center of gravity for a flood of visitors, the waypoint for all of the new ships arriving and, with Nimitz's penchant for greeting and talking with all the new commanding officers, it was getting hard to find time to do his job. As one staffer noted, "you rarely saw him except in a conference or when he called for you to ask questions."[14]

CHAPTER NINETEEN

A DIFFERENT SORT OF WAR

There was growing talk that after the war the armed services would be merged. Interservice rivalries would disappear; control and coordination would be enhanced; and the national defense would be ensured at a greatly reduced cost as "efficiencies" were introduced.

The talk had been initiated by Army Chief of Staff General George C. Marshall in November 1943, was briefly explored in congressional hearings the following spring, and was being encouraged by the Army, which had long been frustrated by the Navy's clout with Congress and the president. In 1939, for example, the Navy spent more money on one battleship than was in the Army's entire equipment budget and the Army did not understand why. Now, the Army was winning the war in Europe, where the Navy was only a bit player. And the Army looked forward to major changes, with the Army in charge. Indeed, the Army Air Forces wanted to absorb or replace all naval aviation. Had not Billy Mitchell proven that warships were obsolete when he sank the captured World War I battleship *Ostfriesland?* In the race for public and congressional support, the Navy—jokingly called the silent service—was fast being eclipsed. The Army was grabbing the headlines, and the generals, the glory—as with MacArthur's "Jovian pronouncements" after the Battle of the Bismarck Sea, when he suggested that control of the seas no longer required a Navy.

News coverage of the invasion of France—June 6, 1944—gave the Army its biggest boost ever. D-Day was covered almost in real time by print, photo, and newsreel. Rules of censorship had been laid down far in advance and were so well understood by the press that, for example, only one word was changed in a 5,000-word story for the *Saturday Evening Post*.

At the very same time, Nimitz had launched the invasion of the Marianas with that fleet of 535 ships and defeated the Japanese at the Battle of the Philippine Sea, in the largest air battle of the Pacific war—all with barely a mention in the American press, a trickle compared with the torrents coming from the beaches of Normandy. In the Pacific, security was tight, old habits and prejudices died hard, and because of enforced radio silence and the sheer volume of information, even with the improved press-support guidelines Nimitz put in place at Tarawa, most news reports from the Navy still took between eight and fourteen days to reach mainland newspapers.

At the request of Assistant Secretary of the Navy for Air Artemis Gates, *New York Herald Tribune* reporter Emmet Crozier conducted an informal survey of newsmen and naval officers who had dealings with the Pacific Fleet public relations office. He found multiple complaints of needless delay of press copy, unreasonable and arbitrary censorship, and bitterness and tension in the relationship between the working press and public relations officer Waldo Drake (now a captain), especially during 1942 and 1943. Things were improving, Crozier noted, but not much.

And he added, taking on Navy public relations as a whole, "there is no clear conception at this critical period in the war of the Navy's informational obligation to the American people or of the sound advantages to the Navy of an enlightened, constructive public relations policy. . . . The Navy has failed to give the American people a clear, comprehensive picture of its work and its problems. It has failed to tell, or permit others to tell, the human story of the men who are fighting and dying in its service. It has failed to tell . . . the great story of naval air power. If the American people sit by impassively after the war, while the Navy's air arm is wrenched away . . . the blame can be laid squarely on the present lack of a constructive public relations policy in the Navy."[1]

James Forrestal, recently appointed secretary of the Navy following the death of Frank Knox on April 28, 1944, invited the Office of War Information (OWI) to take a more formal look at the Pacific Fleet and offer some recommendations. George W. Healey Jr., a former reporter serving as director of OWI's domestic branch, was given the task, assisted by the head of Navy public relations, Rear Admiral Aaron S. "Tip" Merrill.

The two men sat down with Nimitz to review overall practices and procedures. Also, following Crozier's lead, Healey focused on Captain Drake and heard from scores of correspondents that they felt bottled up. Most of them said Drake was not trying to move news along but was trying to slow it down. Even though he was of the profession, Drake didn't know how to work with newsmen, and many simply didn't like him. *Time* described him as "brusque."[2]

Healey soon had a taste of Drake's style. They were having lunch at a popular club in Honolulu, when one of the civilian pool photographers wandered in, obviously alone. Healey asked Drake, why don't we invite him to join us? Whereupon Drake replied, "He's nothing but a goddamn photographer."[3]

Nimitz agreed that, under the circumstances, Drake should be replaced. He believed that Drake, as a witness to the Pearl Harbor attack of December 7, 1941, might be obsessed with security. However, he was a fine officer and any transfer would not be approved unless Drake received orders to a billet with as much authority and dignity as the one he had at Pearl Harbor. Healy had the solution: There was a vacancy at OWI, which already had several senior naval officers on staff, for a deputy director.

Healy reported to Forrestal, who agreed and asked OWI head Elmer Davis to send a letter to the Navy Department, formally requesting a captain with public relations experience to serve as deputy director of the agency. Davis did so and sent a note to Healy, "George, I signed the letter to Forrestal—hope you have arranged through Merrill or otherwise to see that we get Waldo [Drake] and not some old rooster they merely want to get rid of." (Waldo, indeed, they got, and Waldo earned promotion to rear admiral while serving at OWI.)[4]

Nimitz and Merrill developed new ground rules. Reporters could be landed with the troops—after the fifth assault wave. Members of the PR staff would be forward-deployed and handle censorship duties on the spot, approved copy would be carried by air with a goal of reaching the West Coast within 24 hours of leaving the scene of action. More radio time would be allotted for transmission of press copy and for live broadcasts. One sticky issue they were unable to resolve: accreditation of female reporters. Nimitz was adamant. Appropriate facilities were, simply, unavailable.

While Drake's orders were being processed, Forrestal selected Captain Harold B. "Min" Miller as his relief. Miller, of the Naval Academy class of 1924, was a pioneer naval aviator and a former assistant naval attaché in London. He was the author of several magazine articles and at least one book about naval aviation, but he had no experience with public relations and was puzzled by this new assignment. He wanted to go back to sea, he needed a carrier command to be in line for promotion, and here he was being shunted off to a desk job. He made so bold as to ask Forrestal, "Why?" The secretary delivered a little speech, snippets of which Miller later recalled. "We've got problems in the Pacific. We see the end of the war. We know when we're going to close this war out. And MacArthur's winning the war. When this war is over, no one will ever know the Navy was in it. It's been a Navy war the whole time. No one will ever know it. If we don't get something done about our public relations job in the Pacific, I can't go to Congress. We'll get no funding, no allocations, or anything. We've got to change the whole atmosphere." As an incentive, Forrestal indeed promised Miller command of a carrier, when the job was done.[5]

Greatly to his discomfort, Miller's change of duty orders, which directed him to report to CINCPAC, did not specify that he was Drake's relief as staff public relations officer. As far as the CINCPAC administration office was concerned, he was just another staffer. He checked in with the PR office and discovered that Drake was escorting six newsmen some 4,700 miles out in the Pacific. Drake had left a sign on his office door saying "Keep Out," directed at wandering newsmen. Someone told Miller that Nimitz didn't know that he had been sent in to relieve Drake, so he wasn't sure what he should do next. After sitting around for a while, he said to himself, "I'd better do something!" So he took down the "Keep Out" sign, threw it in the wastebasket, took over the office, and began introducing himself to the staff and the newsmen working around the headquarters.

The dynamic was interesting, to say the least. On the one hand, here was Miller, assuming responsibility but not quite in charge. On the other hand, there was a press contingent looking for someone to lead them out of the wilderness. Frank Kelly of the *Chicago Tribune* took the lead as spokesman for the local press contingent. "Min," he said, "we want to see the Admiral." Miller, who had only met Nimitz in a routine "Glad to have you with us" sort of session, agreed. He asked for an audience for a gaggle of reporters. Nimitz said, "Fine, bring the boys in." As Miller later said, "He was such a salt of the earth. He was so wonderful. So I led about twenty of them in like the Judas goat and he said, 'Gentlemen, sit down.' We sat down, and I didn't know what the hell they wanted to talk about. Kelly stood up and said, 'Well, Admiral, I am the spokesman for this group, and we're here to tell you that we want Min Miller to be your public relations man.'" Miller thought he was going to die, and as soon as possible, he escorted the newsmen out of the office and went running back, and said, "Admiral, all I can say is I had no idea what they were up to. I knew nothing about it." Nimitz replied, "Oh, forget about it, no harm done."[6]

What Miller really did not know was that Forrestal had informed Nimitz that Miller was his personal choice to replace Drake. Nimitz was simply watching to see how Miller would handle the situation. Drake returned a couple of days later; to say he was surprised to see a stranger sitting at his desk would be an understatement. Two days later, he was on his way to Washington.

On September 1, 1944, some two weeks after Miller arrived at CINCPAC but before he could have much impact, Forrestal wrote in his diary, "I have been telling King, Nimitz and Company it is my judgment that as of today the Navy has lost its case and that, either in Congress or in a public poll, the Army's point of view would prevail." The Navy, he wrote, could not "be in the position of merely taking the negative . . . but must come up with positive and constructive recommendations."[7]

Indeed. When he formally took over the office, Miller told all reporters, "It will be our policy while I am here to tell you just what the hell is going on. If national security is involved, we will tell you that, too, and try to explain why. My office has three doors, and all of them will be open all day."[8] Nimitz agreed that responsibility for censorship should be a separate staff function, manned at headquarters or in the field, as required by the flow of traffic. Also, all major commands and commanders should have public relations officers on staff or on call. The effort was real and the growth was exponential. On September 1, 1944, there were 13 public relations officers on the CINCPAC staff and 8 more on duty in the forward areas. By the end of the war, just a year later, 90 officers and 250 enlisted men were assigned to the CINCPAC public relations section and more than 400 full-time Navy public relations officers were elsewhere in the Pacific.

Much of the day-to-day effort was devoted to a new approach: "hometown" press releases, sent to selected papers around the nation, which put a focus on local Navy men (and managed to mention the admiral, as well; not necessarily to his liking, but the logic was sound). Something such as: "Seaman So-and-So, son of Mr. and Mrs. So-and-So of this city, was honored today for his participation in the invasion of Island X, one of the last Japanese holdouts in the Pacific. Admiral Chester W. Nimitz, USN, commander in chief of the Pacific Fleet, said 'The contributions of men like Seaman So-and-So continue to pave the path to victory.'"

It was a highly effective mass-communications tool; the mere mention of a small-town hero made the Navy a winner with the locals—and with the sailor. By the end of the war, almost 2 million releases had been sent out to perhaps 12,000 media outlets. As volume grew, management of the program was shifted to the Great Lakes Naval Station. The program continues, to this day.

CHAPTER TWENTY

THE "RETURN"

T he Joint Chiefs had been debating the question since the Pearl Harbor conference in July 1944, but couldn't make up their collective mind: Should the next major target be the Philippines or Formosa? Nimitz sent a friendly warning: He was about to run out of authority to do anything and needed their guidance. Then, on September 12, a *Hornet* pilot, rescued after ditching near Leyte, learned from the locals that the Japanese did not have a large garrison on the island, and Halsey, noting the limited opposition his pilots were reporting, recommended a change in plans. Nimitz handed the opportunity to the Combined Chiefs of Staff, just then meeting with FDR and Churchill in Quebec. By September 16, Mindanao was off the table and the December 20 invasion of Leyte was moved up to October 20, 1944. And so it came to pass that MacArthur would, indeed, return to the Philippines, with timely authority to do so and most of the transportation and air cover provided, courtesy of the U.S. Navy.

On September 23, CINCPAC took over the sparsely inhabited atoll of Ulithi, some 850 miles east of the Philippines and 1,300 miles south of Japan. Ulithi was ideally suited as a support base for the fleet: 40 small islands surrounded a huge lagoon, 20 miles long, 10 miles wide, with water depths of 80 to 100 feet—big enough to hold more than 700 ships. But Ulithi was not just a place to park the ships while they were waiting for the next big operation: The Navy moved in a fully equipped floating service station: Service Squadron 10, made up of repair ships, tenders, and floating dry docks big enough to host a battleship, all manned by some 6,000 artisans. One ship produced drinking water and baked pies; a floating barge made 500 gallons of ice cream a day. Nimitz was taking care of the small boys—the ships that were not equipped to provide all the comforts of home. Scattered among the larger of the islands the Seabees built a 3,500-foot airstrip, a 1,200-seat theatre, a 500-seat chapel, and a recreation center that could accommodate 9,000 men a day.

Service Squadron 10 was Nimitz's "secret weapon," and so sensitive that he would not even allow the name "Ulithi" or the purpose of Service Squadron 10 to be included in any press dispatches. The secret was finally revealed, a month after the end of the war.[1]

On October 16, Nimitz stepped out of his comfort zone and delivered by radio a fifteen-minute address to a forum organized by the New York Herald Tribune, broadcast over a nationwide network. He began by recounting recent victories—none of which came from great battles, and all of which were representative of day-to-day operations in the Pacific: "Since the 9th of October," he said, "we have sunk 73 Japanese ships and destroyed approximately 670 Japanese aircraft." There would have been more, but the fleet was running out of targets. During one air attack on October 13, "only five operational enemy aircraft were observed on the ground, and none were seen in the air." He paid tribute to the design and construction of his warships, to the supply forces that kept the fuel, food, and ammunition coming, and to "the great superiority of [American] carrier-based aviation to anything which the enemy can mount against us." However, he warned, "it would be a grievous error" to "hope that there will be any early end to our war with Japan."[2]

Radio Tokyo had its own version of those same actions: The Japanese Navy sank 11 American carriers, 2 battleships, and 3 cruisers. There was, Radio Tokyo added, great celebration in the streets and warm congratulations from Adolf Hitler and Benito Mussolini. On October 19, Nimitz was happy to inform the world that he had received from Admiral Halsey "the comforting assurance that he is now retiring toward the enemy following the salvage of all the Third Fleet ships recently reported sunk by radio Tokyo."[3]

On October 20, right on schedule, troops landed on Leyte in the morning and MacArthur waded ashore in the afternoon. All of the landing craft were engaged so he headed toward the beach in a standard-issue ship's boat, which grounded in shallow water some distance from the water's edge. He would have motored over to a pier, but most of the piers had been destroyed in the bombardment, and the one man on the island who knew the location of an undamaged pier, the Navy beachmaster, was busy, and according to one account, he "growled 'Let 'em walk.'"[4] So walk they did. It was pure serendipity: The photos of the general and his party sloshing through the surf made great PR. Actually, he waded ashore twice. Newsreel cameras were not around for the first take, so he did it again the next day.[5]

If the Japanese were caught off-guard, it was not for long. The garrison was quickly reinforced, and the Japanese Navy pounced with fury, leading to a series of violent clashes collectively known as the Battle of Leyte Gulf. The Japanese lost three battleships, four carriers, ten cruisers, and nine destroyers. The United States lost one light carrier, two escort carriers, two destroyers, and one destroyer escort. Outnumbered and overpowered, the Japanese Navy—as reported by Halsey—"has been beaten, routed, and broken."[6] He was right.

The Allies had more ships in the battle than the Japanese had airplanes. In desperation, the Japanese came up with "kamikaze" tactics, in which the airplanes themselves became flying-bomb suicide missions.[7] Since so few of their pilots had been returning from their missions, the Japanese decided, why not give someone just enough skill to follow a leader and dive his explosive-laden airplane into an enemy ship? The first strikes were on October 25 and 26 and throughout the Philippine campaign, fifty-five airplanes ploughed into forty-seven ships, sinking an escort carrier and five smaller ships, and causing heavy damage to most of the rest.[8]

Admiral Halsey missed most of the show at Leyte Gulf. He had been lured out of position by a decoying group of Japanese carriers—the ships were real, but they had been stripped of airplanes and were given the role of sacrificial lambs. On October 25, Halsey was headed north in pursuit with a group of ships, designated Task Force 34, leaving the landing forces at Leyte open to attack. The commander of the landing force, unaware of Halsey's movements, called for support several times. When a puzzled Nimitz saw the messages, he wondered why Halsey wasn't already on-scene and asked a staffer to get Halsey's location. This simple question was forwarded by classified dispatch. To confuse enemy cryptographers, a random bit of nonsense opened and closed every classified

message, separated from the text by double consonants. Also—normal practice—important elements were often repeated, not for emphasis but in case
some letters were garbled. As transmitted, the message to Halsey read:

> TURKEY TROTS TO WATER GG FROM CINCPAC ACTION COM THIRD
> FLEET INFO COMINCH CTF SEVENTY-SEVEN X WHERE IS RPT WHERE
> IS TASK FORCE THIRTY FOUR RR THE WORLD WONDERS

The man who decrypted the message on Halsey's flagship properly deleted
the opening phrase "turkey trots to water" but did not strip out the bit after the
double consonant "RR," uncertain as to whether or not it was meant as part of
the text. The message as handed to Halsey came across as an insult, a sarcastic
slap in the face, "Where is, repeat, where is Task Force Thirty Four? The world
wonders."[9]

Halsey erupted, shouted an obscenity, and threw his cap to the deck. Chief
of staff Robert Carney grabbed his arm: "Stop it. What the hell's the matter with
you?" Halsey thrust the dispatch at Carney, then grabbed it back, threw it on the
floor and stomped on it. "What right," he yelled, "does Chester have to send me
a God-damn message like that?"[10] It took some hours before Halsey could calm
down. It was several months before he would have a chance to see Nimitz—who
was, well, surprised to learn of the issue. He asked his communications officer
to check it out. It turned out that an ensign may have been too creative in his
choice of padding. He was given a different job.

Early in December, a British fleet of 4 fleet carriers, 2 battleships, 5 cruisers,
and 15 destroyers was en route to take station in the Pacific, with headquarters
at Sydney, Australia. Under an agreement between FDR and Churchill, Admiral Sir Bruce Fraser would have administrative control of his forces, and they
would largely operate independent of the Americans—to avoid tactical confusion, especially with maneuvering in large formations. But they would report to
Nimitz for operations.

Nimitz and Fraser had met once before, back when Nimitz was CO of the
Augusta and they were both captains. Now, he invited Fraser to fly up for a
conference. One of the first questions Nimitz asked was, how long could the
British fleet remain at sea? Fraser said, in effect, don't worry, they had their

own logistics train including oilers, although they were not as proficient as the Americans at underway replenishment. Nimitz wanted something a bit more specific; Fraser said they could operate eight days out of every month. As Nimitz described the conversation in a December 13, 1944, letter to King, "Admiral Fraser and I had a long conversation. . . . He felt he could operate for eight days a month, and we compromised on twenty."[11] Next, the British needed a mission. Nimitz suggested a raid on the Japanese-held oil fields in Sumatra. Fraser suggested that was not exactly what they had in mind. After some staff coordination, they were assigned to the forthcoming invasion of Okinawa, scheduled for April 1, 1945.

Admiral Fraser had a nonoperational request: The officer who had been assigned to CINCPAC for the past year as the British liaison officer, a commander, should be replaced by a vice admiral. Nimitz thought the commander had been doing a good job, why pull him out? Because to the protocol-sensitive British, he wasn't senior enough. Nimitz said, promote him to admiral. That was a bit too radical, but the Brits made him an "acting captain," which served the purpose.

In the middle of December, Nimitz and six other officers were promoted to a newly approved five-star rank. Marshall, MacArthur, Eisenhower, and Arnold were made "generals of the Army," and Leahy, King, and Nimitz became fleet admirals. There was one open slot in the Navy that eventually went to Halsey. (King thought it was unfair to promote Halsey and not Spruance, but the Act of Congress allowed only eight, total, appointments.) Nimitz was sworn in on December 19.

Throughout November, Halsey's force made seven strikes against the main Philippine island of Luzon, MacArthur's next target. Halsey destroyed almost 800 aircraft, 3 destroyers, 5 transports, and 10,000 soldiers. His next mission was to support MacArthur's landings on Mindoro, scheduled for December 15. This didn't quite work out, but the reason was not the Japanese. It was the weather.

There were warnings—a falling barometer, increasing wind, and historic data on weather patterns at that time of year—but Halsey's aerographers offered ambiguous predictions that they updated frequently with great inaccuracy. Thus, Halsey sailed his fleet directly into the heart of a typhoon. Some of the ships were in no condition to fight a storm at sea and the weather prevented last-minute refueling of the most vulnerable, the destroyers. Without the weight of fuel to enhance stability, and with some skippers lacking the skill or experience to know that empty fuel tanks could be filled with seawater, many of the ships lacked critical ballast.

Halsey changed the fleet course three or four times, each more hazardous than the last. Some commanding officers saw the danger and broke formation the better to ride out the storm; others felt duty-bound to stay on the course as ordered by the force commander. With hundred-mile-an-hour winds and mountainous seas, three destroyers sank, nine other ships were damaged, more than one hundred aircraft were smashed or washed overboard, and 790 men were killed. There was a court of inquiry. Nimitz was in attendance. The court found that Halsey was responsible, but did not recommend sanction.

Nimitz approved the findings of the court, noting that Halsey's mistakes "were errors in judgment under stress of war operations and stemming from a commendable desire to meet military requirements." King agreed, but softened the blow by changing "commendable desire" to "firm determination" and, after "judgment," inserted "resulting from insufficient information."[12] Nimitz sent a cautionary message to all commanding officers in the fleet, reminding them that the skill and judgment of professional seamen must always take precedence over often arbitrary "orders" from higher authority. "No rational captain," he wrote, "will permit his ship to be lost fruitlessly through blind obedience to plan or order since by no chance could that be the intention of his superior. . . . The time for taking all measures for a ship's safety is while still able to do so. Nothing is more dangerous than for a seaman to be grudging in taking precautions lest they turn out to have been unnecessary. Safety at sea for a thousand years has depended on exactly the opposite philosophy."

He added the pointed comment that attention to weather had been the responsibility of men in command since seafaring began, and with all of the advanced technology and knowledge available today, seamen "should be better at forecasting weather at sea."[13]

Six months later, Halsey again took his fleet into a typhoon; this time ships were damaged but none lost. Seventy-five planes were destroyed, seventy badly damaged. Six men were killed. There was another court of inquiry; it recommended that Halsey be given another job. Nimitz—and King, on review—disagreed and kept him on, a reward for tangible success, certainly, but also a nod to public opinion. It would not be prudent to punish the hero of the Pacific in the middle of the war.

On December 26, 1944, MacArthur announced, "the campaign [for Leyte] can now be regarded as closed except for minor mopping up." Perhaps, if killing another 27,000 Japanese on the island between then and May 1945 can be called "mopping up."[14] Nimitz paid a call on MacArthur to discuss support for the forthcoming invasion of Luzon, scheduled for January 9, 1945. Nimitz was wearing his new five-star insignia, custom-built by metalsmiths at Pearl Harbor. MacArthur, who was not so adorned, was openly irritated. He ordered an aide to see that this oversight was corrected by morning.

On January 9, MacArthur did, indeed, invade Luzon—where more than 250,000 Japanese troops were waiting. By June 30, 200,000 defenders had been killed. MacArthur's casualties totaled 8,310 killed and 29,560 wounded.

At the end of January, Nimitz and key members of the CINCPAC headquarters staff began the move to Guam. This was carefully planned to ensure continuity of operations should anything happen to the contingent on Guam. Admiral Towers and the bulk of the staff—logisticians, communicators—remained at Pearl Harbor. Copies were made of all important documents, so that the staffs at both CINCPAC locations could be on the same page. An encrypted teletype link connected the two so they could teleconference in real time. Special one-time-only tapes were run at either end for each conference, so decryption by the enemy was impossible.

Nimitz was in place and ready to work by January 27, 1945.

Next on the schedule: the invasion of Iwo Jima, February 19, 1945.

CHAPTER TWENTY-ONE

IWO JIMA

Three Japanese airfields on Iwo Jima, about halfway between Japan and the new U.S. B-29 base on Tinian, had to be neutralized to permit the bombers safe passage to and from their targets. Then, once Iwo Jima was in American hands, those airfields would provide a base for Army Air Forces escort fighters that would fly protective cover for the bombers and would serve as an emergency landing field for bombers in distress.

The softening-up of Iwo Jima began in August 1944, with some 2,800 sorties flown by B-24 bombers in the following six months. During the two days before the scheduled February 19, 1945, landings, a task force with 16 carriers, 8 battleships, and 5 cruisers launched some 1,200 planes against air bases in Japan from which bombers could attack the invasion force. More than 300 of the enemy's planes were shot down, and almost 200 were destroyed on the ground. This was the first carrier attack on Japan since the Doolittle-*Hornet* raid in April 1942. The Associated Press called this latest raid "one of the boldest operations in naval history," and noted a small departure from Nimitz's usual quiet demeanor: "A twinkle of the eye—no more, no less—is the cue in these calm headquarters of big things happening."[1]

In planning for the assault on Iwo Jima, the Marines asked for ten days of heavy shore bombardment. Admiral Richmond Kelly Turner, commanding the invasion force, said that was impossible because the ships couldn't carry enough ammunition for a ten-day sustained operation—and the nearest point of resupply was nine hundred miles away. Since the island was only eight square miles and had been so heavily pounded by the B-24s, he was certain that a three-day bombardment would be sufficient. He estimated that the Marines would conquer Iwo Jima in another four days. The Marine commander offered his own more conservative estimate: He would take the island in ten days.

The Japanese recognized the strategic importance of Iwo Jima and had been working on defenses for almost a year. Some of those had been spotted by aerial surveillance, but unseen were the caves and tunnels that sheltered troops, ammunition, and other supplies deep enough to be untroubled by any bombardment. Command headquarters itself was seventy-five feet below the surface. The Japanese knew they could not win the battle, but vowed to make it as costly as possible.

The first wave of landing craft headed ashore on February 19 and ran into the first surprise: a narrow but violent surf zone and beaches of volcanic ash in which vehicles could not get traction and the Marines could not get footing. The landings were a mess—a traffic jam of broached or destroyed landing craft.

The main fighting lasted for thirty-five days and skirmishes would continue until June. The Marines' weapons of choice became flamethrowers, grenades, and satchel charges to seal off the tunnels and entomb the defenders. At one point, Nimitz considered but rejected an Army recommendation to use poison gas. While some argued that it was a more humane weapon than the flamethrower, most of the world had agreed to outlaw poison gas soon after the trench-warfare horrors of World War I. Even so, it would not have been a violation of international law for the United States to use gas, since neither the United States nor Japan were signatory to the treaty that outlawed gas warfare. However, President Roosevelt's chief of staff, Admiral Leahy, advised the president that the use of poison gas (or bacteriological warfare, also then being considered) "would violate every Christian ethic I have ever heard of and all of the known laws of war. It would be an attack on the noncombatant population of the enemy."[2] FDR agreed, and gas was off the table.

On the matter of ethics, Christian or otherwise, the U.S. government was, at best, confused. At that very moment, the noncombatant population of the enemy was being incinerated by the thousands. Just two B-29 raids against Tokyo on March 9 and 10 destroyed some 250,000 houses, killed 83,793 people, and left 1 million homeless.

There were more than 20,000 defenders at Iwo Jima; all but 1,000 were killed. The Marines landed 70,000 men, and of those 5,521 were killed and some 17,000 wounded. A *Life* magazine reporter called Iwo Jima "a nightmare in hell."[3] Admiral Nimitz saluted the Marines: "Uncommon valor," he said, "was a common virtue." He wished that he might have been less skittish about the use of poison gas. Failure to do so, he confessed privately, "cost a lot of good Marines."[4]

Iwo Jima proved valuable as a safe haven for crippled or fuel-starved bombers—thirty-six actually landed even before the island had been secured and fighting was still underway. By the end of the war, some 2,400 B-29s had landed on Iwo Jima, but only about 20 percent of those were for "emergency." The rest were more precautionary—for minor maintenance, refueling, or perhaps to avoid bad weather. The escort function proved problematic—it was a long nine-hour-slog for the fighters, which were cramped, cold, unpressurized, and not designed for that purpose; only three escort missions from Iwo Jima were actually flown before that concept crumbled under the weight of reality and the bombers shifted to nighttime missions.

Iwo Jima was the real test of CINCPACs improved press relations and support. Photos of the operation were flown to Guam for processing and review and reached San Francisco less than a day after the first landings. Notable among them was perhaps the most famous photo of the war, AP photographer Joe Rosenthal's iconic shot of Marines raising the flag on Mt. Suribachi. It was a Pulitzer Prize winner and would be rendered immortal by Felix de Weldon's classic Iwo Jima Memorial statue at Arlington, Virginia.[5]

Radio reports and printed dispatches were censored on-scene and released immediately for transmission. *Time*'s report of March 5, 1945, was laudatory: "It was another notable step toward bringing the Navy's public relations up to its fighting arm's high standards."[6]

San Francisco Examiner publisher William Randolph Hearst, however, was not impressed with the improved coverage, or with the Navy in general. He issued a thinly veiled blast at Nimitz: "General MacArthur is our best strategist . . . he wins all his objectives . . . he outwits and outmaneuvers and outguesses and outthinks the Japanese. He saves the lives of his own men . . . why do we not give him supreme command in the Pacific war, and utilize to the utmost his rare military genius of winning important battles without excessive loss of precious American lives?"[7]

This time, the Navy was not asleep at the switch. *Time* reported, "The Navy took special pains to explain to the press and public why the capture of Iwo was vital to the progress of the war, even though it had been especially costly in terms of casualties."

Newsweek was more direct: "The Navy, knowing from experience MacArthur's grip on the imagination of the American people . . . began to see red last week as stories appeared in the daily press contrasting MacArthur's landings, made at small cost on undefended or lightly defended shores, with frontal assaults on such heavily fortified bastions as Tarawa, Peleliu, and Iwo Jima—all Marine Corps operations . . . under the command of Fleet Admiral Nimitz."[8]

Iwo Jima also was a victory, of sorts, for women. After years of resisting pressure to allow female journalists into a combat zone, Nimitz finally agreed. With so many nurses and Red Cross women now in the Pacific, he couldn't continue the argument that facilities were inadequate. Freelance reporter Dickey Chapelle and Barbara Finch of Reuters were allowed to fly into Iwo Jima with the first planeload of nurses, without incident. Later, at Okinawa—the next major push in the Pacific—Chapelle pushed her advantage to the point where she managed to get ashore before most of the Marines; none of the foolishness of waiting for "the fifth wave of the assault." When the boat in which she was riding touched sand, she was over the side and headed inland. Vice Admiral Richmond Kelly Turner, the amphibious force commander, sent a terse note to CINCPAC: "Get that woman out of here!"[9] She was pulled out of Okinawa, sent back to the United States, and banned from the Pacific for the rest of the war. Well, Ms. Chapelle had *her* own agenda and made a career out of proving that a woman could cover any story that a man could. She was probably right: Twenty years later, she was killed by a land mine in Vietnam.

Right in the middle of the battle for Iwo Jima, Nimitz went to Washington to plan out the rest of the war. The Joint Chiefs had just returned from the Roosevelt-Churchill-Stalin conference at Yalta, where it seemed clear that the war in Europe was fast coming to a close, and they could turn their full attention to the Pacific. On Monday, March 5, Nimitz, along with his operations officer, Forrest Sherman, outlined the plan for the invasion of Okinawa. The Navy would cover the landing force and also provide cover between Okinawa and the southernmost home island, Kyushu; the British fleet would be working between Okinawa and Formosa. Four Army and three Marine divisions would be under the command of Army Lieutenant General Simon Bolivar Buckner. Nimitz hoped the conquest would go quickly, as his ships would be exposed to attack from fifty-five Japanese airfields on Kyushu, 370 miles to the northeast, and sixty-five on Formosa, 365 miles to the southwest. The enemy might be able to muster as many as 4,000 airplanes for the effort.

The Joint Chiefs accepted the plan for Okinawa, and after some discussion also agreed on a timeframe for the invasion of Japan, which they targeted for November 1. After the meeting adjourned, Nimitz and Forrestal had lunch at the White House. Nimitz was shocked by the president's appearance; FDR would live only five weeks longer.

This was Nimitz's second and final visit to Washington during the war. It was the only visit at which he was able to attend the wedding of a daughter: Kate, to Commander James Lay (one of the *Augusta* ensigns). They had been engaged for several months and the main event had not been planned for this visit, but, since all of the principals happened to be in town at the same time, why not? However, when the happy couple went to get the marriage license on Tuesday, they discovered there was a three-day waiting period. The ceremony could not be held until Friday, and Nimitz and Catherine had to be in San Francisco on Sunday to watch 13-year-old daughter Mary christen a destroyer. There were a few nervous moments but it all worked out.

At the same time, Admiral Merrill's health was declining and Forrestal told Nimitz that he was bringing Min Miller back from the Pacific to take over as director of public relations. This was fine with Nimitz; things had obviously turned around and his PR staff was well organized and fully functional. But Miller himself objected; he made a trip to Washington to remind Forrestal that he had been promised command of a carrier when his service on Nimitz's staff had ended. Forrestal responded, "Oh, hell, I can get anybody to fight a carrier. Things are going well out there and I've got plans for you." Miller reported aboard April 23, 1945, and was promoted to rear admiral, making him at age 42 the youngest in the Navy—ever.[10] His relief at CINCPAC was Captain (later vice admiral) Fitzhugh Lee.

The Joint Chiefs announced a command restructuring in the Pacific. The division into areas was abolished, and Nimitz was put in command of all naval forces and MacArthur of all army forces, wherever they were operating. The

War Department engineered the change because, under the old arrangement, MacArthur could not lead the army into Japan. He would have been limited to operations in the SOWESPAC area and could not operate north of the Philippines. Japan was Nimitz territory.

Such was the political power of the Army Air Forces, that JCS-member General "Hap" Arnold had unique control of the B-29 fleet. Major General Curtis LeMay, commander of the Pacific-based B-29s, reported neither to Nimitz nor to MacArthur but directly to Arnold. However, LeMay was required to respond to requests for assistance from Nimitz. He did so, but not always willingly.

On paper, the new command structure seemed logical, but it had not been very well thought out. There were issues; for example, should MacArthur immediately take control of army assets then under Nimitz's command—such as the garrisons manning the captured islands? That would have become a logistical nightmare. After a month of staff-level meetings, with scant resolution, Nimitz flew off to MacArthur's new headquarters in Manila, and they worked it out. Operations already underway, as well as in-place command and support relationships, would continue, but new operations would follow the revised plan. The coming invasion of Japan would be handled much like the recent island invasions, with the Navy in charge until the troops were ashore, the Army thereafter.

Nimitz soon rearranged his own assets; thanks to a steady stream of new ships arriving in the Pacific, he could split the combined Third/Fifth Fleet back into separate entities, each vastly larger than their original version. The Fifth Fleet was slated to support landings on Kyushu, the Third Fleet to support operations on Honshu.

But first, Okinawa.

CHAPTER TWENTY-TWO

OKINAWA

The Americans assembled a fleet of some 1,400 ships, including 40 carriers, 18 battleships, and 200 destroyers. The British added another 50 warships. After the usual bombardment of the beaches, the Okinawa landings began on schedule, April 1, 1945. While the troops on the ground were advancing faster than ever before, offshore enemy air attacks against the fleet were brutal. Between March 31 and June 10, there were kamikaze attacks almost every day—at least seven were mass air raids involving some 1,500 planes, along with almost 450 individual attacks.

Nimitz asked LeMay to hit the Japanese airfields from which the kamikaze attacks were coming. LeMay thought his bombers were better employed in fire-bombing Tokyo, but he was obligated to respond. The airfields were attacked, to great effect, but the damage was being repaired so quickly that LeMay was forced to stay the course and continue striking the airfields. Heavy Japanese raids continued on April 6 and 7, resulting in another B-29 mission on April 8. Afterward, when Nimitz still denied LeMay's request to be released, LeMay fired off a blistering memo to Arnold, saying that Nimitz was hampering the war effort. Arnold complained to King, who suggested that, if the AAF was not willing to support the Navy off Okinawa, the Navy might have to pull out, which would leave the ground forces to fend for themselves. That ended the discussion.[1]

A second kind of kamikaze was soon to be confronted: a suicide fleet, consisting of the world's largest battleship, the *Yamato*, along with one light cruiser and eight destroyers. They sailed for Okinawa on April 6 with just enough fuel for a one-way voyage and orders to ground themselves in shallow waters off the beach and serve as coast-defense artillery. This Japanese fleet was spotted by a submarine and attacked by carrier aircraft. All but four destroyers were sunk. The U.S. Navy lost ten airplanes and twelve airmen.

Admiral Richmond Kelly Turner sent a message to Nimitz, "I may be crazy but it looks like the Japs have quit the war, at least in this section." Nimitz replied, "Delete all after 'crazy.'"[2] A lot more Pacific war was still to come.

By mid-April, some of the Marines, moving through lightly defended territory, had taken most of their objectives, but the advance of the Army and the rest of the Marines now had ground almost to a halt. On April 23, a very frustrated Nimitz flew in to take a look—while the Army was creeping forward perhaps 300 yards a day, he was losing a ship and a half every day to the kamikazes. He warned the Army commander, General Simon Bolivar Buckner, "If this line isn't moving within five days, we'll get someone here to move it so we can get out from under these stupid air attacks."[3] There was not much movement in five days and not much Nimitz could do about it; in fact, it took another month to crack the enemy's defenses and the island wasn't secured until June 21.

But someone leaked the story of "Army-Navy dissention" to a reporter. Washington-based syndicated columnist David Lawrence took it up a notch: "Certain high Navy officers here feel that a major mistake was made in handling the Okinawa campaign. . . . Did the Army officers who handled the campaign adopt a slow course? . . . . Why were the Marine Corps generals who had far greater experience in handling amphibious operations not given opportunity to carry on another type of campaign that, might, perhaps have meant . . . a quicker all-around result . . . ?" In a later column, he called Okinawa "a worse example of military incompetence than Pearl Harbor."[4] That sent everyone to general quarters. The last thing the Navy or the Army needed was a distraction when they were getting ready for the invasion of Japan. Nimitz called in the press and praised the Army's role at Okinawa.

In the end, the problem was not the Army's ground game; it was the superbly entrenched resistance by Japanese troops who would die before surrender. The enemy had early on given up trying to defend the beach, knowing it would be torn up in the bombardment. Instead, they let the troops get ashore and used the kamikaze attacks to sink the ships that supplied the Americans.

Then, as the U.S. forces moved inland, they were stymied by a system of caves, tunnels, and hidden gun emplacements.

Ultimately, about 125,000 Japanese soldiers, sailors, and militia were killed, along with 140,000 civilians.[5] On the American side 12,513 were killed and almost 40,000 wounded. More than one-third of the American casualties at Okinawa were from the kamikaze attacks, which sank twenty ships and damaged more than two hundred, twenty of which were beyond repair. Nimitz tried to keep the kamikazes under wraps—he did not want the Japanese to know how successful they were—and he had managed to control the information during the earlier attacks in the Philippines. But there was no way to hide the devastation at Okinawa. After about two weeks, the press was allowed to report on the kamikaze raids.

Something even bigger was being kept under wraps: the atom bomb. Nimitz had been informed about the weapon back in February, when a very sweaty and disheveled young commander arrived with an urgent need to see the admiral. Lamar was skeptical—most visitors usually put on a clean uniform before calling—but Nimitz agreed to see him. When Lamar had left the room, Commander Frederick L. Ashworth opened his shirt, to reveal a very damp money belt from which he extracted a similarly damp envelope, which he handed to a by now slightly amused Nimitz. Inside the envelope was another, marked "Top Secret," and inside that, a letter from Admiral King.

Amusement was replaced by wonder and perhaps a touch of horror. King reported the ongoing development of a weapon with the explosive power of 20,000 tons of TNT, which would be ready for use around August 1. Nimitz could ask Commander Ashworth for technical details and was to tell no more than one staff officer. Nimitz immediately called for his chief of staff, Rear Admiral Charles H. "Soc" McMorris, and showed him the letter.

Ashworth was eager to explain the bomb, but Nimitz did not seem interested in the details. "Young man," he said, "this is all very interesting but August is a long way off and in the meantime I have a war to fight." He added, "Please tell Admiral King that I cannot abide by his requirement to inform only one officer on my staff if he expects me to provide the support I am sure will be needed." Ashworth later said that Nimitz turned in his chair and gazed out of the window for a moment, then rose and said, "Thank you very much. You know, I guess I was born just a few years too soon."[6]

Secretary of the Navy Forrestal continued to push for more and better public relations. If Nimitz thought he could escape distractions by shifting his head-quarters to Guam, he was mistaken. The secretary sent a never-ending stream of visitors, most of them civilians, including members of Congress, labor leaders, industry leaders, prominent authors, and, especially, publishers of magazines and newspapers. Back in January, Admiral King had written to Nimitz, "The Secretary feels that it would be beneficial to give the publishers the opportunity to observe for themselves the tremendous problems involved in the Pacific war, since they, rather than the correspondents, establish the policies which govern the editorials and handling of stories concerning the Pacific."[7] Democrat FDR, however, would not approve that plan, presumably because most publishers were Republicans and he did not want to give them an opportunity to criticize his management of the war. After Roosevelt died on April 12, Forrestal con-vinced President Harry Truman of the merits of such visits—but Truman in-sisted that the guest lists be scrubbed to ensure inclusion of an equal number of card-carrying Democrats. They stayed at Nimitz's guest house on Guam, were entertained at dinner, given tours of some front-line activities, and briefed by senior officers. Some of those officers, we might note, were rather cool to this duty, and complaints soon reached Forrestal, who passed them to King, who warned Nimitz, "The number of prominent visitors to your area will increase, and it is important that they be treated with courtesy." The offending officers were removed from the duty roster.[8]

Beginning in May 1945, there were rumors that Japan might be willing to sur-render; by early July, the rumors were widespread and being reported with skep-ticism in American newspapers. But the rumors were true. In July, the head of the American Office of Special Services (OSS), Allen Dulles, met with Japanese diplomatic officials in Switzerland, who indicated that Japan would consider terms of surrender, with the condition that the emperor not be removed. This was discussed by Truman and Josef Stalin at the July 16 Potsdam conference, and in his diary entry for July 18, Truman referred to "the telegram from the Jap Emperor asking for peace." There is some uncertainty in the documentary record as to whether or not the Allies were interested. In any event, they did not pursue the opening, and on July 26 the governments of the United States, Great

Britain, and China issued the Potsdam Declaration, which laid out their terms of peace for Japan: unconditional surrender of all Japanese forces, surrender of all territories then occupied except the home islands, submission to occupation by the Allies until such time as an acceptable government had been established by free elections. The alternative was "prompt and utter destruction."[9] Two days later, the Japanese prime minister issued an ambiguous comment that the Allies took as a rejection of the peace terms.

Naval ordnance expert Captain William Parsons arrived at CINCPAC headquarters in Guam with movie footage of the first atomic test, which he showed to an awed audience including Nimitz, Spruance, and LeMay. He then flew up to Tinian, where the bomb-carrying B-29s were based and where the cruiser *Indianapolis* had just arrived with some components of the bomb. Parsons was the man in charge of putting it all together.[10] By August 2, all necessary parts for two bombs had arrived on Tinian, and the first "special bomb" drop was ordered "as soon as weather will permit visual bombing after about 3 August."[11]

At 2:45 A.M. on August 6, 1945, a B-29 dubbed "Enola Gay" (in honor of pilot Paul Tibbets's mother), accompanied by two observer B-29s, took off from Tinian with Captain Parsons aboard to assemble the bomb en route to the target, Hiroshima. The bomb was dropped at 9:15, the planes were back on Tinian by 3:00 P.M. Perhaps 66,000 people were killed; there has never been a definitive estimate.

On August 8, the Soviet Union invaded Japanese-held Manchuria, and rushed to declare war on Japan while they still had the opportunity to do so. On August 9, another B-29 dropped an atomic bomb on Nagasaki, killing perhaps another 39,000 people. On August 11, King sent a "peace warning" message to Nimitz; the Japanese would accept the terms of the Potsdam agreement if the emperor could remain as sovereign. The United States was willing, but Truman would not issue a cease-fire order until the United States had concurrence from Britain, the Soviet Union, and China, lest the Japanese be encouraged to change their minds. On August 13, Halsey made a raid. On August 15, he was about to launch another when Nimitz ordered, "Suspend attack air operations."

The war was over.

CHAPTER TWENTY-THREE

SURRENDER

For some people it was a time to rejoice, jump up and down, and cheer. When he got the word, Nimitz simply sat down and smiled. Then he sent instructions out to the fleet: Stand down but remain alert, and in any future contact with the Japanese, all officers and men were to conduct themselves as gentlemen. Halsey picked up the theme in his own way and sent a message to his forces to be on guard against kamikaze attacks: "Investigate and shoot down all snoopers—not vindictively, but in a friendly sort of way." Overall, Japanese forces that were in communication with headquarters obeyed the orders of the emperor and Nimitz could relax, a bit; the Japanese seemed to be living up to their end of the agreement.[1]

Then, a personal blow: Truman appointed General Douglas MacArthur Supreme Commander of the Allied Forces, to arrange for the surrender ceremonies and the official signing of the documents of peace. "Well, this does it!" muttered Nimitz, greatly annoyed. The Navy and Marines had taken the brunt of the battles in the Pacific, and won them, and now the Army was being given the credit, albeit indirectly. It seemed that whenever MacArthur demanded the limelight, he got it.[2]

Nimitz expressed his professional disappointment to COMINCH Admiral King and Secretary of the Navy Forrestal, who suggested to the president that if an Army general was going to be in charge and represent all of the combatant forces, then a naval officer—Nimitz—should represent the United States and the ceremony should be held aboard a Navy warship. Thus, Halsey's latest flagship, the battleship *Missouri,* became a key player in the event. Some folks thought the honor should go to a more battle-scarred veteran—the *Missouri* was a Johnny-come-lately with only some eight months in the war zone. But Forrestal knew Truman could not deny the honor to this ship named for his home state, a ship christened by his daughter Margaret back when he was still a senator, and thus a selection that would be hard for anyone to contest.[3]

It was a brilliant move. Had the ceremony been ashore in some Tokyo hotel under the total direction of MacArthur, the American-casual brand of history would have recorded the Army, forever, as winner of the Pacific. The *Missouri,* one of the most substantial warships ever built, with a long and distinguished postwar career, is moored today in Pearl Harbor, one of the biggest tourist attractions in Hawaii. And, nose to tail with the *Arizona* memorial, she keeps the focus of the Pacific war on the Navy.

Captain Stuart S. Murray (the submarine skipper who had trouble parking his boat back in 1920) had been the *Missouri*'s commanding officer for just three months, but to him fell the honor of hosting the final event of the Pacific war. The date of the formal surrender was set for September 2, 1945, and Murray had less than two weeks to prepare. He had the crew touch up parts of the superstructure that were in desperate need of cosmetic refreshment and strip off a wartime coating of paint that had been applied to the teak decks and scrub them down to the classic prewar-era look.

The first wave of occupation troops flew in to the Tokyo area on August 28, with great anxiety but no opposition. The *Missouri* and other ships of the fleet dropped anchor in Tokyo Bay, just off the Yokosuka naval base, the morning of August 29. There were no problems, but the Americans put out boat patrols and UDT swimmers just in case. Nimitz flew in by seaplane that afternoon and set up shop on the battleship *South Dakota.* Soon after, Halsey came by to tell him that there were Japanese POW camps near Tokyo, and conditions were deplorable, but apparently MacArthur had put out the word that no POWs were to be released until the Army was ready to participate. Halsey had a hospital ship standing by and asked Nimitz what to do. Nimitz said, "Go ahead, General MacArthur will understand."[4] By midnight, nearly 800 prisoners had been brought out. MacArthur flew in the next day. If he had any comment, it was not recorded.

On September 1, 1945, Nimitz sent letters home, including this to daughter Kate:

> Yokohama is like a dead city with very little activity. There are Japanese police and gendarmes on duty . . . and they act as if we were not in sight. They are not sullen or amazed, as one might expect. They simply do not see us.

Nimitz noted that the fleet was standing by, ready to send in airplanes should anything untoward happen, especially during the surrender ceremony scheduled for nine o'clock the next morning. And, he wrote, he was about to pay a call on his friend Admiral Bruce Fraser, Royal Navy, aboard the *Duke of York* anchored close by. The call was "partly on official business, partly because I like him, and mostly to get a scotch and soda before dinner."[5] As a British contribution to the ceremonies and to provide a symbolic surface on which the surrender documents might be executed, Admiral Fraser sent over a very fine, very polished mahogany table that had survived the Battle of Jutland. The table was standing ready aboard the *Missouri*.

Someone suggested that the *Missouri* should be on the exact spot where Commodore Matthew Calbraith Perry had been anchored in 1854, when he negotiated the opening of trade and diplomatic relations with then-isolationist Japan. The position was easily determined from the log of his flagship. The Naval Academy museum sent on loan the flag that Perry had flown at that time, and it was mounted on a bulkhead in the ceremonial area. The National Geographic Society asked Nimitz for permission to send a team of experts to determine, in the interests of history, the exact position of the *Missouri* when the surrender documents were signed. Nimitz deemed the *Missouri's* navigator competent to handle that routine task and denied their request. However, since a ship at anchor will swing with the movement of the tides and current, as much as 100 or 200 yards in almost any direction, the position had to be plotted exactly at the moment. The navigator took several sets of bearings and then turned off power to every gyro compass repeater on the ship, to forestall efforts by any visitor or eager amateur to make his own (inaccurate and therefore sure to become controversial) plot.

MacArthur insisted on absolute precision. The ceremony would start at 9 A.M. But Foreign Minister Mamoru Shigemitsu had a wooden leg, and it might take him longer than expected to come aboard the *Missouri* and then up the ladder to the ceremonial area. Captain Murray organized a "Shigemitsu board-ing party test," a time trial in which a sailor with a swab handle stuck down a trouser leg and strapped in place, maneuvered along the route. The wooden leg was not an issue after all.

Nimitz had the Seabees on Guam dress up a landing boat decorated in Army colors, which was carried to Tokyo Bay and offered to MacArthur for transport from shore to ship for the ceremonies. Call this a Nimitz miscalcula-tion. He didn't realize that MacArthur would be coming from his headquarters in Yokohama, not from a nearby pier at the Yokosuka naval base. MacArthur took one look at the boat and said, reasonably, "I'm not going to ride 20 miles in that thing." He preferred to have a destroyer.[6]

MacArthur also let it be known that he would like to have his five-star Army flag flown from the *Missouri* as a special honor. This raised a sticky issue. Navy protocol and practice was to fly the flag of the senior *naval* officer aboard a ship, and never to fly the flags of two officers of equal rank on the same ship at the same time. Lamar, sensitive to the fact that MacArthur was the senior (by two weeks), asked Nimitz, "What do we do now?" Nimitz said, "You're the flag lieutenant, that's your problem." Lamar, a Nimitz-trained delegator, passed management of the problem to the ship's company, which installed a pair of hoists to fly both flags, Nimitz to starboard, MacArthur to port, at the exact same height.[7]

September 2, 1945, aboard the *Missouri* began—as did every day in the Navy—with "attention to colors." A clean set was pulled out from the spares and hoisted, national ensign on the stern, Navy jack at the bow.[8] Nimitz came over to the *Missouri* shortly after eight. The destroyer carrying MacArthur came alongside to port and, about 8:40, MacArthur came aboard and went in to Ad-miral Halsey's flag quarters to await his big moment. Also arriving with Mac-Arthur was an Army colonel who had flown out from Washington with the surrender papers, two copies (one for the Allies, one for the Japanese). These were to be signed in turn by the Japanese and then the representatives of the Allied parties. The documents were quite large, about 40 by 20 inches and were to be laid side by side on the table. Admiral Fraser's beautiful mahogany antique was much too small.

A team of sailors began a scramble to find a suitable table. The officer's wardroom mess was close by—but the tables were bolted to the deck. Off in a rush to the crew's mess where they found a folding table but no tablecloth, not a standard item in the crew's mess. Back to the wardroom to grab a somewhat stained green baize tablecloth, then out to the deck for set-up with minutes to spare.

The ceremony was going to be crowded, with perhaps 225 news correspondents, 75 photographers, and 75 senior officers representing 8 nations—and everyone wanted to have the best view of the signing. The immediate area was divided into standing room spots, each assigned to a specific visitor. The rest of the topside surface went to the crew, at least those who were not on duty or manning the antiaircraft batteries. For the military observers, rank and protocol took care of the placement; the newsmen and photographers drew lots. Escorts were appointed to take each visitor to his assigned spot as they came aboard. A few of the escorts for the newsmen and photographers remained with their guests to discourage casual wandering. The precaution was warranted, especially as it applied to photographers, never known as a docile breed. One photographer who tried to get right up close to the signing was caught and towed back.

Things were more or less on time, but the Japanese were nervous and moved slowly—which had nothing to do with the foreign minister's wooden leg. At one point, MacArthur popped out of the door expecting everyone to be in place. They were not, so he turned around and went back in. A few minutes later all was ready, and MacArthur, Nimitz, and Halsey made a formal entrance.

The ceremony was brief. The chaplain delivered an invocation, the band played "The Star-Spangled Banner," and MacArthur made a brief speech, expressing, "the hope of all mankind" that these ceremonies would lead to lasting worldwide "freedom, tolerance, and justice."[9] He then directed the representatives of the Imperial Japanese Government and Imperial Japanese Staff to come forward and sign. Shigemitsu was clearly disoriented—not surprising, under the circumstances. He limped over, sat down, took off his hat and gloves, dropped his cane, picked it up, fumbled in his pocket looking for a pen. One of his aides stepped forward and handed him a pen. Shigemitsu was confused and didn't know where to sign. MacArthur said to his chief of staff, "Sutherland, show him where to sign." General Richard Sutherland did so. General Yoshijiro Umezu, chief of the army general staff, leaned over the table and signed, standing up.

MacArthur signed, with Lieutenant General Jonathan Wainwright and Lieutenant General Sir Arthur Percival standing symbolically behind him. Both men had been prisoners since 1942—Wainwright, captured with the fall of Bataan and Percival at the fall of Singapore. Then Nimitz signed for the United States, and was followed by the representatives of Great Britain, China, the Soviet Union, Australia, Canada, France, the Netherlands, and New Zealand.

MacArthur had one last word, "Let us pray that peace be now restored to the world and that God will preserve it always."

The war had lasted almost four years; the surrender ceremony took about twenty-three minutes. On signal, an armada of perhaps 450 Navy and Army warplanes flew overhead. Some had been airborne for some time, on security patrol against opportunists. There was one last-minute glitch, however. The members of the Japanese delegation were not the only folks confused; the Canadian representative signed on the wrong line on the Japanese copy of the document, skipping his allotted space and signing one line down so the following signers were one line off and the last, the New Zealander, had to sign in a blank space at the bottom. As they were about to leave the *Missouri*, one of the Japanese started a commotion. Layton translated: "The document is invalid!" MacArthur called out: "Fix it." Sutherland crossed out the mismatched country names and inserted, by hand, those that coincided with each signature, leaving the original space for the Canadian blank, and adding "Dominion of New Zealand Representative" under the last signature at the bottom.[10] The Japanese accepted the revised copy (if they had a choice, it wasn't apparent), and the war had officially ended.

When Nimitz got back to the *South Dakota*, he sent a message of congratulations to the crew of the *Missouri*. The Nimitz touch: He did so by flag hoist so that all other ships in the harbor would see the compliment. Then, after lunch, he made a trip ashore to see the great Buddha at Kamakura, a few miles out of town. He took Layton along as translator, cultural interpreter, and bodyguard (earlier, Nimitz had verified Layton's skill with a firearm, just in case). As they drove through the countryside, Marine escorts, riding in jeeps in front and behind, were blowing their horns to clear the way, and peasants were dropping to their knees by the roadside. Nimitz was curious. Layton explained that the only person with an electric horn in Japan is the emperor, and the sound of a horn said he was coming, down on your knees and cover your eyes.

Along the way Nimitz stopped at a military hospital. He thought it would be a nice gesture to visit wounded Japanese servicemen but found them scared to death. They were told the American "head man" was coming in and they were sure he was going to behead all of them. Nimitz also paid a visit to Togo's flagship from the Battle of Tsushima, the *Mikasa,* which had been set up as a national monument but was now in a sorry state. It had already been picked over for souvenirs by American servicemen—including Admiral Halsey, who had pinched off the flag, which he sent to Admiral King for presentation as a trophy to the Russians. Nimitz ordered that a Marine guard be placed at the *Mikasa.*

Meanwhile, back aboard the *Missouri,* the guests had left and the crew was tidying up when someone asked, "Where's the table?" After all, it was a bona fide artifact of history, to be preserved for the ages. It had been returned to the mess deck and the tablecloth lay crumpled up against a bulkhead. Both were retrieved—it was just in time for the table, as it was about to be set up for the crew's lunch and would have disappeared into anonymity. Table and cover were sent off to the Naval Academy Museum.

Captain Murray arranged to have printed souvenir cards, one for each person aboard at the signing, attesting to their brush with history. An adequate quantity was made in advance, authenticity affirmed by facsimile signatures (included with permission) of MacArthur, Nimitz, and Halsey, and hand-signed by Murray. These were given to all attendees, crew, and guests, at the ceremony. Afterward, a number of people asked for extra copies; among them was Nimitz, who wanted a few for the secretary of the Navy and some other officials. Murray said "No, as it says on the card, 'Certifying the Presence of . . .'" Nimitz quickly affirmed that restriction and told Murray, "If anyone tries to put pressure on you, I will back you up." All unused cards were burned and the printing plate thrown over the side.[11]

CHAPTER TWENTY-FOUR

HOMECOMING

Forces were lining up for that next big fight: the battle between the Army and the Navy over the shape of national defense. At first, Nimitz thought that "unification" seemed like a good idea. He saw it as a follow-on to the very effective unified management of his forces in the Pacific; he had even offered a positive response to a Joint Chiefs of Staff poll of senior officers taken back in December 1944.

However simple the original scheme, the devil was in the details, and as it developed, the details were astounding. The proposed Unified Armed Forces would be headed by the Army. The Marine Corps would disappear. There would be a separate Air Force, whose long-range bombers, it was assumed, would eliminate the need for aircraft carriers. Indeed, some supporters of unification argued that the advent of the atomic bomb had rendered most of the Navy obsolete. Whatever remained would provide transportation.

The move was being championed by senior Army officers, including the aviators who had fought the war in Europe with masses of ground troops and easily obtained air support, and had attacked Germany's industrial base with medium-range bombers. With ever-improving technology, they believed, wars of the future would be won from the air.

On the other side were senior naval officers, most of whom had fought in the Pacific where the targets were islands that could be approached only from the sea and were so far apart that air support was usually unavailable except from aircraft carriers. More important, those officers were steeped in the vital concept of control of the seas, whereby the Navy kept the sea lanes open for an ally—whether for commercial transport or the movement of military forces—and blocked their use by an enemy.

The opening moves of this warriors' dance were subtle. An internal Army Air Forces memo suggested "the AAF has been and is the idol of the American public. The public's acceptance and support must be carefully planned and jealously guarded."[1] AAF commander General Henry H. "Hap" Arnold pledged that he would "scour the country to provide you with the men most capable of putting into words the achievements of the Army Air Forces."[2] Once the war had ended, those "men most capable"—advertising and public relations professionals—were at work, providing guidance and assistance to senior AAF officers. A simple example: slipping pro-air-power propaganda into meetings of professional engineering societies and business advisory councils—many of which had a strong interest in possible development, manufacturing, training, or support contracts with the AAF.

Commanders returning from the war were being treated to grand celebrations, but at this point, they were Army men: the victorious Eisenhower, the heroic Wainwright, saluted by millions in New York and Washington. MacArthur would soon join the parade. Secretary of the Navy James Forrestal wanted Nimitz to take advantage of this public interest, to step onto the stage and tell the *Navy* story.

At first, Nimitz was reluctant. It was not his style to play the conquering hero or future hope, but he finally agreed to serve as surrogate for all of the men who had served under his command and who merited the salute.

Time offered a simple perspective:

> Americans were inclined to be a little vague about the U.S. Navy's white-haired, pink-cheeked Fleet Admiral Chester W. Nimitz, who had directed the Battle of the Pacific from a desk. He had never courted publicity. He had accumulated stiff titles like CINCPAC or CINCPOA instead of nicknames. And he had spent most of the war at Pearl Harbor and Guam. Also the public had been welcoming Army heroes on a production-line basis and was a little throat-weary. Nevertheless the Navy was determined to see that its senior hero got his due.[3]

During the first week in October, Nimitz, accompanied by his operations officer Forrest Sherman and his flag lieutenant Hal Lamar, headed to events in San
Francisco, Washington, D.C., and New York City. At San Francisco City Hall he
hit on the theme he would replay over the following days: the vital role played
by the Navy in defeating Japan and the imperative for maintaining a strong
Navy. He also spoke of the need for continuing research in advanced weapons.
"New weapons such as the atomic bomb may change the character of warfare
but it will not change the fact we must have control of the sea. We have it now.
We have the power and the resources now. We must keep them." Nimitz was
given the key to the city. "What," he wondered, "wouldn't Yamamoto have given
for this?"[4]

October 5, 1945, was designated as "Nimitz Day" in Washington, and quite
a day it was. Nimitz rode in a parade escorted by six bands, five thousand sailors, Marines, WAVES, and one hundred Coast Guard sentry dogs, past cheering
crowds estimated to be as large as one million. Marine Corps artillery and captured Japanese aircraft were towed along behind. One thousand Navy aircraft
flew overhead, some in a formation that spelled N I M I T Z in letters one block
long. The *New York Times* called the parade "by far the most elaborate staged in
Washington since the war."[5]

In what might be called the opening naval salvo of the next battle, Nimitz
gave a joint session of Congress a short but telling tutorial on sea power.

"I wish to give you a brief report," he said, "on the job we are just bringing
to an end. . . . Five weeks ago today I was in a land of hunger and defeat and
disillusionment. Five weeks ago today I was in Japan."

A land of hunger, defeat, disillusionment, yes, but, as Nimitz told the assembled members of Congress, Japan was at the time maintaining a widespread
army of some five million men, larger than at the time of Pearl Harbor, and
had six thousand combat aircraft, twice as many as on December 7, standing
ready for battle. Why then, he asked, "did Japan sue for peace [in July] before
the introduction of the atomic bomb and before the entry of Russia into the
war? . . . Because Japan, a maritime nation, dependent on food and materials
from overseas, was stripped of her sea power."

"Five weeks ago today," what remained of the once-mighty Japanese
Navy? "One battleship, damaged. Four aircraft carriers, all damaged. Two

heavy cruisers, damaged, and two light cruisers, one of which was damaged. . . . Not one of these ships had a crew aboard." Japanese industry was
strangling, people were at the point of starvation, and Japan lacked oil for
ships and gasoline for aircraft.

"We gave Japan," Nimitz said, "the single choice of surrender or slow but
certain death."

Nimitz next gave a speech to a huge crowd at the Washington Monument
and touched on another of his themes. "Perhaps it is not too much to predict,"
he said, "that history will refer to this present, not as the ending of a great conflict, but as the beginning of a new atomic age." He hoped that at some time
in the future atomic power would be "tamed and harnessed" for "industrial
and humanitarian uses." And he reiterated his pitch to the Congress: "The
introduction of atomic power has given new importance to seapower. . . . Our
defense frontiers are no longer our own coastlines. . . . Today our frontiers are
the entire world."[6]

Neither Congress nor the general public were paying much attention.
The warm glow of victory blanketed rational thought like a friendly fog.
However, the AAF propaganda team most certainly was listening. In at least
two speeches that came after Nimitz Day, General Carl A. "Tooey" Spaatz asserted to one and all that we were in the "air age," whose primary force is air
power: "As sea power was the dominant factor in the destiny of nations in the
nineteenth century, so today the dictate is air power." While once the Navy
protected U.S. shores from enemy invasion, he said, in a great leap of faith, "in
the air age only air power could defend the United States from the devastation
wrought by an enemy air force."[7]

Following his speech at the Washington Monument, Nimitz went over to the
White House, where the president awarded him a Gold Star in lieu of a third
Distinguished Service Medal. Nimitz accepted the award on behalf of the more
than two million men who served under him in the Pacific, "those who had
made the victory possible." Most of the Nimitz family—Catherine and the three
daughters—was in attendance; Truman, a well-known poker-player, compli-
mented Nimitz on his "three of a kind." Kate later said that the dapper president
looked just as she would have expected "for a former haberdasher."[8]

The Nimitz family rounded out the day at a gala dinner.

The following morning, the admiral paid a call on Secretary of the Navy Forrestal. He wanted to be named chief of naval operations, to cap a memorable career from the top of the profession. However, he now found himself in the awkward position of having to ask for the job from a man who had not volunteered the assignment, and with whom he often had issues. This reflected an enmity going back to Nimitz's refusal to give a commission to Forrestal's friend with a prison record, aggravated by Nimitz's reluctance, against the urging of Forrestal, to appoint aviators—most of whom had little experience with naval operations other than flying—to important command posts.

To further roil the waters, Nimitz heard a rumor that Forrestal once tried to have Admiral King—with whom Forrestal rarely got along—appointed as CINCPAC to replace Nimitz, which would have accomplished the twin goals of getting King out of town and sticking a finger in Nimitz's eye.

Now, the war was over, King was above the mandatory retirement age of 64, and it was time for a change. Congress decreed that five-star officers would be on active duty for life, but this was a ceremonial posting that did not involve day-to-day conflict and decision. Nimitz, only 61, elected not to beat around the bush: He told Forrestal outright that he would like to succeed King.

Forrestal was just as forthright in his opposition. He had battled King too long and too often and didn't want to have to deal with another intransigent naval officer. Besides, he suggested, Nimitz should bask in the glory he had achieved. He should either remain as CINCPAC or take a position as chairman of the General Board, that collection of wise men who recommended but did not command. By this point in history, the once-powerful board had so little influence that by 1951 it would be disbanded.

Unpersuaded, Nimitz repeated his request, that he would like to be considered for the job of CNO. He did not press for an immediate answer and headed off to New York for another grand parade, this one along a route lined with 4 million spectators and doused by 274 tons of tickertape and scrap paper. The parade ended at City Hall Plaza, which at that moment was under heavy cloud cover until the irrepressible Mayor Fiorello LaGuardia pointed to the sky and said, "Come out sun." And sun there was, to the delight of 350,000 cheering New Yorkers. Nimitz was made an honorary citizen. Master of the local touch, he noted, "Some of our best sailors had no more previous experience at sea beyond a ride on the Staten Island ferry."[9]

At a press conference a short time later, Nimitz touched on the unification controversy: "I am a strong advocate of unity of command in a theatre of operations [as was the case in the Pacific], and I do not favor merging the War and Navy Departments into a single department."[10]

The day closed with a banquet at the Waldorf-Astoria hotel attended by two thousand guests, who paid $15 each for the privilege (about $176 in today's money). LaGuardia was host and Nelson Rockefeller introduced the guest of honor. Nimitz gave the crowd their money's worth, especially when he began with a bit of humorous doggerel entitled "Nimitz and Halsey—and Me." A sample:

> Me and Halsey and Nimitz
> Have sure got the Japs on the run.
> We're driving them wacky
> In old Nagasaki
> We're setting the damn risin' sun.

The *New York Times*—which printed the full text—credited the author as an "unnamed naval officer in the Pacific."[11] In truth, the verse was courtesy of Captain William G. Beecher, Jr., one of the first naval officers to sail into Tokyo Bay.[12]

After he had warmed up the crowd, Nimitz delivered his key remarks, calling the Navy the largest single force for the preservation of peace. "Our enemy has seen his fleet destroyed, his sea lanes cut . . . his vital supply sources closed— all by our control of the sea—on it, over it, and beneath it. . . . Japan faced the logical and ultimate result of our blockade—starvation at home."[13]

New York City was careful not to play favorites when celebrating war heroes. On June 19, General Eisenhower had enjoyed what was reported to be an identical reception. But Eisenhower's banquet remarks were not as entertaining; he was all business and all over the place. He was a simple soldier "coming home from the wars," but acknowledged "we are still at war." He encouraged the diners to support the USO and the Red Cross, warned that "Civilization itself, in the face of another catastrophe . . . would tremble, possibly decay and be destroyed," and in closing, affirmed that "No man can tell me that America with its glorious mixture of races, of creeds, its Jews, its Catholics, its Protestants—it cannot lose."[14]

Nimitz was all Nimitz. As he had done so many times before, he used humor to disarm and prepare his audience, whether a couple of staffers or two thousand slightly inebriated diners, for the real, focused message.

The next day, it was back to Washington and another meeting with Forrestal, who seems to have reconsidered Nimitz's request. He had been helped along by a nudge from Congressman Carl Vinson and a note from Admiral King, which pointed out that Nimitz was "the officer clearly and definitely indicated" to be the next CNO.[15] Forrestal told Nimitz he would pass a positive recommendation along to the president, but only on the condition that the tour would be for two, not the usual four, years. That was fine with the admiral, and he headed back to Pearl Harbor by way of Texas—where the number of celebrants was irrelevant because Nimitz would be in his element.

Nimitz spent Friday in Dallas and Austin, met by happily cheering crowds. The next day, as his cavalcade approached Kerrville, Nimitz was taken from his borrowed undertaker's limousine and perched atop a horse-drawn buckboard for the ride into town. It would have been just like the old days—except for the mounted escort of cowhands and ranchers, hugs from cousins and former teachers, and the huge "Welcome Home Chester" banners. The 80-year-old former high school principal, one of the team who had coached him for the Annapolis exams, presented Chester with the diploma he never quite earned. This was followed by a visit to Fredericksburg, where he made ceremonial homage to his birthplace, was appointed an "Admiral in the Texas Navy" by Governor Coke Stevenson, and let the crowd know the role of Texas in the surrender negotiations. "One of my principal worries," he said, was "that I would not be able to persuade Texans to stop fighting. However, a satisfactory agreement was arrived at between Tokyo and Austin."[16]

CHAPTER TWENTY-FIVE

THE ROCKY
ROAD TO CNO

Octber 27, 1945, was Navy Day in New York City, and Nimitz had planned to ride the *Missouri* into the harbor for a grand celebration. For reasons unknown, President Truman, who was scheduled as the headliner for the Navy Day event, did not want Nimitz involved, so Nimitz went back to Hawaii to await orders for his new job. Truman had a good day in New York: He gave a speech in Central Park, presided at commissioning ceremonies for the carrier *Franklin D. Roosevelt* at the Navy Yard, had lunch aboard the *Missouri,* and held a fleet review from the deck of a destroyer.

Back in Hawaii, Nimitz got word that Navy Secretary Forrestal might have changed his mind about the CNO job. At the same time, the *New York Times* of November 2 briefly noted:

> The Army and Navy bulletin predicted tonight that Adm. Nimitz would succeed Adm. King as chief of naval operations. The service Journal said that a move was under way in Congress to give Adm. Nimitz the post. It added that Adm. R. S. Edwards, deputy CNO, was the choice of Secretary Forrestal while Adm. King supported Adm. Spruance, Fifth Fleet commander.[1]

This was curious, but the last sentence was patently specious—Edwards was a submariner and Forrestal clearly favored aviators, and King had already recommended Nimitz. But, something was wrong; Nimitz's orders should have arrived many days earlier. Perhaps Truman—who ultimately controlled the appointment—was pulling the strings; he had once said, "When Roosevelt was here, [the White House] was like a wardroom. As long as I'm here the admirals will never get in again."[2]

By great and grand coincidence, freshly minted Rear Admiral Waldo Drake was passing through Hawaii on his way to Japan with his new boss, oilman and Democratic powerhouse Ed Pauley. Although Nimitz had accepted Forrestal's diktat to replace Drake as the CINCPAC public relations officer, the move was made in accordance with Nimitz's request that Drake not be penalized, but be given an equally prestigious new job. Call it bread cast upon the waters.

Nimitz described his problem to Drake: He would really like to be CNO, but he seemed to be getting nowhere with Forrestal. Drake suggested that Pauley, who was very close to the president, might have some influence, and he brought Pauley out to meet Nimitz. After several hours' conversation, Pauley got on the phone with Truman and made the pitch. Truman said, "Well, I'd like to help him Ed, but Forrestal insists he's just a stubborn Dutchman and he doesn't rate the job and he doesn't want him to have it." Ed said, "I know him pretty well and I've had a long talk with him. I think he should have it."[3]

If this did not seal the deal, it certainly didn't hurt.

Meanwhile, Congress had scheduled another series of hearings on the unification of the armed forces. Forrestal brought in a group of Navy and Marine Corps Medal of Honor winners, stars to shine in the hearing room. But things were getting ugly. Lieutenant General James Doolittle challenged Nimitz's earlier statement that "It was our sea power which ultimately compelled Japan to ask for peace." What about, asked Doolittle, the thousands of tons of bombs the B-29s dropped on Japan, and the "sacrifices of the heroic B-29 crews?"[4]

In a hearing on November 9, Doolittle was scornful. "It was not sea power that compelled Japan to ask for peace, and . . . it was not carrier superiority that won the air war. . . . [O]ur B-29 boys are probably resting uneasily in their graves. . . ." He added, the carrier is "going into obsolescence, having reached the peak of its usefulness." The carrier, he said, had two attributes: It can move about, and it can be sunk.[5] "When we get aircraft with sufficient range we will not need carriers."[6] To make his point, the AAF sent a B-29 on a nonstop, 8,198-mile flight from Guam to Washington, D.C. Of course, the B-29 range with a full crew and load of bombs was well under half that, but why spoil a good stunt with the facts?

Forrestal was not going to expose the Medal of Honor winners to political mud-slinging, so he changed his plan. He called Nimitz back to Washington to appear before the Senate Committee on Military Affairs on November 17. This was an awkward moment for Nimitz. The committee was quick to remind him of that informal JCS survey of senior officers, taken just a year earlier, in which Nimitz said he thought unification could be a good idea. Nimitz was not fazed. "That was then," he said. "I now believe that the theoretical advantages of such a merger are unattainable, whereas the disadvantages are so serious that it is not acceptable. For this change of opinion I make no apology, since it represents my conviction based on additional experiences and further study of the proposal and its current implications."[7]

After leaving the hearing, he headed to the White House, as he told an inquiring reporter, for "a very personal call" on President Truman.[8] There appears to be no record of the meeting or why it came about. A few contributory bits have surfaced, the most significant of which is contained in King's autobiography. Since Forrestal would not agree that Nimitz should be CNO, King addressed a letter to the president urging the appointment, to be delivered via the secretary of the Navy.[9] When Forrestal refused to endorse the letter and send it along to the White House, King made a personal call on the president, in which, it has been reported, he said that if the president did not appoint Nimitz chief of naval operations, he would have to explain his failure to do so to the American people.

On November 20, the White House announced a series of appointments: General Dwight Eisenhower was to succeed General George Marshall as Army Chief of Staff, Admiral Chester Nimitz was to succeed Admiral Ernest King as Chief of Naval Operations, and Admiral Raymond Spruance would become Commander in Chief of the Pacific Fleet.

Four days later, Nimitz turned command of the Pacific Fleet over to Spruance; symbolically, he did so on the deck of a submarine, just as he had assumed command in 1941. Spruance was to hold the job for only two months. He had long made it known that for his last posting he would like to be president of the Naval War College. That job unexpectedly became available, and as Spruance had only two years before reaching mandatory retirement, he jumped at the chance to make the move. Forrestal, who long wanted an aviator in the fleet job, replaced Spruance with John Towers.

Nimitz headed for duty in Washington, and for the first time in years, he was not accompanied by Hal Lamar, who, looking for new experiences, had asked for duty in China. Nimitz and Catherine moved into the CNO quarters on the grounds of the Naval Observatory on Massachusetts Avenue—distance to the office, 3.25 miles, just right for frequent brisk walks to and from work. (He would be the last CNO to work out of Main Navy; his successor would be the first to set up shop in the Pentagon.) Nimitz found that the turnover schedule seemed a bit rushed; in his memoir, King suggested a reason: "Mr. Forrestal was sufficiently irritated about the whole matter to order the change of command to be moved up to December 15."[10]

In the meantime, Forrestal's group of Medal of Honor winners was disbanded. One of the group was Commander Gene Fluckey, the submarine skipper who earlier had impressed Nimitz with his proposal for a mining operation. Fluckey was scheduled to go on a month-long, boost-the-Navy, public speaking tour when he got a call: Admiral Nimitz wanted to see him. Nimitz had pulled his name out of that "mental filing cabinet."

Nimitz asked Fluckey to come aboard as his personal aide. Fluckey was flattered, admitted this was "kind of out of my field," but said he was sure he could learn. He asked, "Is there anything special I should know, mistakes to avoid?" Nimitz said, "I'm going to give you one order, and this is the last order I will give you: Never offend anyone."[11]

King was in his last few weeks as CNO and, according to Fluckey, was "barreling around the office like a bull in the china closet, scaring people half to death." The relationship between King and Nimitz was proper although not necessarily warm. They understood each other even if they hadn't always agreed with each other, even down to the change of command ceremony. King wanted it to be private, no reporters. Nimitz insisted otherwise; he won. Perhaps the usually unflappable King had reason for wanting to exclude the press. As the December 16, 1945, *New York Times* reported, King was overtaken by "the emotion of the moment," skipped over two paragraphs when reading his prepared remarks, and dropped a sheaf of papers when he turned to shake hands with Nimitz.[12]

Three weeks later, Nimitz held his first press conference as CNO, to introduce his new deputies and outline his plans "for bringing the Navy abreast of developments occurring in atomic energy and other new weapons," and for keeping the Navy out in front, "supreme among the navies of the world." Some of the attendees seemed surprised at his candor; he noted that, now that the war was over, he could be more open in discussing "matters of public interest." The *New York Times* lauded the effort: "At no period during recent years had so much 'brass' been assembled in one room to talk about Navy plans and no conferences yet arranged by the War Department have paralleled the Navy discussion."[13]

The issue of unification of the U.S. military forces was front and center, but it was hardly the only problem the Navy was facing. The public was clamoring to bring the boys home—a monumental task, for there were some twelve million in the armed services who were spread across the world. A sailor stationed in San Diego but whose "home" was Boston was just as eager for a move as a soldier in Okinawa. Most of the servicemen wanted to be discharged as soon as possible, leading, especially for the Navy—the most broadly technical of the forces—to serious imbalances in specialties and skill levels. At one point, a squadron of destroyers in San Diego was lucky to scrape together enough people to send one ship to sea once a week. The battleship *New Jersey* was being manned by a crew of 400, less than one-fourth the wartime complement: according to Bill Leverton, then serving as its executive officer, "about enough people to sweep the decks a couple of times a week."[14]

The wartime fleet of almost 7,000 ships had to be cut down to size without sacrificing the ability to meet mission commitments. There were thousands of ships to be sold, transferred to other navies, put in reserve, or scrapped, while at the same time the Navy was evaluating and incorporating the latest war-developed technology into new construction. Much of this work was not in the CNO portfolio, but the CNO was the public face of the Navy and the work load was immense. There were meetings to be held, proposals to be pondered, politicians to be coddled, three to four hundred phone calls and fifty to sixty personal letters to be answered each day. Working hours were 7:30 A.M. to 7 P.M., seven days a week. There was no money to pay overtime to the civil service secretarial staff, but the hard-working women would stay on well past their normal quitting time. Other civil servants on their way home at 4:30 would come by the office and yell "Scabs!" driving them to tears. Nimitz had a solution: He brought in WAVES—who would work whatever hours were necessary—to replace the civil service workers. He had changed his mind about women in uniform.

One evening, while having dinner at home with guests Gene Fluckey and his wife, Margery, Nimitz asked what he thought was a socially gracious question: "Well, Margy, how do you enjoy shore duty?" She hesitated, then said that she saw more of her husband during the war. Nimitz got the message. He changed the schedule, a bit, by dropping Sunday as a workday, and not long after started closing shop at 4 on Saturday.[15]

Nimitz made quick judgments about people. He needed a new Marine Corps driver, and before he had started the formal process, the incumbent brought over a friend, Leo Cozard, who might be interested. After a few minutes conversation, Nimitz asked the 24-year-old Marine if would he like the job, Cozard said he would, and Nimitz said, "Well, I'll tell you what, why don't you just wait around and drive me home today." When Cozard dropped him off, many hours later, Nimitz said, "Pick me up tomorrow morning." And that was that. Cozard continued as Nimitz's driver throughout his tour as CNO, and then again from 1949 until his own retirement from the Marine Corps in 1961.[16]

Nimitz honored as many invitations as feasible, giving up to three speeches in a day—in Washington or out of town. When offered an honorarium, he told the host to make the check out to a charity. Fluckey served as an adjunct speechwriter, organizing the points he knew Nimitz wanted to make and providing the obligatory social amenities in which a speaker thanks the host and recognizes dignitaries in the audience. Fluckey put everything on a few 3" × 5" cards that Nimitz could put in his pocket.

It was a good system—when Nimitz let it work. One time, just before he was to address a large military service organization, Fluckey handed Nimitz the cards and began to give a quick briefing about the group, their philosophy, their current projects, and Nimitz brushed him aside. "Gene," he said, "You don't need to tell me about that organization. I was the granddaddy of it when I was chief of BUNAV." It was about two minutes into the talk when Fluckey realized that the boss thought he was talking to the USO—which just happened to be the main rival of their host. His talk finished, Nimitz was making his manners to the president of the host organization when he caught a bit of the next speaker's remarks and realized he had made a terrible mistake. He tried to apologize: "I know your organization, it's a wonderful organization." The president, a most gracious lady, kissed him on the cheek and said, "Admiral, we're just so happy to have you here; we know your real feelings." In the car, after a few moments of tense silence, Nimitz slapped Fluckey on the thigh and said, "Gene, the next time I say to you that I'm the granddaddy of any organization, will you just say, 'Shut up and take these cards and listen.'"[17]

Nimitz was incredibly popular, easily recognized, and often given movie-star treatment. Once he was even followed into the men's room by a throng of adoring women. He latched himself inside a stall, stood on the toilet, and said, to the suddenly embarrassed but laughing intruders, "Is there any place we can *go?*" When traveling for a convention or banquet the local hosts would typically give Nimitz a hotel suite where they might join him for a bit of post event socializing; Fluckey would be assigned to an unlisted room. As bedtime approached and the last guest had been nudged out the door, Nimitz and Fluckey would swap rooms so that Nimitz would not be disturbed by the inevitable return visit by any revelers not ready to call it a day.[18]

They developed a few survival tactics. To speed them through a mob of well-meaning well-wishers, Fluckey carried a bunch of autographed cards, freely handed out: "Best wishes, Fleet Admiral Chester W. Nimitz USN." If Nimitz wanted to sneak out of the house and go to a movie, he would dress like the gardener, cover his brilliantly white hair with an old hat, and use a rear gate that was hidden from the street. If he got a dinner invitation in which he was not interested, he would not offer an excuse that wasn't legitimate. But he might ask Fluckey, "Gene, wouldn't you like to have us over for a potluck supper and poker with a couple of your neighbors?" The neighbors were always delighted and somewhat in awe, that they were actually playing poker with Admiral Nimitz.[19]

Before his appointment as CNO, Nimitz's relationship with President Truman could be categorized as "ambiguous." After, Nimitz quickly developed a cordial friendship with the president. They were about the same age, came from humble beginnings (Truman was the son of a farmer), and discovered shared interests. One was music, another was Truman's interest in pitching horseshoes—a sport about which he was enthusiastic but not adept. One day, a man identifying himself as the world champion horseshoe pitcher showed up at the CNO's office, wondering if he might get an autographed photo of the admiral. When Nimitz had satisfied himself that the man's claim was true, and found him to be an amiable sort, he picked up the direct line to the White House and soon had Truman on the line. "Hey, Harry," he said, "I've got the champion horseshoe pitcher of the world over here. Let's come over to the White House and show you how he can pitch horseshoes." Within fifteen minutes, they were out in the back garden learning some trick moves.[20]

Nimitz, knowing of the president's limited knowledge of the Navy and devotion to the Army, did impose some not-too-subtle propaganda on their friendship, including visits to a couple of aircraft carriers and a ride on a submarine. In November 1946, when he learned that Truman's doctor ordered him to vacation in some warm climate, Nimitz offered quarters at the Key West Naval Station in a building that once was home to the base commandant. There, Truman could vacation in comfort and safety, and over the course of his administration, he stayed in what became known as the winter White House for some 175 days. It may have kept Nimitz on the good side of Truman, but there is no evidence that it softened Truman's opinion of the Navy.

CHAPTER TWENTY-SIX

SKIRMISHES

Nimitz's speeches got attention—audiences listened and local newspapers dutifully reported his sea-power message. The AAF campaign, however, had a broader reach. One example: a book published in March 1946, *The Case Against the Admirals: Why We Must Have a Unified Command.* Right up front, author William Bradford Huie said his goal was "to attack the cabal of admirals which is obstructing consolidation of our armed services."[1] *Time* called it "an air-power fanatic's assault."[2] The Navy obtained advanced galleys of *The Case Against the Admirals,* and Nimitz sent a note to his Army counterpart, General Dwight Eisenhower. "The net result of publication," he wrote, "will be harmful to both services and particularly unfortunate at this time when further evidence of disunity between the services can be used to our national disadvantage."[3] Eisenhower, unaware that AAF officers were conducting a behind-the-scenes campaign, sent a March 9, 1946, memo to his senior staff: The War Department "does not approve of methods intended to discredit another service; we must be objective, logical, and public minded. . . . The job of the officer is not that of a political conniver."[4]

At the same time, in secret, some of the Joint Chiefs were trying to strip the Marine Corps down to the bone, replacing their ability to conduct land-combat operations with a bare mission to protect United States citizens ashore in foreign countries and to provide an interior guard for naval ships and naval shore establishments. Eisenhower proposed that no Marine unit should be larger than a regiment—which would ensure that no Marine officer would ever again be in a position to lead Army troops into battle.[5] Nimitz accused the Army of trying to eliminate the Marine Corps as an effective combat element, reducing it to the status of a naval police unit.

On June 15 President Truman let everyone know where he stood on one issue, when he sent a directive to the secretaries of War and Navy: "Land based planes for naval reconnaissance, anti-submarine warfare and protection of shipping can and should be manned by Air Force personnel."[6] General Carl A. Spaatz wanted Congress to deny the Navy money to purchase any land-based aircraft; he feared the Navy would go into the bombing business. Navy patrol aircraft, he said, were too "similar in character to the long-range bomber which is the backbone of our strategic Air Force."[7]

Later in the year, another player entered the fray: AAF Brigadier General Frank A. Armstrong, the senior air advisor at the Armed Forces Staff College in the Navy bastion of Norfolk, Virginia. In a talk to a businessman's group, Armstrong put himself in the record book for dumb after-dinner comments:

> You gentlemen had better understand that the Army Air Force is tired of being a subordinate outfit. It was a predominant force during the war, and it is going to be a predominant force during the peace . . . and we do not care whether you like it or not. The Army Air Force is going to run the show. You, the Navy, are not going to have anything but a couple of carriers which are ineffective anyway, and they will probably be sunk in the first battle. Now as for the Marines, you know what the Marines are, a small bitched-up army talking Navy lingo. We are going to put those Marines in the Regular Army and make efficient soldiers out of them.[8]

As this game was playing out, the Navy was assessing the impact of the atom bomb on the future of sea power. Four months before Nimitz was sworn in as CNO, Captain Lewis Strauss, assigned to the Bureau of Ordnance, had sent a private memo to Secretary of the Navy Forrestal, proposing a test of the bomb against naval warships. He wrote, "If such a test is not made, there will be loose talk to the effect that the fleet is obsolete in the face of this new weapon," and the Navy would likely be denied funding to keep the fleet at fighting strength.[9] Strauss had a keen interest in nuclear issues and would eventually head up the Atomic Energy Commission.

A week later—unaware of the Strauss memo—Senator Brien McMahon of Connecticut, chair of the newly created Senate Special Committee on Atomic Energy, called for just such a test, but his goal was to show the Navy's vulnerability. "The resulting explosion," he said, "should prove to us just how effective the atomic bomb is when used against the giant naval ships."[10]

The Navy announced their plans at the end of October, and invited Army participation. However, in a bit of stupidity, they established an all-Navy panel to evaluate the results. Senator McMahon complained to Truman that the Navy should not be "solely responsible for conducting operations which might well indeed determine its very existence."[11]

In February, the president called in six key players: CNO Nimitz, Navy Secretary Forrestal, Secretary of War Robert P. Patterson, General Eisenhower, Truman's chief of staff Admiral Leahy, and Secretary of State James F. Byrnes. He said he trusted them to be objective, but that was not enough. The public had to believe that the tests were objective. He didn't want a latter-day Billy Mitchell mucking up the process. There was a straightforward solution: To the group of observers already scheduled by the Navy, a few members of the House and Senate could be added, with the whole to be constituted as a special commission reporting directly to the president. At a press conference, Nimitz introduced the head of the CNO Special Weapons Division, Vice Admiral W. H. P. Blandy, who would be running the tests. Blandy assured the newsmen that this would be a thoroughly joint effort, not a contest between the Army and Navy.[12]

The tests were conducted at Bikini Atoll in the Marshall Islands, a sparsely inhabited (population 167) speck of land with a deep-water lagoon. With the code name Operation Crossroads, the tests included more than 150 active (not target) ships and 42,000 participating Navy and Army personnel and observers. The 167 islanders were relocated.

There were ninety target ships: older capital ships, surplus destroyers, cruisers, auxiliaries, and three captured German and Japanese warships. The ships were moored in a density much tighter than any logical commander would allow, but the goal was to measure damage from ground zero, not to replicate the impact on actual cruising formations. Some critics warned that the test would be invalid because it was only against equipment, not people, so 200 pigs, 60 guinea pigs, 204 goats, 5,000 rats, 200 mice, and tubs of grains containing insects were added to assess the impact on life forms. Whereupon some animal rights activists complained—to no avail. The operation went on as scheduled.

There were two tests, Able and Baker. Able was a July 1, 1946, air drop from a B-29, with the bomb detonating 520 feet above the target area. However, the aim was poor and the bomb was dropped almost half-a-mile off the bull's-eye, the battleship *Nevada*—which was not much affected. Yes, five ships were sunk—two transports, two destroyers, and one Japanese cruiser, none of them considered important in the grand scheme of things. Residual radioactivity was negligible. But how, indeed, could an experienced B-29 crew so grandly screw up such an important assignment? There was an investigation. Blame was placed on a flaw in the plane's stabilizer.

For Baker, on July 25, 1946, a bomb was suspended ninety feet beneath one of the target ships. Eight were sunk, and everything for miles around was bathed in a radioactive spray. The atoll itself, through contamination of the land and especially the sources of the food supply, was rendered uninhabitable.

Some of the surviving target ships were too radioactive to be salvaged and were scuttled. However, after thorough decontamination—for some, as simple as a high-pressure hosing—many of the surviving ships were sailed back to the United States by their original crews. Most of those ships, already scheduled for destruction, became test targets for conventional weapons. A few were even returned to active service. One result of the Bikini Atoll test was the installation of anticontamination wash-down systems on all Navy ships.

Toward the end of 1946, Navy leadership decided that continuing to block a separate air force would get them nowhere; Secretary of the Navy Forrestal was given assurances from some of the AAF champions that they would not infringe on naval aviation roles and missions. By mid-January 1947, Forrestal and Secretary of War Patterson sent a joint letter to the president: they had reached agreement. Among other things, responsibility for Navy air recon-naissance, anti-submarine warfare, and protection of shipping would remain with the Navy. There were other signs of cooperation: the Naval Academy would train Air Force students until a formal Air Force Academy could be established. However, issues remained, especially the status of the Marine Corps. The Marines took charge of that problem and enlisted the aid of some influential congressmen who slipped protective language into the pending legislation.

The National Security Act of July 26, 1947, created the National Military Establishment (with the unfortunate initials, NME, which, when sounded out, sounded like "enemy"; that defect was remedied in 1949 when the NME was redesignated the Department of Defense, DOD). The Navy got most of what it wanted and the Marine mission was enshrined in law, especially for "the conduct of such land operations as may be essential to the prosecution of a naval campaign."[13] In his diary, Eisenhower wrote that the Marines were "so unsure of their value to their country that they insisted on writing into the law a complete set of rules and specifications for their future operations and duties. Such freezing of detail . . . is silly, even vicious." The Marines were "unsure" because everyone, including Eisenhower, had been trying to take away most of those "operations and duties."[14]

There were now three co-equal armed services—Army, Navy, and Air Force—each headed by a military chief of staff (CNO for the Navy) and a civilian secretary. Overall direction came from a civilian secretary of defense, assisted by the joint chiefs of staff. James Forrestal became the first secretary of defense; the assistant secretary of the Navy, John L. Sullivan, succeed him as Navy secretary. There were some chain-of-command issues: until the 1949 modification of the Act, the service secretaries continued to have free and unfettered access to Congress and the president.

As a collateral duty, the CNO served as president of the U.S. Naval Institute. Nimitz enjoyed his participation, treating it as a welcome break from the pressures of his day-job, and he was not shy to offer editorial comment and correction on books and articles that had been submitted for consideration. On his own, he wrote articles for some half a dozen business, military, and news magazines. Most were focused on the basic message—the Navy is peace insurance—but in the June 1946 *National Geographic,* he stepped out of the present and into the future:

> The capital ship of tomorrow . . . may very well become the submarine. Not
> the submarine as we know it—a surface ship which makes its approach and
> retreat under water—but a truly underseas warship capable of circumnavigating

the world without surfacing. This monster . . . would approach an enemy coast under water and, remaining a hundred fathoms down, bombard the shore with self-guided atomic missiles.[15]

Whether by coincidence or plan, just as that article was being prepared for publication, physicist Philip H. Abelson of the Naval Research Laboratory proposed development of a high-speed nuclear-powered submarine, free of the constraints of the air-breathing, diesel-electric power plant, and free to roam the depths, submerged for extended periods of time. The American fleet boats of the day had maximum submerged speed of 9 knots and underwater endurance of 48 hours at 2 knots.[16]

A high-speed submarine with great underwater endurance had been demonstrated experimentally by the Germans, but using a different source of energy. Physicist Hellmuth Walter showed that the controlled decomposition of highly concentrated (95 percent) hydrogen peroxide, H_2O_2, released sufficient quantities of superheated steam to drive a turbine, along with oxygen that could support conventional combustion or be used for respiration by the crew. Eight prototype hydrogen-peroxide boats were constructed, incorporating a sophisticated hull shape that allowed underwater speeds as high as 28 knots, but were never put into production.

Abelson proposed marrying the Walter hull with a nuclear energy source. Radical or visionary? As a start, the Navy sent a team of engineering officers, headed by Captain Hyman G. Rickover, to study with experts at the Manhattan Project Laboratory (home of the atom bomb) at Oak Ridge, Tennessee. Within the CNO's office, the topic was controversial because it could waste scarce resources on an unproven concept. Nimitz thought the idea had merit and asked for an assessment. The report was sobering: Increasingly sophisticated antisubmarine techniques required deeper-diving, long-endurance boats. The assessment urged further investigation of hydrogen peroxide and nuclear power plants. Nimitz approved the report, and Rickover assembled a study group to undertake that further investigation. The group affirmed that nuclear power was feasible and that only nuclear power could deliver the required speed and endurance. In a memo to Nimitz, eighteen months after the *National Geographic* article, Rickover predicted that with appropriate effort, a nuclear-powered submarine capable of launching a nuclear-tipped guided missile could be fielded by the mid-1950s. As one of his last official acts as CNO, Nimitz approved the recommendation and sent it on to Secretary of the Navy Sullivan, who forwarded it with approval to Secretary of Defense Forrestal. The world's first nuclear-powered submarine, the *Nautilus* (SSN-571) went to sea in January 1955. Her first extended voyage was more than 1000 miles—all underwater.

Some time later, Nimitz was asked to comment on a statement naming Rickover as "Father of the Nuclear Navy." Well, did the concept of "father" include the men who conceived the idea, or the men who approved the program (himself among them), or the congressmen who provided the money, or the shepherd who helped bring it to maturity? He thought about it for a moment, then offered, "Give credit where credit is due," thus neatly ducking the issue.[17]

One other end-of-tour item was the CNO's positive recommendation for a proposed supercarrier, the *United States*—almost twice the displacement of the latest class of carrier, the *Midway,* which had entered service late in 1945. The *United States* would handle the very heavy planes required to carry a 5-ton atom bomb. Of course, this was a capability claimed as an exclusive right by the Air Force, but Nimitz told Navy Secretary Sullivan that, despite Air Force propaganda, their new dreamboat B-36 bomber—soon to enter service—could not reach all possible targets in the Soviet Union unless it had overseas bases, which could prove problematic. The Navy could fill in the gaps of coverage with the supercarrier. Congress was in favor, but the Air Force objected. Forrestal held a meeting of the JCS, which agreed, albeit reluctantly, that the Navy should be allowed to attack any targets, with any weapons, in order to accomplish any assigned mission. Therefore, the Navy should be allowed to build bigger carriers. In July 1948, the president approved construction of *United States* and four more supercarriers.

CHAPTER TWENTY-SEVEN

THE LAST BATTLE

W hile it seemed that the U. S. defense organization had been settled, the new Air Force had not abandoned the dreams of old to absorb or replace naval aviation, and behind the scenes, the Army still did not support a Marine Corps. Not quite a month after passage of the National Security Act of July 26, 1947, the War Department circulated "Final Report: The War Department Policies and Program Review Board." This was meant to offer internal guidance for negotiation and coordination with the Navy in setting up the new National Military Establishment—but the War Department had some peculiar ideas about Navy roles and missions. The Report listed five: control of sea areas (especially through antisubmarine warfare); amphibious lift; support and protection of amphibious forces and convoys; maintaining outlying bases; and mobilization. There was no mention of offensive operations or what troops would provide the assault force carried in those amphibious ships. In fact, the Report asserted:

> For the foreseeable future there will be no naval threat to the United States in any portion of the world except by the submarine . . . . the determination of the relative proportion between naval and land-based aviation . . . should be based on the most careful considerations of roles and missions, and strict evaluation of characteristics and capabilities.[1]

This triggered a Nimitz rebuttal, a CNO valedictory as his tour would end on December 15, 1947. Originally, the valedictory was intended only for review and discussion by the Joint Chiefs, but once the text was in hand, Nimitz changed his mind. If delivered to the JCS, it would be given a cursory glance and end up in a file, never again to be seen. He wanted the paper to be given wide distribution. Accordingly, the draft was sent through proper channels for security review, and published about three weeks after the CNO change of command as "The Future Employment of Naval Forces."

This was not limited to, but was, of course, a rationale for and justification of naval aviation. Since a naval task force could remain at sea for months, he wrote, "the art of concentrating air power within effective range of enemy objectives" had been raised to the high point. Naval aviation would be the head of the spear until the Air Force could begin operating from captured land bases abroad.

> The net result is that naval forces are able, without resorting to diplomatic channels, to establish offshore anywhere in the world, airfields completely equipped with machine shops, ammunition dumps, tank farms, warehouses, together with quarters and all types of accommodations for personnel.
>
> Such task forces are virtually as complete as any air base ever established. They constitute the only air bases that can be made available near enemy territory without assault and conquest; and furthermore, they are mobile offensive bases that can be employed with the unique attributes of secrecy and surprise— which attributes contribute equally to their defensive as well as offensive effectiveness.

To counter charges that new "supersonic weapons" threaten the existence of the carriers, Nimitz affirmed that the Navy was well ahead in developing and deploying countermeasures "in the form of propulsion, armament, and new aircraft weapons." He predicted that the Navy of the future would be able to launch missiles from surface vessels and submarines, and to deliver atomic bombs from carrier-based planes. And then he made his main point:

> It is improbable that [Air Force] bomber fleets will be capable, for several years to come, of making two-way trips between continents, even over the polar routes, with heavy loads of bombs.

It is apparent then, that in the event of war within this period, if we are to project our power against vital areas of an enemy across the ocean before beach-heads on enemy territory are captured, it must be by air-sea power; by aircraft launched from carriers, and by heavy surface ships and submarines projecting guided missiles and rockets.[2]

When he wrote "air-sea," he meant the coordination of the Air Force and the Navy, as recent experience had shown the merits of such teamwork. But he emphasized that in the future, the Navy would be out front and carry the war to the enemy, not wait for war to come to it.

The paper kicked up quite a storm; as Nimitz wrote to Vice Admiral Forrest Sherman, it got him "in hot water with the authorities in Washington." But he assured Sherman that, "Even if I have been properly spanked, I believe I have done a public service in speaking as I did."[3]

Editorially, the *New York Times* said "Future Employment" was a "well-balanced and persuasive argument for the continued maintenance by the United States of a strong naval establishment." However, the *Times* warned, it was not a blank check for proponents of a big Navy and a strong naval establishment should not be pursued at the expense of air power. The *Times* also noted that the Navy probably had more ships in the water and under construction than it needed, and further suggested that the shipbuilding industry might better be switched to "construction of fast, modern passenger and cargo vessels, which are just as necessary to the defense of this country as battleships and aircraft carriers."[4]

As for the Air Force, on the same day the *Times* editorial appeared, General Spaatz sent a note to Secretary of the Air Force W. Stuart Symington:

> Although we have a separate Air Department, we haven't established firmly in the minds of some people, particularly the Navy, that there is only going to be one Air Force. . . . If the Navy is trying to spend hundreds of millions of dollars building aircraft carriers of a hundred thousand tons to move 36 bombers somewhere close to the hostile shores to deliver devastating attacks, it shows an utter lack of realization of what the hell strategic air and what air power is.[5]

The debate was further enlarged that first week of January with the publication of "Survival in the Air Age," the report of President Truman's Air Policy

Commission. Created back in July and headed by Thomas K. Finletter, the commission was tasked to make an "objective inquiry" into national aviation policies and problems. The report warned that the "military establishment must be built around the air arm" and called for a downgrade of traditional Army and Navy forces. It argued for a massive buildup of some 20,000 new aircraft. Naval aviation was included in that equation, to a point, but so effective were the Air Force public relations efforts that to the public and to the Congress, "air arm" and "air power" meant "Air Force." Finletter would later become the second secretary of the Air Force.

In the meantime, Symington began to press Congress for greatly increased Air Force appropriations. The Air Force had a lot of friends in Congress. At one point, the public relations staff proposed, "our campaign for unification should be aimed with a rifle at the 531 senators and congressmen who are actually going to vote on unification rather than with a shotgun at the 140,000,000 citizens who are not."[6]

Successful? A Navy staff analysis of the Congressional Record for January through March 1948 focused on material that had been inserted by members of Congress. It found eleven pro-Navy and eleven anti-Navy items; twenty-eight items were pro–Air Force and none were against.[7]

The headline-grabbing stunts continued. On April 12, just as Congress was considering the Air Force budget, thirty B-29s flew nonstop from Kansas to Germany. On September 18—Air Force Day, the first anniversary of the establishment of the Air Force—fifty B-29s traveled nonstop from Europe, Hawaii, and Japan on mock bombing runs over 25 American cities, two planes each. Many of the runs were timed to coincide with well-attended public air shows. Brilliant.

By this time, Chester Nimitz was long gone from the scene. On December 15, 1947, he was given a fine send-off on the steps of Main Navy, with the band playing and an honor guard honoring as he and Catherine (along with daughter Nancy) got into the family's almost-ten-year-old Chrysler for a drive to California, to make Berkeley their new home.

Congress had decreed that the five-star military officers would never "retire," that they would always be considered on active duty with an annual salary of $15,000. Because of a strange edict, however, the salary was fixed, never to be adjusted for the cost of living. This active duty had no duties except to answer mail and, on occasion, be ceremonial. Nimitz did wear his uniform when appropriate, but hated the dress sword, which turned both sitting and standing into awkward maneuvers. He pretended to hide his sword, putting it under the bed. He told his Marine driver, George Cozard, "If I can't find it, I won't have to wear it."[8] All of the five-stars were allowed an office (Nimitz's was in the San Francisco Federal Building) and a staff of eight. Unlike his peers, Nimitz elected to have only three: a secretary, an aide, and a driver. It wasn't long before he dropped the secretary and the aide, and Cozard assumed the duties of all. Nimitz did not go into the office all that often; instead Cozard brought the office to the house, including the mail to be answered and letters to be signed.

Nimitz settled into a pleasant but frustrating life, in which for the first time in his life he had few responsibilities and most of the challenges had to do with gardening.

Nimitz had suggested Admiral William Blandy as the next CNO, but the job went to Admiral Leahy's favorite, Louis Denfield. Nimitz was satisfied with the Navy's efforts during his tenure as CNO; downsizing had gone about as well as could be expected and the fleet was still at a respectable size. The unification of the military services, he believed, was evidence that men of goodwill could work out their differences. Even a year later, he told a friend that he was a "great booster of the National Security Act of 1947."[9]

Within the military establishment, however, things were not so sanguine. As Nimitz was offering praise, one journalist told his editor, "Forrestal's staff is very frank in saying that unification is not working and they are putting the blame on the Air Force, which has great ambitions. The administrative setup is absolutely impossible because any of the department secretaries can bypass Forrestal and go either to the White House or Congress."[10] It was just then, December 1948, that Forrestal began to fray around the edges, showing signs of undiagnosed mental illness. A month or so later, the president told Forrestal that he was going to be replaced on May 1 by Louis Johnson. Forrestal rapidly decompensated, barely able to function. Truman moved up the change and on March 1 forced Forrestal's resignation. Johnson took over as secretary of defense on March 28, 1949. Forrestal was sent to Bethesda Naval Hospital, where he could be protected from prying newsmen. He fell or jumped from the sixteenth floor of the hospital tower on May 22.

Soon after taking office, Secretary Johnson proclaimed, "There's no reason for having a Navy and Marine Corps. General Bradley tells me that amphibious operations are a thing of the past. We'll never have any more amphibious operations. That does away with the Marine Corps. And the Air Force can do anything the Navy can do nowadays, so that does away with the Navy."[11]

Johnson, the chief fund-raiser for Truman's 1948 election campaign, was by profession a lawyer who served as an Army officer in World War I and assistant secretary of war from 1937 to 1940. The Navy's worst nightmare had come true: a rabid Army-partisan calling the shots as head of the merged armed forces. He had been in the job for only a month before he canceled construction of the supercarrier *United States*. He was under some pressure to cut budgets and save money, and was convinced that the nuclear-armed B-36 was about all the nation needed to keep any enemy at bay. Secretary of the Navy Sullivan resigned in protest; he was replaced by a Johnson crony who knew nothing about the Navy, Francis P. Matthews.

In June, some senior naval officers began an organized assault on the B-36, in a move that became known as the "Revolt of the Admirals." The B-36 was a prewar design; the prototype XB-36 didn't even have first flight until the summer of 1946—by which time the AAF had already ordered a hundred, sight-unseen. At first flight, the general in charge of the newly created Strategic Air Command recommended cancellation of the contract because aircraft development had moved on, and while the B-36 might be bigger, it wasn't as advanced as the latest model Air Force bomber, the B-50.

Entrenched interests rose up in protest: the contractor, the members of Congress whose districts benefited from the B-36 program, the reputations of those officers who were pushing for it, and even Secretary Johnson himself, who had been a director of the company that was building the B-36—although he didn't think this was a conflict.

In August 1949, as the infighting continued and hearings were held, the Soviet Union tested its first atom bomb. This was a huge surprise to American defense planners. The Air Force quickly asserted that the B-36 was now the only hope, that the B-36 had the range and capacity to fly round-trip from the United States, to carry an atom bomb to hit key targets in the Soviet homeland. Perhaps, perhaps not. Some of the range and payload estimates turned out to be just that, unproven estimates. The Air Force believed that the B-36 flew so high—40,000 feet—that it was invulnerable to attack. It may have been invulnerable to attack by any U. S. Air Force fighter of the day, but several Navy fighters could reach B-36 flight altitude in plenty of time to intercept the bomber. Secretary Johnson refused to test that proposition in the name of "national security."[12]

The controversy grew, and late in October, in the dark and in over his head, Secretary Matthews asked Nimitz to meet him at a private, off-site location; he needed some advice. He was having problems with CNO Denfield, he said, and actually asked Nimitz, "How can I get rid of Denfield?"[13] Nimitz, out of power and trying to be an honest broker, told Matthews that if he really believed he couldn't work with Denfield, he should write a letter to President Truman asking to have the CNO reassigned to some other duty.

Matthews did just that and soon thereafter Truman called Nimitz. According to Nimitz's notes of the conversation, Truman said that he was "being pressured" to bring Nimitz back as CNO, and asked for his reaction. Nimitz told Truman that it would be a mistake to return an officer beyond retirement age to that job, especially in time of peace, when there were plenty of able young officers from whom to pick. He said that he would take the job only if the president so ordered. Truman said he would never do that unless Nimitz agreed in advance and then asked, who would he recommend? Nimitz suggested his longtime associate, Vice Admiral Forrest Sherman, who, as it turned out, was already under consideration and was quickly appointed.[14]

In the meantime, Secretary Johnson charged ahead, taking aim at his next target. He began downgrading the Marine Corps—starting with a petty but symbolic move: He took away the car and driver assigned to the commandant. Of greater significance, he blocked the commandant from attending any sessions of the Joint Chiefs, even if Marine Corps matters were under discussion. Then he began cutting funding, mothballing amphibious ships, and scrapping or selling landing craft.

It took the outbreak of another war—Korea, June 1950, just over fourteen months after Johnson took office and some seven months after Denfield had been fired—to demonstrate the folly of putting all of the Department of Defense budget eggs in the Air Force atom bomb basket. Air support from Navy carriers and those amphibious operations that had been declared "a thing of the past" saved the day in Korea, and the demonstrated capabilities of new Soviet jet fighter aircraft put an end to the B-36 program. By September 19, 1950, John-son was out as secretary of defense, and the more rational George C. Marshall was in. The Navy budget soon included a new class of supercarriers, every bit as capable as the *United States*. The lead ship in the class was named *Forrestal*, laid down in 1952.

CHAPTER TWENTY-EIGHT

TWILIGHT

Nimitz may have been out of sight in Berkeley, but he wasn't out of mind in Washington. In March 1949, about the same time that Louis Johnson became secretary of defense, Nimitz accepted a United Nations appointment as plebiscite administrator for the disputed territory of Kashmir. His job was to arrange and monitor a popular election to settle a bloody stalemate between India and Pakistan, at a salary of $26,000 (in addition to his Navy pay). He had a multinational staff and an office at the UN headquarters at Lake Success and housing in Port Washington, both on New York's Long Island. He had plenty of opportunity for swimming . . . and not much to do. The job looked great on paper—but in the real world, India would agree to put allegiance up to a vote only if Pakistan withdrew its army while the Indian army remained. Naturally, Pakistan would not accept such an arrangement. After a year, the plebiscite team was dissolved but Nimitz stayed on with the UN for another two years, giving speeches as a roving ambassador.

After the two years were up, Nimitz and Catherine were ready to go home to Berkeley, where family and friends had kept their house in good order during their absence. Once back, Nimitz soon took on some chores beyond housework—he became a regent of the University of California, a position that gave the university a great deal of wise counsel and gave the admiral a great deal of satisfaction. He was offered any number of other well-paying jobs, especially ones in which his fame might bring in donations (as president of UCLA) or investors (as a director of the American President Line), but he was not interested. He felt that any such job would demean his service during the war, and would suggest to the many people who had lost friends and relatives under his command that he had just been punching his ticket, building a great resume so he could later cash in. Many of his peers accepted such posts. He would not.

Many of those peers also rushed to ensure that *their* side of the war was preserved in print for the ages, among them Bradley, Eisenhower, Halsey, Kimmel, King, LeMay, MacArthur, Marshall, J. O. Richardson, Holland Smith, and Spruance. The diaries of some others were published, and many more cooperated with biographers. But not Nimitz. He did not want to capitalize on the war in any fashion, and "Sampson-Schley" was never far from his mind.

He *was* memorialized in his home town of Fredericksburg, Texas, when the old Nimitz Hotel—which had been modernized by a more recent owner—was restored to its 1890 appearance and turned into the "Admiral Nimitz Center." But Nimitz thought the effort should salute not just him, but all who had served in defeating Japan. Thus was created the "National Museum of the Pacific War," which long ago outgrew the hotel and today boasts more than 50,000 square feet of indoor exhibit space and an outdoor park for oversized equipment.[1]

Catherine became a member of the San Francisco Symphony board, and they were regular patrons of the weekly concerts. They made a trip to Europe—their first since the working honeymoon of 1913. Nimitz accepted an invitation to serve as co-editor with USNA professor E. B. Potter of a comprehensive naval history text, *Sea Power;* he donated his fee to a Naval Academy building fund. He went to the 50th anniversary of the Naval Academy class of 1905, but always the gentleman, he did not want his exalted rank to drive the program. He asked the superintendent to have the 1905 class president, Captain A. B. Court, take the honors when the brigade of midshipmen marched passed the reviewing stand. Moreover, to ensure that his presence would not interfere, Nimitz stayed away from the event until the review had been completed.

Nimitz learned that Togo's flagship, *Mikasa,* had fallen further into disrepair—it had even, for a time, been roofed-over and converted into a dance hall. He volunteered to write an article for a popular Japanese magazine to express his admiration for Admiral Togo and to encourage restoration of the *Mikasa*— not as a symbol of militarism but as a monument to a turning point in Japanese history. He asked that the author's fee not be paid to him and instead be given to a preservation fund. At that point, there was no such fund, but his donation became the seed money and one was quickly established. The *Mikasa* was restored and opened to the public on May 27, 1961—the anniversary of the Battle of Tsushima Straits.

In a bit of a stretch, Nimitz served as technical adviser for the 1959 movie *John Paul Jones*. He did not appreciate the marketing aspects of movie-making: He thought accuracy was paramount. He suggested that the leading man should look like John Paul Jones, short and red-haired, not the tall, dark, and handsome actor Robert Stack. His suggestion was ignored.

And he would often meet with groups of children, scouts or students, to tell them a bit about the Navy. He got their attention with card tricks and held their attention with stories. Once, a young girl asked, how did he feel when he found out he was going to be commander-in-chief of the fleet? He replied, "Lonely."[2]

His own children had moved on but not out of his life. Chester Jr. retired as a rear admiral in 1957 and went on to a career in business; he became president and chairman of scientific-equipment manufacturer Perkins-Elmer. He and his wife Joan had three children, all girls. Kate left the Washington, D.C. library for the job of housewife, and she and Junior Lay had three boys. Nancy became a Harvard-trained Russian-studies expert and rounded out her career as the Russian agriculture specialist at the Rand Corporation. Mary, to the surprise—but with the support—of her generally nonreligious parents, became a Catholic nun. She earned a PhD from Stanford, went into teaching, and in 1970 became head of the Department of Biology at Dominican College, San Rafael.

Nimitz maintained his friendships, and his friendships maintained him. His neighbors in the Bay Area included Admirals Spruance, Lockwood, and Turner. His house guests included his old boss, Admiral Robison, and Dr. Ralph Bunche, winner of the 1950 Nobel Peace Prize with whom he worked at the United Nations. There was a grand 75th birthday party, packed with at least twenty-five flag officers who had flown in from around the world. A surprise guest was Francis Cardinal Spellman, the archbishop of New York, who had served as military vicar of the Armed Forces for Catholics and whom Nimitz had met back in the war.

Age was creeping up, but pride was intact. His fetish for punctuality became an obsession. If he and Catherine had a dinner date at a restaurant before a concert, he might have Cozard drive around the block, sometimes more than once, in order to arrive precisely at the time set. He did not want to be late and

keep people waiting, or to embarrass them by arriving too early. A minute either side was too late or too early.

His dinner-party repartee seemed as sharp as ever; one of his granddaugh-
ters, however, discovered a little book in which he had written down the punch
lines of most of his jokes. He kept the book in the bathroom, ready for a refresher while he was washing his hands.

His walks were a little slower, and every once in a while he would stop to
examine a rock or admire the view—he would never admit that he was resting
for a moment. One time, when they were playing horseshoes, a friend stooped
down to pick up both shoes and Nimitz waved him off. "Don't do that," he said,
"That's part of the exercise, and I'll pick up my own shoes."[3]

But his health was failing. Catherine's was also in steep decline; afflicted
with arthritis, she needed two canes to walk and climbing stairs was a major
challenge. In 1963 the senior officer's quarters at the nearby Treasure Island
Naval Station became vacant. It was a large house with an elevator and a staff,
which the Navy turned over to Nimitz and his wife. Over the next two years, the
admiral suffered through several surgeries, pneumonia, a series of small strokes,
and was more or less bed-ridden by the end of 1965.

Nimitz, the ultimate planner, planned the ultimate event of his life. In 1949
he picked out his burial plot at the Golden Gate Cemetery in San Bruno, south
of San Francisco. By arrangement, he and his wife would be buried alongside
his longtime companions Spruance, Turner, and Lockwood and their wives. An
administrative officer at the Treasure Island Naval Station—a WAVE—was the
designated "Nimitz funeral officer." The operations manual, dictated by Nimitz, was half-an-inch thick, every detail spelled out: the draft obituary, the time
of day for the funeral service and the burial, plus the name of everyone who
should be invited—all decided well in advance. The book was updated, from
time to time, to take out the names of friends who had passed on.

Fleet Admiral Chester W. Nimitz died in his quarters on February 20, 1966.
The funeral service was held at the Naval Station chapel. There was a 100-car
motorcade to the cemetery, a 70-plane Navy flyover, and a 19-gun salute; Rear
Admiral James W. Kelly, chief of chaplains, conducted the graveside service.
Cardinal Spellman offered a prayer. Secretary of the Navy Paul Nitze presented
the national colors and the admiral's personal flag to Catherine.

It was February 24. It would have been his 81st birthday.

EPILOGUE

When sixteen-year-old Chester William Nimitz went off to Annapolis in 1901, his Navy had more in common with the Phoenicians than with the Navy he left behind in 1966. Most of the growth and change, of course, was the result of advancing technology, but Nimitz was very much involved in operational and educational innovations that contributed to greatly increased effectiveness. Diesel engines for submarines, underway refueling, the NROTC, the circular formation, integration of the carrier with the fleet, adoption of practical landing craft, innovative officer training programs, nuclear power for warships, and notably, the unsung legacy of his tour as CNO is that "monster submarine," hiding in the depths "with self-guided atomic missiles."

Today, one of those ballistic missile submarines could be parked in New York harbor or (more likely) hidden anywhere in the Atlantic Ocean for months on end. On signal, she could hit, say, both Pyongyang and Tehran at the same time with a multitude of nuclear warheads. The 1940s Air Force vision of strategic bombing, so much a matter of bitter contention with the Navy of Chester Nimitz, was long ago rendered inoperative. And, despite the dire warnings of the Army aviators, aircraft carriers remain one of the most valued assets in the defense arsenal. In 1972, Nimitz's daughter Catherine (Kate) Lay was honored to christen the world's second nuclear-powered aircraft carrier, lead ship of a new class—the *Nimitz*.

It was a fitting salute to a great man.

May he rest, in peace.

NOTES

CHAPTER ONE: TEXAS

1. Twelve years younger than Chester, Otto would follow his half-brother into the Navy and retire, in ill-health, as a captain.
2. Dora Nimitz Reagan, interviewed by E. B. Potter, U.S. Naval Institute, DVD, March 12, 1970, p. 12.
3. Gunther Henke, interviewed by E. B. Potter, U.S. Naval Institute, DVD, March 14, 1970, p. 14.
4. Dora Nimitz Reagan, interview by E. B. Potter, p. 17.
5. Ibid., p. 18.
6. Chester Nimitz, "My Way of Life," *Boys' Life*, Jan. 1966, 56:1. This article appeared one month before Nimitz's death in February 1966.
7. Ibid.
8. Some ten years later another Texan, Dwight Eisenhower, wanted to go to the Naval Academy but was above the age limit, so he ended up at West Point.

CHAPTER TWO: NAVAL ACADEMY

1. Nathan Miller, *Theodore Roosevelt, A Life* (New York: Quill/William Morrow, 1994), p. 337.
2. "Cadets" were re-designated as "midshipmen" in 1902 and from 1912 onward, graduates were directly commissioned as "ensign."
3. Chester Nimitz, "My Way of Life," *Boys' Life*, Jan. 1966, 56:1.
4. John Davis Long, *The New American Navy*, vol. 2 (New York: Outlook Company, 1903), p. 210. Schley found some redemption in the popularity of his subsequent autobiography, *Forty-Five Years under the Flag* (New York, 1904).
5. E. B. Potter, *Nimitz* (Annapolis, MD: Naval Institute Press, 1976), p. 344.
6. Potter, *Nimitz*, p. 55.

CHAPTER THREE: A PHILIPPINE ADVENTURE

1. This process began with the 1852-1854 visits of Commodore Matthew C. Perry, who arranged some trade agreements that opened Japan to the outside world.
2. E. B. Potter, *Nimitz* (Annapolis, MD: Naval Institute Press, 1976), p. 56.
3. Masuii Miyakawa, *Powers of the American People, Congress, President, and Courts: According to the Evolution of Constitutional Construction* (Baker & Taylor, 1908).
4. Annual Address of the President of the United States, Dec. 3, 1906.
5. When the Spanish surrendered to Admiral Dewey, they ceded only Manila. The population at large thought that meant freedom. The United States was in the throes of its own dreams of expansion and wanted all of the Philippines, all 7,000 islands, so after some wrangling, the United States paid Spain $20 million for clear title (and got the Pacific island of Guam as part of the bargain). The population at large, not much interested in being sold, created the Philippine Republic and declared war on the United States. That war officially ended July 4, 1902, but some independent guerrilla actions continued until 1913.
6. Dede W. Casad, and Frank A. Driscoll, *Chester W. Nimitz: Admiral of the Hills* (Austin, TX: Eakin Press, 1983), p. 74.

7. Potter, *Nimitz*, p. 58.
8. 1907 State of the Union message, Dec. 3, 1907, reprinted in George Percival Scriven, *The Service of Information, United States Army* (Washington, DC: Government Printing Office, 1915), p. 66.
9. "The Fleet Will Go, Says Roosevelt," *New York Times*, Sept. 27, 1907.
10. Potter, *Nimitz*, p. 59.
11. Ibid., pp. 60-61.
12. Ibid., p. 61.
13. Ibid.

CHAPTER FOUR: CHANGE OF COURSE

1. Jan S. Breemer, "Chasing U-Boats and Hunting Insurgents: Lessons from an Underhand Way of War," *Joint Forces Quarterly*, no. 40 (1st Quarter 2006), 60.
2. *Nova*, PBS, retrieved May 1, 2011, http://www.pbs.org/wgbh/nova/lostsub/hist1900.html.
3. In 1776 David Bushnell's *Turtle* made the first (but unsuccessful) submerged attack: on a British warship in New York harbor. In 1800 American inventor Robert Fulton built his *Nautilus* for the French Navy, which really didn't want it. Inventor Lodner D. Phillips offered a proven design to the U. S. Navy just before the Civil War; he was told the ships of "our Navy go on, not under, the ocean." The Confederate boat *Hunley* became the first of the breed to actually sink a warship although it was operating on the surface at the time. For the rest of the nineteenth century, submarine development, worldwide, was impressive. See the author's website, www.submarine-history.com.
4. Chester Nimitz, "My Way of Life," *Boys' Life*, Jan. 1966, 56:1.
5. At first, the U.S. Navy named submarines just like any other warship, but in 1911 the boats were symbolically demoted to, roughly, the status of harbor tugboats. The names went away, and submarines were identified by class and order of birth. Thus, *Plunger* became A-1, *Snapper*, C-5, *Narwhal*, D-1, and *Skipjack*, E-1. Names came back in 1924, and in the Navy way, most of the earlier names were recycled in later boats.
6. Chester W. Nimitz, U.S. Naval Institute *Proceedings*, July 1912.

CHAPTER FIVE: THE GREAT WAR

1. E. B. Potter, *Nimitz* (Annapolis, MD: Naval Institute Press, 1976), pp. 125-126.
2. Admiral Sir Percy Scott, "Letter to the Editor," *Times of London*, June 15, 1914.
3. "Text of Germany's Note to the United States," *New York Times*, Feb. 1, 1917.
4. A case could be made—and has been made—that the Confederacy lost the American Civil War for a similar reason. The South had plenty of food, but not much else. It was an agricultural region, with minimal manufacturing capacity, that, once the war began, was dependent on overseas supply of munitions and a great deal more. The Union Navy's 3,500-mile blockade of both coastline and rivers choked the armies of the Confederacy but neither created headlines nor took up much space in the history books.
5. Stuart S. Murray, Admiral, USN (Ret.), eight interviews, 1970-1971, by Etta-Belle Kitchen, U.S. Naval Institute, DVD, compiled in 2001, p. 48.
6. "Commodore" was a naval rank in the eighteenth and nineteenth centuries but, in most of the twentieth century and yet today, has more often been the honorary title for a squadron, division, or flotilla commander, whether he was an ensign watching over mine-sweeping boats or a captain with a group of destroyers.
7. Murray, interviews 1970-1971, p. 47.

CHAPTER SIX: CHANGE AND CHALLENGE

1. *The Independent*, March 12, 1921, vol. 105, p. 259.
2. By 1925 Mitchell's agitation led to a court-martial for "conduct prejudicial to good order and military discipline." He was found guilty. In an effort to defuse the controversy, President Calvin Coolidge appointed a special board to recommend aviation policy, headed by Dwight W. Morrow, an attorney by trade. The Morrow Board did not support a separate air force, dashing the near-term hopes of the Army aviators, but instead recommended that the Army air arm should be organized as a branch of the Army (just like the Army's Signal Corps or the Quartermaster Corps) and that naval aviators should be integrated with the regular line of the Navy, as were the submarine officers.

3. E. B. Potter, *Nimitz* (Annapolis, MD: Naval Institute Press, 1976), p. 136.
4. Ibid.
5. Albert A. Nofi, *To Train the Fleet for War: The U. S. Navy Fleet Problems, 1923-1940* (Washington, DC: Government Printing Office, 2010), p. 68.
6. "Defense of Hawaii Inadequate to Meet the Strain of War," *New York Times,* May 7, 1925.
7. *Washington Post,* Nov. 30, 1924.
8. "Tokio Papers Call War Game a Menace," *New York Times,* May 3, 1925.
9. "Japanese Press Expresses Much Alarm Over Plans to Extend Defenses of Hawaii," *New York Times,* May 16, 1925.

CHAPTER SEVEN: THE PROFESSOR

1. E. B. Potter, *Nimitz* (Annapolis, MD: Naval Institute Press, 1976), p. 144.
2. Potter, *Nimitz,* p. 144.
3. J. Joseph Chase, interviewed by Etta-Belle Kitchen, U.S. Naval Institute, DVD, Oct. 19, 1969, p. 3.
4. C. W. Nimitz, "The Naval Reserve Officers Training Corps." U.S. Naval Institute *Proceedings,* June 1928, vol. 54, no. 304.
5. Catherine Nimitz Lay, interviewed by John T. Mason, U.S. Naval Institute, DVD, Feb. 16, 1970, p. 37.
6. Potter, *Nimitz,* p. 153.
7. Ibid.

CHAPTER EIGHT: THE *AUGUSTA*

1. Lloyd M. Mustin, Vice Admiral, USN, interviewed by John T. Mason, U.S. Naval Institute, DVD, March 10, 1970, pp. 65-68.
2. Any flag officer rank above rear admiral (identified by the two stars on his personal flag) was "temporary" and applied only while serving in a billet that called for either the rank of vice admiral (three stars) or admiral. It was not uncommon for a three- or four-star flag officer to revert to his "permanent" rank of rear admiral when shifted to an active duty billet of lesser stature; he would, at some point, be retired in the highest rank satisfactorily held.
3. Sam P. Moncure, Captain, USN (Ret.) interviewed by John T. Mason, U.S. Naval Institute, DVD, July 30, 1969, pp. 10-11.
4. J. Wilson Leverton, Jr., Rear Admiral, USN (Ret.), interviewed by John T. Mason, U.S. Naval Institute, DVD, August 22, 1969, p. 7.
5. Odale D. Waters, Rear Admiral, USN (Ret.), interviewed by John T. Mason, U.S. Naval Institute, DVD, July 14, 1969, p. 136.
6. James T. Lay, Captain, USN, interviewed by John T. Mason, U.S. Naval Institute, DVD, Feb. 16, 1970, p. 4.
7. Odale D. Waters, interview by John T. Mason, p. 10.
8. E. B. Potter, *Nimitz* (Annapolis, MD: Naval Institute Press, 1976), p. 160.

CHAPTER NINE: IN TRAINING

1. The name would be changed in May 1942 to Bureau of Naval Personnel (BUPERS).
2. In fact, the Navy became a campaign issue when FDR's team spread a rumor that Hoover planned to abolish the Marine Corps.
3. William M. McBride, *Technological Change and the United States Navy, 1865-1945* (Baltimore: Johns Hopkins University Press, 2000), p. 167.
4. Preston V. Mercer, Rear Admiral, USN (Ret.), interviewed by John T. Mason, U.S. Naval Institute, DVD, Oct. 18, 1969, p. 9.
5. We might note that Towers twice had been passed over for promotion to rear admiral; he didn't fit the pattern that line officer selection boards expected—as in, command at sea. He finally made flag in 1939. There was a rumor that FDR made it happen.

CHAPTER TEN: PREPARING FOR WAR

1. To encourage enlistments of siblings, Nimitz announced that, when possible, brothers who enlisted together would be assigned to the same ship. The poster family of the day was the Patten brothers, six on *Nevada,* based in Pearl Harbor. A seventh brother had just entered recruit training

but already had his orders to the same ship. The policy was a big mistake. The Pattens—all at Pearl Harbor on December 7, 1941—survived the war, but another set of brothers—the five Sullivans— were killed together in November 1942 when their ship was sunk. The policy was changed.

2. J. Wilson Leverton, Jr., Rear Admiral, USN (Ret.), interviewed by John T. Mason, U.S. Naval Institute, DVD, Aug. 22, 1969, p. 25.

3. Ibid.

4. Nathan Miller, *War at Sea: A Naval History of World War II* (New York: Oxford University Press, US, 1997), p. 197.

5. "264 New Ensigns Get Commissions," *New York Times,* Nov. 15, 1940.

6. "NAVY: Broad Stripe for Mustangs," *Time,* Mar. 31, 1941. V-7 was followed by the similar V-5 and V-12 programs. Laugh, they might, but had they lived long enough, the members of Congress, circa 1945, would have been astounded with one grand example. V-12 graduate Samuel Gravely, commissioned December 1944, was one of the first African-Americans to become a naval officer and he was the first to reach flag rank. He retired as a vice admiral in 1980. Today only about half of Navy flag officers are Naval Academy graduates; most of the rest come from the NROTC. Onnie Lattu, University of California class of 1930, was among the first three NROTC graduates to make flag, in 1955. The NROTC unit at Holy Cross can claim perhaps sixteen flag officers, to date, and from the class of 1945 one secretary of the Navy—J. William Middendorf, II, who served from 1974 to 1977.

7. Ibid.

8. E. B. Potter, *Nimitz* (Annapolis, MD: Naval Institute Press, 1976), pp. 170, 171.

9. H. Arthur Lamar, Captain USNR (ret), interviewed by John T. Mason, U.S. Naval Institute, DVD, May 3, 1970, pp. 26-29.

10. Draper Kauffman, Jr. email to Dr. Eric Berryman, copy in author's possession.

11. Preston V. Mercer, Rear Admiral, USN (Ret.), interviewed by John T. Mason, U.S. Naval Institute, DVD, Oct. 18, 1969, p. 6.

12. "Asks Congress Act to Hold Navy Men," *New York Times,* June 27, 1941.

CHAPTER ELEVEN: WAR

1. Address by the President of the United States, Dec. 8, 1941, in *Declarations of a State of War with Japan, Germany, and Italy,* Senate Document No. 148 (77th Congress, 1st Session), p. 7.

2. E. B. Potter, *Nimitz* (Annapolis, MD: Naval Institute Press, 1976), p. 6.

3. The Naval War College 1941 annual war game recommended that in the event of war, all waters of the Far East should be declared as war zones in which all merchant ships would enter at their peril. The General Board said "war zones" were not recognized in international law. Therefore, in a bit of word-twisting, all Japanese shipping was defined as being in the service of the military, wherever found, and thus fair game. "Unrestricted" submarine warfare had become part of the standing war plan.

   Five years later the qualifier "unrestricted" would become a key element of the Nuremburg War Crimes trial of pioneer submariner and German Navy commander in chief, Admiral Karl Doenitz. He was charged with violation of law and custom for authorizing "unrestricted submarine warfare." A witness for the defense, by deposition: Admiral Chester Nimitz affirmed that the United States had done likewise. Doenitz was found guilty, but not on that charge. By the end of the war, Doenitz had become the head of the government and since the Nuremburg tribunal couldn't punish Hitler—who had committed suicide—they treated Doenitz, who had no hand in any of the unethical actions of the Nazi party—as a surrogate. He was sentenced to ten years in prison.

4. On the first day of the war, twenty-eight American submarines had been in position around the Philippines—more than half of all American submarines in the Pacific, more submarines than had ever been assembled for one battle, anywhere, at the same time. They might as well have been in San Diego. On December 21, seven of them confronted a fleet of seventy-six Japanese troop and supply ships—and sank two. There were reports of too-timid commanders and faulty torpedoes. It would get worse: At the end of a three-week campaign, only one more Japanese ship had been sunk. By the end of 1942, almost one-third of the U.S. submarine commanders were replaced as incompetent. It took a bit longer to fully resolve the problems with torpedoes.

5. Potter, *Nimitz,* p. 9.

6. Ibid.
7. H. Arthur Lamar, Captain USNR (ret), interviewed by John T. Mason, U.S. Naval Institute, DVD, May 3, 1970, p. 2.
8. Potter, *Nimitz*, p. 9.
9. Catherine Nimitz Lay, interviewed by John T. Mason, U.S. Naval Institute, DVD, Feb. 16, 1970, p. 47.
10. "President Confers with Top Officers," *New York Times*, Dec. 19, 1941.
11. "The U. S. At War, Shake-Up," *Time*, Dec. 29, 1941.
12. H. Arthur Lamar, interview by John T. Mason, p. 21.
13. Paul Stillwell, *Air Raid, Pearl Harbor: Recollections of a Day of Infamy* (Annapolis, MD: Naval Institute Press, 1981), p. 261.
14. "World: Hoomanawanui," *Time*, Jan. 12, 1942; Potter, *Nimitz*, p. 19.
15. Potter, *Nimitz*, p.19.

CHAPTER TWELVE: OPENING GAMBIT

1. As commander in chief U.S. fleet, King thus became the military head of the Navy, even senior to the chief of naval operations (CNO). Soon, because of tension between King and CNO Harold Stark, FDR added "CNO" to King's portfolio and shifted Admiral Stark to duty as commander, U.S. Naval Forces Europe. In light of the Pearl Harbor debacle, King wisely elected to drop the usual acronym "CINCUS," pronounced "sink us," and replaced it with an almost unpronounceable "COMINCH."
2. In his diary, General Dwight D. Eisenhower noted his frustration with the "grotesquely brusque" Admiral King whose policies, he believed, were endangering the war effort. "One thing that might help win this war," he wrote in his diary, "is to get someone to shoot King. He is the antithesis of cooperation, a deliberately rude person . . . a mental bully." Gerard H. Clarfield, *Security with Solvency: Dwight D. Eisenhower and the Shaping of the American Military Establishment* (Westport, CT: Praeger, 1999), p. 5.
3. John B. Lundstrom, *Black Shoe Carrier Admiral* (Annapolis, MD: Naval Institute Press, 2006), p. 55.
4. E. B. Potter, *Nimitz* (Annapolis, MD: Naval Institute Press, 1976), p. 36.
5. "Girding of Pacific Speeded by Nimitz," *New York Times*, Jan. 31, 1942.
6. Potter, *Nimitz*, p. 37.
7. *New York Times*, Feb. 2, 1942.
8. "Answer to 'Where's the Fleet,'" *New York Times*, Feb. 3, 1942.
9. In the U.S. Civil War, a brief telegraphic newspaper alert about a battle, "Fighting—Joe Hooker" was transmogrified into the nickname "Fighting Joe" when a typographer left out the em-dash. Hooker didn't like it. He thought it made him seem impetuous. Perhaps he was.
10. Potter, *Nimitz*, p. 41.
11. Ibid.
12. Ibid.
13. Ibid.
14. Lundstrom, *Black Shoe*, p.76.
15. Douglas MacArthur, *Reminiscences* (New York: McGraw-Hill, 1964), p. 145.
16. Lundstrom, *Black Shoe*, p. 102.
17. Ibid., p. 103.
18. Ibid.

CHAPTER THIRTEEN: THE CODE-BREAKERS

1. John Ford, Commander USNR, interview in box 10 of World War II Interviews, Operational Archives Branch, Naval Historical Center. Highlights at http://www.history.navy.mil/faqs/faq81-8b.htm, accessed Jan. 10, 2011.
2. W. J. Holmes, *Double-Edged Secrets: U. S. Naval Intelligence Operations in the Pacific during World War II* (Annapolis, MD: Naval Institute Press, 1979), p. 90.
3. Robert J. Cressman, *A Glorious Page in Our History: The Battle of Midway, 4-6 June, 1942* (Missoula, MT: Pictorial Histories Publishing, 1990), p. 34.
4. E. M. Eller, Rear Admiral, USN (Ret.), interviewed by John T. Mason, U.S. Naval Institute, DVD, Dec. 19, 1974, p. 535.

5. John Ford, Commander USNR, interview in box 10 of World War II Interviews, Operational Archives Branch, Naval Historical Center.
6. E. B. Potter, *Nimitz* (Annapolis, MD: Naval Institute Press, 1976), p. 95.
7. Potter, *Nimitz*, p. 99.
8. Joseph J. Rochefort, Captain, USN (Ret.), interviewed by Etta-Belle Kitchen, U.S. Naval Institute, DVD, Aug. 14, 1969; declassified version issued August 1983, p. 227.
9. Edwin T. Layton, Rear Admiral, USN (Ret.), interviewed by E. B. Potter, U.S. Naval Institute, DVD, March 19, 1970, p. 448.

CHAPTER FOURTEEN: FALLOUT

1. "'Midway' Spurs Pun by Admiral Nimitz," *New York Times,* June 7, 1942.
2. "'No Limits to Nimitz' Is Slogan in China," *New York Times,* June 8, 1942.
3. Robert J. Casey, *Torpedo Junction* (Garden City, NY: Halcyon House, 1943), pp. 14, 15.
4. "Asks Congress Act to Hold Navy Men," *New York Times,* June 27, 1941.
5. Commander Seligman's career came to a dead end, and the incident added to a traditional mistrust of the press on the part of many naval officers. A paragraph was added to the U.S. Government's Code of Wartime Practices for the American Press: "To the end that the enemy may not have information concerning any success the U.S. may attain in deciphering his encoded or enciphered communications, no mention should be made of available or captured enemy codes or enemy ciphers, or about the intelligence gained from intercepting and studying enemy radio messages." A popular business newsletter applauded the change and noted: "As between an ethical professional requirement that a journalist hold nothing back and a patriotic duty not to shoot one's own soldiers in the back, we have found no difficulty in making a choice. Freedom of the press does not carry with it a general license to reveal our secret strengths and weaknesses to the enemy." *Whaley-Eaton American Letter,* Dec. 26, 1942.
6. "Big Bombers Won," *New York Times,* June 12, 1942.
7. Ibid.
8. "Yorktown Was Hit in Midway Melee," *New York Times,* July 15, 1942.
9. Edwin T. Layton, Rear Admiral, with Captain Roger Pineau USNR (ret) and John Costello, *And I Was There: Pearl Harbor and Midway—Breaking the Secrets* (New York: William Morrow and Co., Inc., 1985), p. 450.
10. Stephen Budiansky, *Battle of Wits: The Complete Story of Codebreaking in World War II* (New York: Free Press, 2002), p. 23.
11. Layton, *And I Was There,* p. 469. For a fascinating study of the fight between Rochefort and Op-20-G, see Frederick D. Parker, "How Op-20-G Got Rid of Joe Rochefort," *Cryptologia,* July 1, 2000.
12. Budiansky, *Battle of Wits,* p. 3.

CHAPTER FIFTEEN: THE NIMITZ STYLE

1. By the end of the war, there were 82,000 women in the Navy, 11,000 in the Coast Guard, 20,000 in the Marine Corps, and 85 percent of enlisted personnel assigned to Marine Corps Headquarters were women.
2. George W. Healy Jr., *A Lifetime on Deadline* (Gretna, LA: Pelican Publishing, 1976), p. 144.
3. Onnie P. Lattu, Rear Admiral, USN (Ret.), interviewed by John T. Mason, U.S. Naval Institute, DVD, July 17, 1969, p. 17.
4. E. B. Potter, *Nimitz* (Annapolis, MD: Naval Institute Press, 1976), p. 222.
5. H. Arthur Lamar, Captain USNR (ret), interviewed by John T. Mason, U.S. Naval Institute, DVD, May 3, 1970, p. 96.
6. Ibid., p. 42.
7. Stuart S. Murray, Admiral, USN (Ret.), eight interviews, 1970-1971, by Etta-Belle Kitchen, U.S. Naval Institute, DVD, compiled in 2001, p. 449.
8. Chester Nimitz Jr., Rear Admiral, USN (Ret.), interviewed by John T. Mason, U.S. Naval Institute, DVD, April 14, 1969, p. 41.
9. Ibid., p. 13.
10. H. Arthur Lamar, interview by John T. Mason, p. 84.
11. Brigadier General S.L.A. Marshall, U.S. Naval Institute *Proceedings,* July 1966.

12. Stuart S. Murray, interviews by Etta-Belle Kitchen, p. 214.
13. Mel A. Peterson, Rear Admiral, USN (Ret.), interviewed by Etta-Belle Kitchen, U.S. Naval Institute, DVD, May 24, 1969, p. 12.
14. Eugene B. Fluckey, Rear Admiral, USN (Ret.), interviewed by John T. Mason, U.S. Naval Institute, DVD, Oct. 20, 1971, p. 16. A typical Nimitz joke: A nervous young Marine was facing his first parachute jump. "Don't worry," said his sergeant, "Count to ten and pull the rip cord; if that doesn't work, pull the cord on the emergency chute." The Marine nodded his understanding, then asked, "How will I get back to camp?" His sergeant said that a station wagon would be waiting at the landing zone. The Marine jumped. He pulled the rip cord—nothing happened. He pulled the cord for the emergency chute. Nothing happened. Looking down at the ground, he said, "Damn! I'll bet that station wagon won't be there, either."
15. H. Arthur Lamar, interview by John T. Mason, p. 3.
16. Ibid., p. 4.
17. Catherine Nimitz Lay, conversation with the author.

CHAPTER SIXTEEN: ON THE OFFENSIVE

1. E. B. Potter, *Nimitz* (Annapolis, MD: Naval Institute Press, 1976), p. 111.
2. Ibid., p. 112.
3. Ibid., pp. 113-114.
4. Ibid., p. 181.
5. William Waldo Drake, Rear Admiral USNR (Ret.) interviewed by Etta-Belle Kitchen, U.S. Naval Institute, DVD, June 15, 1969, p. 53.
6. Ibid., p. 52.
7. Samuel B. Griffith, *The Battle for Guadalcanal* (Champaign: University of Illinois Press, 2000), p. 72.
8. Potter, *Nimitz*, p. 189.
9. Ibid., p. 188.
10. Ibid., p. 194.
11. Ibid., p. 197.
12. H. Arthur Lamar, Captain USNR (Ret.), interviewed by John T. Mason, U.S. Naval Institute, DVD, May 3, 1970, p. 88.
13. Potter, *Nimitz*, p 199
14. H. Arthur Lamar, interview by John T. Mason, p. 61.
15. "An Enemy Disaster," *New York Times,* March 7, 1943.
16. "Test of Air Power Looms in the Pacific," *New York Times,* March 14, 1943.
17. William Manchester, *American Caesar: Douglas MacArthur, 1880-1964* (Boston: Little, Brown, 1978), p. 329.
18. Allen G. Quynn, Rear Admiral, USN (Ret.), interviewed by John T. Mason, U.S. Naval Institute, DVD, Dec. 17, 1969, p. 30.
19. Manchester, *American Caesar,* p. 329.
20. *New York Times,* Sept. 4, 1945.
21. The Layton-Nimitz dialogue on Yamamoto is described in E. B. Potter, *Nimitz,* p. 233.
22. Douglas MacArthur, *Reminiscences* (New York: McGraw-Hill, 1964), p. 175.

CHAPTER SEVENTEEN: MIDCOURSE CORRECTION

1. H. Arthur Lamar, Captain USNR (Ret.), interviewed by John T. Mason, U.S. Naval Institute, DVD, May 3, 1970, p. 39.
2. E. B. Potter, *Nimitz* (Annapolis, MD: Naval Institute Press, 1976), p. 261.
3. *Time,* Dec. 6, 1943.
4. Potter, *Nimitz,* p. 280.
5. Ibid., p. 283.
6. Ibid., p 287.
7. William Waldo Drake, Rear Admiral USNR (Ret.) interviewed by Etta-Belle Kitchen, U.S. Naval Institute, DVD, June 15, 1969, p. 36.
8. Potter, *Nimitz,* p. 275.
9. Ibid., p. 278; Carrie Nation was a leader of the temperance movement.

10. Ibid., p. 285.
11. Ibid., p. 289.
12. Ibid.
13. Potter, *Nimitz*, p. 291.
14. Robert R. Gros, interviewed by Etta-Belle Kitchen, U.S. Naval Institute, DVD, July 18, 1970, pp. 24-25.
15. Edwin T. Layton, Rear Admiral, USN (Ret.), interviewed by E. B. Potter, U.S. Naval Institute, DVD, March 19, 1970. In the 1976 *Nimitz* biography written by Nimitz's friend E. B. Potter, the author left out the part about "horse's ass."

CHAPTER EIGHTEEN: THE MARIANAS

1. E. B. Potter, *Nimitz* (Annapolis, MD: Naval Institute Press, 1976), p. 294; E. B. Potter, *Bull Halsey* (Annapolis, MD: Naval Institute Press, 2003), p. 197.
2. Potter, *Nimitz*, p. 352.
3. William Waldo Drake, Rear Admiral USNR (Ret.) interviewed by Etta-Belle Kitchen, U.S. Naval Institute, DVD, June 15, 1969, p. 22.
4. Chester W. Nimitz, Jr., Rear Admiral, USN (Ret.), interviewed by John T. Mason, U.S. Naval Institute, DVD, April 14, 1969, p. 11.
5. H. Arthur Lamar, Captain USNR (ret), interviewed by John T. Mason, U.S. Naval Institute, DVD, May 3, 1970, p. 35.
6. Ibid.
7. Potter, *Nimitz*, p. 295.
8. Ibid., p. 307; *Time*, Sept. 18, 1944.
9. Potter, *Nimitz*, p. 308.
10. Ibid., p. 309.
11. Preston V. Mercer, Rear Admiral, USN (Ret.), interviewed by John T. Mason, U.S. Naval Institute, DVD, Oct.18, 1969, p. 24.
12. Potter, *Nimitz*, p. 318.
13. The tale of the FDR visit to Nimitz's quarters is related in H. Arthur Lamar, interview by John T. Mason, p. 5, the Seabee comment is on p. 86.
14. E. M. Eller, Rear Admiral, USN (Ret.), interviewed by John T. Mason, U.S. Naval Institute, DVD, Dec. 19, 1974, p. 713.

CHAPTER NINETEEN: A DIFFERENT SORT OF WAR

1. Edmund Castillo, "U.S. Navy Public Affairs: The First Hundred Years," unpublished ms. prepared for the U.S. Navy Public Affairs Alumni Association, 2005, p. 46, copy in author's personal files.
2. *Time*, Dec. 6, 1943.
3. George W. Healy, Jr., *A Lifetime on Deadline* (Gretna, LA: Pelican Publishing, 1976), p. 147.
4. Ibid.
5. Castillo, Public Affairs, p. 31.
6. Ibid., p. 32.
7. Gerard H. Clarfield, *Security with Solvency: Dwight D. Eisenhower and the Shaping of the American Military Establishment* (Westport, CT: Praeger, 1999), p. 15.
8. Miller obituary, *New York Times*, May 18, 1992.

CHAPTER TWENTY: THE "RETURN"

1. "ServRon 10: Floating Arsenal," *Popular Mechanics:* 59, November 1945.
2. Oct. 16, 1944 radio link to the *New York Herald Tribune* Forum, broadcast over the Blue Network, typescript in Nimitz family files.
3. E. B. Potter, *Nimitz* (Annapolis, MD: Naval Institute Press, 1976), p. 328.
4. William Manchester, *American Caesar: Douglas MacArthur, 1880-1964* (Boston: Little, Brown, 1978), p. 386.
5. After Chester Nimitz died, his family found a book in his personal library, a biography of Christopher Columbus, with a full-page illustration over the caption, "Columbus wading ashore in the New World." In the margin, in Nimitz's handwriting, a brief note: "An early MacArthur?"

6. Potter, *Nimitz*, p. 343.
7. The Japanese word meaning "divine wind." This was the name given to a typhoon in 1274 that destroyed an enemy fleet and spared Japan from invasion; the Japanese hoped for a symbolic replay.
8. Air attacks had not been much of a problem before, because the number of attackers could be handled by the combat air patrol and antiaircraft batteries. But later in the war, a single kamikaze attack might include several hundred aircraft. They overwhelmed the defenses and the pilots would not back off when under fire. However, the concept was not without a flaw: the excited young men often would dive on the first ship they sighted, usually one of the destroyers or other small ships on picket duty, sparing the major warships.
9. Evan Thomas, *Sea of Thunder: Four Commanders and the Last Great Naval Campaign, 1941-1945* (New York: Simon & Schuster, 2006), p. 301.
10. Ibid.
11. Potter, *Nimitz*, p. 348.
12. Ibid., p. 350.
13. Pacific Fleet Confidential Letter 14CL-45, declassified and reprinted in the U.S. Naval Institute *Proceedings*, Jan. 1956.
14. D. Clayton James, *The Years of MacArthur, 1941–1945*, vol. 2 (Boston: Houghton Mifflin, 1975), pp. 602-603.

CHAPTER TWENTY-ONE: IWO JIMA

1. "Twinkle in Nimitz's Eyes Mark of Fleet's Success" *New York Times*, Feb. 18, 1945, "Toward Tokyo; and a New Blow," Feb. 18, 1945.
2. Barton J. Bernstein. "Why We Didn't Use Poison Gas in World War II," *American Heritage Magazine*, Aug.-Sept. 1985, 36:5.
3. Richard F. Newcomb, *Iwo Jima* (New York: Henry Holt, 1965), p. 136.
4. E. B. Potter, *Nimitz* (Annapolis, MD: Naval Institute Press, 1976), p. 363.
5. For the record, this photo recorded the second flag raising on Mt. Suribachi. The first was not captured by Rosenthal but was watched by Secretary of the Navy Forrestal when he went ashore as an observer, four days after the initial landings. He turned to his escort, General Holland Smith, and said "The raising of that flag on Suribachi means a Marine Corps for the next five hundred years." Time will tell.
6. "The Press: A Tight Lip Loosens." *Time*, March 5, 1945.
7. Newcomb, *Iwo Jima*, p. 240.
8. *Newsweek*, March 5, 1945.
9. Edmund Castillo, "U.S. Navy Public Affairs: The First Hundred Years," unpublished ms. prepared for the U.S. Navy Public Affairs Alumni Association, 2005, p. 40, copy in author's personal files.
10. Castillo, U.S. Navy *Public Affairs*, p. 41.

CHAPTER TWENTY-TWO: OKINAWA

1. E. B. Potter, *Nimitz* (Annapolis, MD: Naval Institute Press, 1976), p. 372.
2. Ibid.
3. Potter, *Nimitz*, p. 375.
4. Ibid., p. 376.
5. That is more than the number of Japanese later killed in the nuclear attacks on both Hiroshima and Nagasaki.
6. Potter, *Nimitz*, pp. 381-382. Ashworth would retire as a vice admiral, after his final job as commander of the Sixth Fleet in the Mediterranean.
7. Edmund Castillo, "U.S. Navy Public Affairs: The First Hundred Years" (unpublished, prepared for the U.S. Navy Public Affairs Alumni Association, 2005; copy in author's personal files), p. 44.
8. Castillo, "Public Affairs," p. 45.
9. Potsdam Declaration, http://www.army.mil/postwarjapan/downloads/Potsdam%20Declaration.pdf, retrieved May 1, 2011.
10. After leaving Tinian, the *Indianapolis* was hit by a Japanese submarine and sank in twelve minutes. Because he had not ordered *Indianapolis* to steer a zigzag course, a tactic to throw

an attacking submarine off its aim, commanding officer Captain Charles B. McVay III was charged with reckless hazarding of his ship; he was the only commanding officer of any ship lost in the war to be held accountable. The captain of the Japanese sub was a witness for the defense: He said that he fired a spread of six torpedoes and would have hit the *Indianapolis* whether or not she had been zigzagging. Nonetheless, McVay was found guilty but did not receive any substantive punishment. On the day the verdict was announced, a newsman asked Nimitz had there ever been an officer who had been court-martialed and still made flag rank? The admiral simply pointed to himself, recalling his embarrassment with the *Decatur,* and said, "Here's one." McVay did retire as a rear admiral, in 1949, but under a rule dating from 1920 that allowed officers with combat decorations to be retired in the next higher rank—a practice known derisively as a "tombstone promotion," which ended in 1959.

11. Potter, *Nimitz,* p. 389.

CHAPTER TWENTY-THREE: SURRENDER

1. Stuart S. Murray, Admiral, USN (Ret.), eight interviews, 1970-1971, by Etta-Belle Kitchen, U.S. Naval Institute, DVD, compiled in 2001, p. 309.
2. E. B. Potter, *Nimitz* (Annapolis, MD: Naval Institute Press, 1976), p. 390.
3. Truman told the skipper of the *Missouri* that he alone had made the choice. Perhaps; accounts differ.
4. Potter, *Nimitz,* p 391.
5. Catherine Nimitz Lay, interviewed by John T. Mason, U.S. Naval Institute, DVD, Feb. 16, 1970, p. 73.
6. Stuart S. Murray, interviews by Etta-Belle Kitchen, p. 228; H. Arthur Lamar, Captain USNR (Ret.), interviewed by John T. Mason, U.S. Naval Institute, DVD, May 3, 1970, p. 64.
7. H. Arthur Lamar, interview by John T. Mason, p. 64.
8. Note well: a clean set of colors pulled out of ship's spares, all published reports to the contrary notwithstanding. The flag had not flown over the Capitol on December 7, had not been flown during the Casablanca Conference in 1943, and was not taken away by MacArthur to fly over his headquarters in Tokyo.
9. Potter, *Nimitz,* p.395.
10. H. Arthur Lamar, interview by John T. Mason, p. 64.
11. Stuart S. Murray, interviews by Etta-Belle Kitchen, p. 282.

CHAPTER TWENTY-FOUR: HOMECOMING

1. Jeffrey G. Barlow, *Revolt of the Admirals* (Washington, DC: Brassey's, 1998), note 94, p. 45.
2. Barlow, *Revolt,* note 96, p. 46.
3. "HEROES: Back to Texas," *Time,* Oct. 22, 1945.
4. E. B. Potter, *Nimitz* (Annapolis, MD: Naval Institute Press, 1976), p. 400.
5. Dede W. Casad and Frank A. Driscoll, *Chester W. Nimitz: Admiral of the Hills* (Austin, TX: Eakin Press, 1983), pp. 238-239; "Nimitz Receives All-out Welcome from Washington," *New York Times.* Oct. 6, 1945.
6. "Nimitz Addresses in Congress and at Monument," *New York Times,* Oct. 6, 1945.
7. Barlow, *Revolt,* note 100, p. 46.
8. Catherine Nimitz Lay, conversation with the author.
9. "City Millions Roar Welcome to Nimitz in Triumphant Trip," *New York Times,* Oct. 10, 1945; "HEROES: Back to Texas." *Time,* Oct. 22, 1945.
10. "Army-Navy Union Opposed by Nimitz," *New York Times,* Oct 10, 1945.
11. "Admiral Twangs His Lyre to Hearer's Glee, For Epic Tale of 'Nimitz, Halsey and Me,'" *New York Times,* Oct. 10, 1945.
12. In June 1946 Beecher was assigned as special assistant for public relations to Secretary of the Navy Forrestal. He retired as a vice admiral in 1955, after serving a tour as the Navy's chief of information. This was a job into which he followed former Nimitz CINCPAC staffers Rear Admiral H. B. (Min) Miller and Commodore E. M. Eller. It's a small world.
13. "Nimitz Urges US to Remain Strong." *New York Times,* Oct. 10, 1945.
14. "Text of Speeches by Gen. Eisenhower, Mayor La Guardia, and Judge Lehman," *New York Times,* June 20, 1945.

15. Potter, *Nimitz*, p. 403.
16. "HEROES: Back to Texas." *Time*, Oct. 22, 1945.

CHAPTER TWENTY-FIVE: THE ROCKY ROAD TO CNO

1. "Says Nimitz Will Succeed King," *New York Times*, Nov. 2, 1945.
2. Robert Debs Heinl, *Soldiers of the Sea: The United States Marine Corps 1775-1962* (Annapolis, MD: Naval Institute Press, 1962), p. 25.
3. E. B. Potter, *Nimitz* (Annapolis, MD: Naval Institute Press, 1976), p. 407.
4. Eugene B. Fluckey, Rear Admiral, USN (Ret.), interviewed by John T. Mason, U.S. Naval Institute, DVD, Oct. 20, 1971, p. 7.
5. For the record, five U.S. fleet carriers of prewar design and six thin-skinned unarmored escort carriers were sunk in all of World War II (out of some 140 of all classes in service), and none, as in "not one," since February 21, 1945.
6. Potter, *Nimitz*, p. 408.
7. Ibid.
8. Potter, *Nimitz*, p. 409.
9. Ernest J. King and Walter Muir Whitehill, *Fleet Admiral King: A Naval Record* (New York: W. W. Norton, 1952), p. 636.
10. Ibid.
11. Eugene B. Fluckey, interview by John T. Mason, p. 7.
12. "Nimitz Succeeds to Navy Command," *New York Times*, Dec. 16, 1945.
13. "Navy Tells Plans for the Atom Age," *New York Times*, Jan. 14, 1946.
14. J. Wilson Leverton, Rear Admiral, USN (Ret.), interviewed by John T. Mason, U.S. Naval Institute, DVD, Aug. 22, 1969, p. 42.
15. Eugene B. Fluckey, interview by John T. Mason, p. 8.
16. George E. Cozard, Master Sergeant USMC (Ret.), interviewed by Etta-Belle Kitchen, U.S. Naval Institute, DVD, Jan. 24, 1970, p. 2.
17. Eugene B. Fluckey, interview by John T. Mason, pp. 13-14.
18. Ibid., p. 23.
19. Ibid., p. 11.
20. Ibid., p. 26.

CHAPTER TWENTY-SIX: SKIRMISHES

1. Jeffrey G. Barlow, *Revolt of the Admirals* (Washington, D.C.: Brassey's, 1998), p. 49, n.120. Huie was a World War II Navy public relations officer who did not seem to care much for the Navy. He may best be known for his novel (and movie), *The Americanization of Emily*, in which a temporarily deranged admiral decrees that, for the great press it would trigger, the first man to die on Omaha Beach must be a sailor.
2. "The Press: In Dubious Battle," *Time*, Nov. 27, 1950.
3. Barlow, *Revolt of the Admirals*, p. 49, n.121.
4. Ibid., p. 49, n.122.
5. It didn't stick. The latest example: in April 2011, Marine General John Allen was designated to relieve Army General David Petraeus as commander of all U.S. Forces in Afghanistan.
6. That order was never carried out. Barlow, *Revolt of the Admirals*, p. 37, n.57.
7. Barlow, *Revolt of the Admirals*, p. 39.
8. Robert S. Burrell, *Ghosts of Iwo Jima* (College Station, TX: Texas A&M University Press, 2006), pp. 167-168. General Armstrong was merely reflecting things his senior commanders had said—for example, President Truman wrote: "The Navy had its own 'little army' that talks Navy and is known as the Marine Corps." [Harry S. Truman, *Memoirs: Years of Trial and Hope*, vol. II (Garden City, NY: Doubleday, 1956), p. 47.]
9. Lewis Strauss, *Men and Decisions* (Garden City, NY: Doubleday, 1962), pp. 208-209.
10. William A. Shurcliff, *Bombs at Bikini: The Official Report of Operation Crossroads* (New York: William H. Wise, 1947), p. 10.
11. Jonathan Weisgall, *Operation Crossroads: The Atomic Tests at Bikini Atoll* (Annapolis, MD: Naval Institute Press, 1994), p. 67.
12. "Navy Tells Plans for the Atom Age," *New York Times*, Jan. 14, 1946.

13. Gordon W. Keiser, *The U.S. Marine Corps and Defense Unification 1944-1947* (Washington, DC: National Defense University Press, 1982), p. 113.
14. Robert H. Ferrel, *The Eisenhower Diaries* (New York: W. W. Norton, 1976), p. 142.
15. Chester W. Nimitz, "Your Navy as Peace Insurance," *National Geographic,* June 1946, p. 685.
16. The idea of nuclear power for a warship had first been proposed by the laboratory's Dr. Ross Gunn in 1939; a science writer for the *Saturday Evening Post* estimated that one pound of the uranium isotope U-235 had the equivalent energy of five million pounds of coal.
17. Admiral James Fife, Jr., interviewed by John T. Mason, U.S. Naval Institute, DVD, May 31, 1969, p. 34.

CHAPTER TWENTY-SEVEN: THE LAST BATTLE
1. Jeffrey G. Barlow, *Revolt of the Admirals* (Washington, D.C.: Brassey's, 1998), p. 53, n.140.
2. Barlow, *Revolt,* p. 54, n.144,; *Armed Forces Staff College Newsletter,* March 1948; "U.S Navy Now Rules the Seas, Says Nimitz; Cites Attack Role," *New York Times,* Jan. 7, 1948.
3. Barlow, *Revolt,* p. 55, n.147.
4. "The Nimitz Report," *New York Times,* Jan. 8, 1948.
5. Barlow, *Revolt,* p. 56, n.150.
6. Ibid., p 50, n.124.
7. Paolo Enrico Coletta, *The United States Navy and Defense Unification, 1947-1953* (Wilmington: University of Delaware Press, 1981), p. 44.
8. George E. Cozard, Master Sergeant USMC (Ret.), interviewed by Etta-Belle Kitchen, U.S. Naval Institute, DVD, Jan. 24, 1970, p. 43.
9. Barlow, *Revolt,* p. 52, n.136.
10. Ibid., p. 53, n.137. That "privilege" would be taken away in the August 1949 re-statement of the department—which lodged all power in one man, the secretary of defense.
11. Victor H. Krulak, *First to Fight: An Inside View of the U.S. Marine Corps* (Annapolis, MD: Naval Institute Press, 1999), p. 120.
12. Barlow, *Revolt,* pp. 209-212.
13. E. B. Potter, *Nimitz* (Annapolis, MD: Naval Institute Press, 1976), p. 447.
14. Ibid.

CHAPTER TWENTY-EIGHT: TWILIGHT
1. In 1976, in gratitude for Nimitz's continuing respect for Admiral Togo and his healing efforts after the war, Japanese military leaders donated an exact replica of Togo's personal garden and meditation center to the museum.
2. Catherine Nimitz Lay, interviewed by John T. Mason, U.S. Naval Institute, DVD, Feb. 16, 1970, p. 93.
3. John A. Sutro, interviewed by Etta-Belle Kitchen, U.S. Naval Institute, DVD, July 12, 1970, p. 17.

BIBLIOGRAPHY

SELECTED SOURCES

Barlow, Jeffrey G. *Revolt of the Admirals.* Washington, DC: Brassey's, 1998.

Bernstein, Barton J. "Why We Didn't Use Poison Gas in World War II." *American Heritage Magazine,* August / September 1985 Vol. 36, Issue 5.

Blair, Clay, Jr. *Silent Victory: The U. S. Submarine War against Japan.* Philadelphia and New York: J. B. Lippincott Company, 1975.

Brinkley, David. *Washington Goes to War.* New York: Alfred A. Knopf, 1988.

Budiansky, Stephen. *Battle of Wits: The Complete Story of Codebreaking in World War II.* New York: Free Press, 2002

———. *The Men, Machines, and Ideas That Revolutionized War, from Kitty Hawk to Iraq.* New York: Penguin, 2005.

Buell, Thomas B. *Master of Sea Power: A Biography of Fleet Admiral Ernest J. King.* Annapolis, MD: Naval Institute Press, 1995.

Burrell, Robert S. *Ghosts of Iwo Jima.* College Station, TX: Texas A&M University Press, 2006.

Casad, Dede W., and Frank A. Driscoll. *Chester W. Nimitz: Admiral of the Hills.* Austin, TX: Eakin Press, 1983.

Casey, Robert J. *Torpedo Junction.* Garden City, NY: Halcyon House, 1933.

Castillo, Edmund. *U.S. Navy Public Affairs: The First Hundred Years.* Unpublished manuscript; copy in author's personal files.

Clarfield, Gerard H. *Security with Solvency: Dwight D. Eisenhower and the Shaping of the American Military Establishment.* Westport, CT: Praeger, 1999.

Coletta, Paolo Enrico. *The United States Navy and Defense Unification, 1947–1953.* Wilmington: University of Delaware Press, 1981.

Craven, Wesley Frank, and James Lea Cate. *Plans and Early Operations, January 1939 to August 1942.* Vol. 1 of *The Army Air Forces in World War II.* Chicago: University of Chicago Press, 1948.

Cressman, Robert J. *A Glorious Page in Our History: The Battle of Midway, 4–6 June, 1942.* Missoula, MT: Pictorial Histories Publishing Company, 1990.

Ferrel, Robert H. *The Eisenhower Diaries.* New York: W. W. Norton, 1976.

Forrestel, E. P., Vice Admiral. *Admiral Raymond A. Spruance, USN: A Study in Command.* Washington, DC: Government Printing Office, 1966.

Frank, L. J. The United States Navy v. the Chicago Tribune. *Historian* 42, Issue 2 (February 1980).

Friedman, Norman. *U. S. Submarines through 1945.* Annapolis, MD: Naval Institute Press, 1995.

Fuchida, Matsuo, and Okumiya Masatake. *Midway: The Battle That Doomed Japan.* Annapolis, MD: U.S. Naval Institute, 1955.

Furer, Julius Augustus, Rear Admiral USN (ret). *Administration of the Navy Department in WWII.* Washington, DC: Government Printing Officer, 1959.

Gilbert, Alton Keith. *A Leader Born: The Life of Admiral John Sidney McCain, Pacific Carrier Commander.* Havertown, PA: Casemate Publishers, 2006.

Gonzalez, Therese. *Great Lakes Naval Training Station.* Mount Pleasant, SC: Arcadia Publishing, 2008.

Griffith, Samuel B. *The Battle for Guadalcanal.* Champaign, IL: University of Illinois Press, 2000.

Healy, George W, Jr. *A Lifetime on Deadline.* Gretna, LA: Pelican Publishing Company, 1976.

Heffernan, John B. ed. *United States Naval Chronology World War II.* Washington, DC: Government Printing Office, 1955.

Heinl, Robert Debs. *Soldiers of the Sea: The United States Marines Corps 1775–1962.* Annapolis, MD: Naval Institute Press, 1962.

Herge, Henry C. *Navy V–12.* Nashville, TN: Turner Publishing Company, 1996

Holmes, W. J. *Double-Edged Secrets: U. S. Naval Intelligence Operations in the Pacific during World War II.* Annapolis, MD: Naval Institute Press, 1979.

Hoyt, Edwin P. *How They Won the War in the Pacific: Nimitz and His Admirals.* New York: Weybright and Talley, 1970.

James, D. Clayton. *The Years of MacArthur: 1941–1945.* Boston: Houghton Mifflin, 1975.

Johnson, William Bruce. *The Pacific Campaign in World War II: From Pearl Harbor to Guadalcanal.* New York: Taylor & Francis, 2006.

Keiser, Gordon W. *The U.S. Marine Corps and Defense Unification 1944–1947.* Washington, DC: National Defense University Press, 1982.

King, Ernest, Fleet Admiral, and Walter Muir Whitehill. *Fleet Admiral King: A Naval Record.* New York: W. W. Norton, 1952.

Krulak, Charles C., Lieutenant General. "Expeditionary Operations." *Marine Corps Doctrinal Publication 3* (April 16, 1998). Headquarters Marine Corps.

Krulak, Victor H., Lieutenant General. *First to Fight: An Inside View of the U.S. Marine Corps.* Annapolis, MD: Naval Institute Press, 1999.

Layton, Edwin T. Rear Admiral, with Captain Roger Pineau USNR (ret) and John Costello. *And I Was There: Pearl Harbor and Midway—Breaking the Secrets.* New York: William Morrow and Co., Inc., 1985.

Lingeman, Richard R. *Don't You Know There's a War On? The American Home Front 1941–1945.* New York: G. P. Putnam's Sons, 1970.

Lundstrom, John B. *Black Shoe Carrier Admiral.* Annapolis, MD: Naval Institute Press, 2006.

————*The First South Pacific Campaign: Pacific Fleet Strategy December 1941–June 1942.* Annapolis, MD: Naval Institute Press, 1976.

MacArthur, Douglas, General. *Reminiscences.* New York: McGraw-Hill, 1964.

Manchester, William. *American Caesar: Douglas MacArthur, 1880–1964.* Boston: Little, Brown and Company, 1978.

Marutollo, Frank. "A Good Bowl of Chowder Saved the Marine Corps." *Marine Corps Gazette* 62 (December 1978).

McBride, William M. *Technological Change and the United States Navy, 1865–1945.* Baltimore, MD: JHU Press, 2000.

Miller, Nathan. *War at Sea: A Naval History of World War II.* New York: Oxford University Press, US, 1997.

Millis, Walter, ed. *The Forrestal Diaries.* New York: The Viking Press, 1951.

Miyakawa, Masuii. *Powers of the American People, Congress, President, and Courts: According to the Evolution of Constitutional Construction.* The Baker & Taylor Co., 1908.

Newcomb, Richard F. *Iwo Jima.* New York: Holt, Reinhart and Winston, 1965.

Nimitz, Chester, Fleet Admiral. "Your Navy as Peace Insurance," *National Geographic,* June 1946.

Parker, Frederick D. "How OP–20-G got rid of Joe Rochefort." *Cryptologia,* July 1, 2000.

Parker, Frederick D. A *Priceless Advantage: U.S. Navy Communications Intelligence and the Battles of Coral Sea, Midway, and the Aleutians.* United States Cryptologic History Series IV, World War II, Volume 5. Center for Cryptologic History, National Security Agency, 1993.

Perez, Louis G. *The History of Japan.* Westport, CT: Greenwood Publishing Group. 1998.

Potter, E. B. *Bull Halsey.* Annapolis, MD: Naval Institute Press, 2003

————*Nimitz.* Annapolis, MD: Naval Institute Press, 1976.

Potter, E. B. and Chester W. Nimitz, Fleet Admiral, eds. *Sea Power: A Naval History.* Englewood Cliffs, NJ: Prentice Hall, 1960.

Shurcliff, William A. *Bombs at Bikini: The Official Report of Operation Crossroads.* New York: William H. Wise and Co., 1947.

Spector, Ronald H. *Eagle against the Sun: The American War with Japan.* New York: Macmillan, 1985.

Stillwell, Paul. *Air Raid, Pearl Harbor: Recollections of a Day of Infamy.* Annapolis, MD: Naval Institute Press, 1981.

Strauss, Lewis. *Men and Decisions,* Garden City, NY: Doubleday, 1962.

Thomas, Evan. *Sea of Thunder: Four Commanders and the Last Great Naval Campaign, 1941–1945.* New York: Simon and Schuster, 2006.

Truman, Harry S. *Memoirs: Vol. II Years of Trial and Hope.* Garden City, NY: Doubleday, 1956.

Weisgall, Jonathan. *Operation Crossroads: The Atomic Tests at Bikini Atoll,* Annapolis, MD: Naval Institute Press, 1994.

Wright, Derrick. *Iwo Jima 1945: The Marines Raise the Flag on Mount Suribachi.* Oxford: Osprey, 2001.

Wukovits, John. *Admiral "Bull" Halsey.* New York: Palgrave Macmillan, 2010.

U.S. NAVAL INSTITUTE ORAL HISTORIES

Anderson, Thomas C., Admiral, MC, USN (Ret.), interviewed by Etta-Belle Kitchen, U.S. Naval Institute, DVD, July 5, 1969.

Archer, James W., interviewed by Etta-Belle Kitchen, U.S. Naval Institute, DVD, August 2, 1969.

Bassett, James, Jr., Captain, USNR, interviewed by Etta-Belle Kitchen, U.S. Naval Institute, DVD, May 28, 1969,

Bauernschmidt, George W., Rear Admiral, USN (Ret.), interviewed by John T. Mason, U.S. Naval Institute, DVD, August 6, 1969.

Brewer, Edward V., interviewed by Etta-Belle Kitchen, U.S. Naval Institute, DVD, January 24, 1970.

Bruton, Chester, Rear Admiral, USN (Ret.), interviewed by John T. Mason, U.S. Naval Institute, DVD, June 18, 1969.

Caldwell, J. Emott, interviewed by Etta-Belle Kitchen, U.S. Naval Institute, DVD, January 25, 1970.

Callaghan, William, Vice Admiral, USN (Ret.), interviewed by John T. Mason, U.S. Naval Institute, DVD, June 30, 1969.

Chase, Joseph, interviewed by Etta-Belle Kitchen, U.S. Naval Institute, DVD, October 19, 1969.

Court, Alvah B., Captain, USN (Ret.), interviewed by John T. Mason, U.S. Naval Institute, DVD, May 14, 1969.

Cozard, George E., Master Sergeant USMC (Ret.), interviewed by Etta-Belle Kitchen, U.S. Naval Institute, DVD, January 24, 1970.

Curts, M. E., Admiral, USN (Ret.), interviewed by Paul L. Hopper, U.S. Naval Institute, DVD, June 19, 1969.

Cuttle, Tracy D., Captain MC, USN, interviewed by John T. Mason, U.S. Naval Institute, DVD, August 28, 1969.

Drake, William Waldo, Rear Admiral USNR (Ret.) interviewed by Etta-Belle Kitchen, U.S. Naval Institute, DVD, June 15, 1969.

Durst, Mrs. Milton, interviewed by E. B. Potter, U.S. Naval Institute, DVD, March 14, 1970.

Eller, E. M., Rear Admiral, USN (Ret.), interviewed by John T. Mason, U.S. Naval Institute, DVD, December 19, 1974.

Fife, James, Jr., Admiral interviewed by John T. Mason, U.S. Naval Institute, DVD, May 31, 1969

Fluckey, Eugene B., Rear Admiral, USN (Ret.), interviewed by John T. Mason, U.S. Naval Institute, DVD, October 20, 1971.

Fox, Charles M., Jr., by E. B. Potter, U.S. Naval Institute, DVD, March 17, 1970.

Gros, Robert R., interviewed by Etta-Belle Kitchen, U.S. Naval Institute, DVD, July 18, 1970.

Henke, Guenther, interviewed by E. B. Potter, U.S. Naval Institute, DVD, March 14, 1970.

Kiehne, Mrs. Charles, interviewed by E. B. Potter, U.S. Naval Institute, DVD, March 13, 1970.

Lamar, H. Arthur, Captain USNR (ret), interviewed by John T. Mason, U.S. Naval Institute, DVD, May 3, 1970.

Lattu, Onnie P., Rear Admiral, USN (Ret.), interviewed by John T. Mason, U.S. Naval Institute, DVD, July 17, 1969.

Lay, Catherine Nimitz, interviewed by John T. Mason, U.S. Naval Institute, DVD, February 16, 1970.

Lay, James T., Captain, USN, interviewed by John T. Mason, U.S. Naval Institute, DVD, February 16, 1970.

Layton, Edwin T., Rear Admiral, USN (Ret.), interviewed by E. B. Potter, U.S. Naval Institute, DVD, March 19, 1970.

Leavell, John, interviewed by E. B. Potter, U.S. Naval Institute, DVD, March 12, 1970.

Leverton, J. Wilson, Jr., Rear Admiral, USN (Ret.), interviewed by John T. Mason, U.S. Naval Institute, DVD, August 22, 1969.

Mercer, Preston V., Rear Admiral, USN (Ret.), interviewed by John T. Mason, U.S. Naval Institute, DVD, October 18, 1969.

Moncure, Sam P., Captain, USN (Ret.) interviewed by John T. Mason, U.S. Naval Institute, DVD, July 30, 1969.

Murray, Stuart S. Admiral, USN (Ret.), eight interviews, 1970–1971, by Etta-Belle Kitchen, U.S. Naval Institute, DVD, compiled in 2001.

Mustin, Lloyd M., Vice Admiral, USN, interviewed by John T. Mason, U.S. Naval Institute, DVD, March 10, 1970.

Nimitz, Chester W., Jr., Rear Admiral, USN (Ret.), interviewed by John T. Mason, U.S. Naval Institute, DVD, April 14, 1969.

Nimitz, Sister M. Aquinas, O.P., interviewed by John T. Mason, U.S. Naval Institute, DVD, June 4, 1969.

Peterson, Mell A., Rear Admiral, USN (Ret.), interviewed by Etta-Belle Kitchen, U.S. Naval Institute, DVD, May 24, 1969.

Plank, David W., Commander, CHC, USN, interviewed by John T. Mason, U.S. Naval Institute, DVD, January 14, 1970.

Quynn, Allen G., Rear Admiral, USN (Ret.), interviewed by John T. Mason, U.S. Naval Institute, DVD, December 17, 1969.

Reagan, Dora Nimitz, interviewed by E. B. Potter, U.S. Naval Institute, DVD, March 12, 1970.

Redman, John R., Vice Admiral, USN (Ret.), interviewed by John T. Mason, U.S. Naval Institute, DVD, June 5, 1969.

Reinbach, Max O., interviewed by E. B. Potter, U.S. Naval Institute, DVD, March 12, 1970.

Rochefort, Joseph J., Captain, USN (Ret.), interviewed by Etta-Belle Kitchen, U.S. Naval Institute, DVD, August 14, 1969; de-classified version issued August, 1983.

Schreiner, Louis, interviewed by E. B. Potter, U.S. Naval Institute, DVD, March 12, 1970.

Sutro, John A., interviewed by Etta-Belle Kitchen, U.S. Naval Institute, DVD, July 12, 1970.

Toepperwein, Herman, interviewed by E. B. Potter, U.S. Naval Institute, DVD, March 11, 1970.

Waters, Odale D., Rear Admiral, USN (Ret.) interviewed by John T. Mason, U.S. Naval Institute, DVD, July 14, 1969.

Wheeler, Joseph, interviewed by John T. Mason, U.S. Naval Institute, DVD, August 4, 1969.

Whiting, F.E.M., Vice Admiral, USN (Ret.), interviewed by John T. Mason, U.S. Naval Institute, DVD, Sept 19, 1969.

INDEX